THE ARKANSAS

Books *by* Clyde Brion Davis

THE ANOINTED
"THE GREAT AMERICAN NOVEL—"
NORTHEND WILDCATS
NEBRASKA COAST
THE ARKANSAS

Other Rivers of America books are:

KENNEBEC by Robert P. Tristram Coffin
UPPER MISSISSIPPI by Walter Havighurst
SUWANNEE RIVER by Cecile Hulse Matschat
POWDER RIVER by Struthers Burt
THE JAMES by Blair Niles
THE HUDSON by Carl Carmer
THE SACRAMENTO by Julian Dana
THE WABASH by William E. Wilson

THE
RIVERS OF AMERICA

Edited by
STEPHEN VINCENT BENÉT
and CARL CARMER

As Planned and Started by
CONSTANCE LINDSAY SKINNER

Art Editor
RUTH E. ANDERSON

THE ARKANSAS

by

CLYDE BRION DAVIS

Illustrated by

DONALD McKAY

FARRAR & RINEHART
INCORPORATED

New York   Toronto

To
My Brother Glen,
Who Knows Arkansas.

Contents

THE ARKANSAS

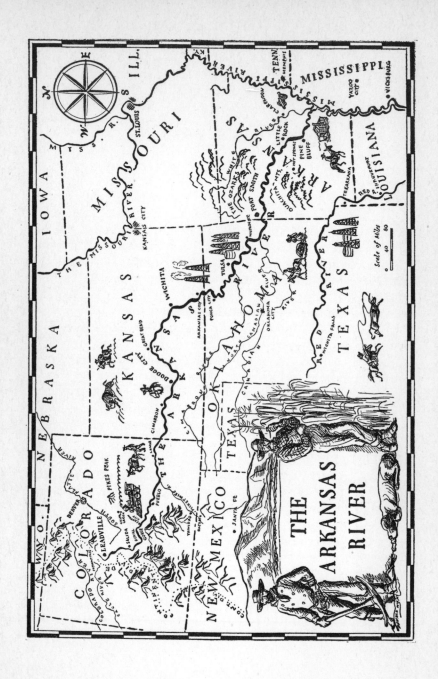

THE ARKANSAS RIVER

CHAPTER ONE

Highborn Brook

THE Continental Divide in the United States pursues a general north and south course from the Alberta border to Chihuahua. Like a crooked ridgepole it wavers south through Montana, Wyoming, Colorado, and New Mexico. In some spots it is merely the crest of a gradual slope on a high plateau. In Colorado, however, it is the roof of the nation.

From the Wyoming line this rocky barrier runs almost directly south along the Rampart, or Front, Range until it reaches a point a dozen miles north of Leadville in central Colorado. Then it abruptly transfers its eminence to the Sawatch, or Saguache, Mountains. Thus, for a matter of thirty or forty miles, the great divide runs east and west instead of its normal north and south.

This sudden jog to the west gives the impression of a slipshod correction to a cosmic surveyor's error. As a matter of fact, the whole region gives evidence of monstrous carelessness. It is as if the coat of the continent failed to fit and a ridiculously clumsy tuck had been taken between the shoulder blades to take care of surplus material.

Traveling southwest from Silver Plume, you have crossed the Continental Divide once in the normal order, moving from east to west at Loveland Pass, 11,992 feet above sea level. Unless you are accustomed to driving in the Rocky Mountains, you have expended a large quantity of nervous perspiration on this pass. No matter how accustomed you are to mountains, you have been impressed with the scenery.

Across Loveland Pass, you know you are on the western slope of the United States. You know that melting snow and other drainage trickles down the rocks to the Eagle River and the Colorado River and eventually finds its way to the Pacific Ocean by way of the Gulf of California.

State Highway 91 now turns south and presently you again are confronted by the Continental Divide at that point where the rampart jogs west to join the Sawatch Mountains. This time you mount the divide at Fremont Pass.

There's nothing spectacular about Fremont Pass. You wouldn't realize it was a pass if it were not for the sign beside the road. You sweep up a brief rise with high mountains on both sides and there is the town of Climax, with the great molybdenum workings behind a wire fence, and the white road sign reading, "Fremont Pass, Altitude 11,320 Feet," and that's all there is to it.

That's all, except that the road in front of you winds south, down to a green valley—green if it's summer. Looking south, down the basinlike valley, the high and rugged Sawatch Mountains are to your right. To your left, sharper cut than any steel engraving, is the Mosquito Range, mostly treeless, seamed pink and gray rock, jagged, austere and self-sufficient as God.

Park your car beside the gravel road here and take a few steps south. Now you are on the eastern slope of the United States and the small boy who has stayed by the car is on the western slope.

Pick up some snow from the side of the road and make it into a snowball. Throw it at the small boy who is thirty or forty feet back on the road and, if he dodges successfully, the snowball will spatter on the rocks, melt in the sun, drain down to the Colorado River and eventually will wash against the shores of Baja California—if it escapes being used to irrigate a farm in the Imperial Valley.

Then the small boy most certainly will pick up some snow from beside the road, make it into a snowball and throw it at you. And, if you dodge successfully, his snowball will spatter on the rocks, melt in the sun and drain down to the Arkansas River, pass by Leadville, turn east at Salida, roar through the Royal Gorge, pass the steel plants of Pueblo and, if it escapes being used to irrigate cantaloupes around Rocky Ford, will travel

1,450 miles through eastern Colorado, Kansas, eastern Oklahoma and then bisect the state of Arkansas past Fort Smith, Little Rock and Pine Bluff, until it mixes with the Mississippi's yellow flood and travels another 600 miles or so past New Orleans to the Atlantic's waters in the Gulf of Mexico.

This is disregarding the possibility that all or a part of both snowballs may be consumed by evaporation or by a thirsty cow.

Looking south from Fremont Pass, down on the green, tundralike, swampy valley, you can see a brook glistening in the mountain sunshine. This brook of cold, clear, glacial water is the infant Arkansas River. Its mother is the Mosquito Range. Its father is the perennial snow.

Surprisingly soon this baby brook of crystal water will grow into one of the most rambunctious of American rivers. It is one of the longest. At times it is one of the most treacherous. And surely no American river has seen more varied or wilder or more incredible history in the making than the Arkansas.

It is the only river I know about that changes the pronunciation of its name in mid-course.

From its mouth to the Oklahoma-Kansas line the river invariably is pronounced as is the state—as if it were spelled Arkansaw. From Arkansas City, Kansas, to Leadville it is more often pronounced as if it were spelled Ar-Kansas. People in Arkansas City, Kansas, don't like to have their municipality called Arkansaw City. In Colorado the watershed from the Royal Gorge to Lamar is usually called the Ar-Kansas Valley. But in the state of Arkansas the pronunciation was fixed legally by legislative action in 1881.

The name Arkansas came from a tribe of Indians.

It was Gallicized by the French explorers and then Anglicized by the supplanting English-speaking settlers.

The first recorded mention of these Indians and this territory comes from Father Jacques Marquette in Louis Joliet's journal of 1673. Father Marquette phoneticized it into Arkansea.

A few years later La Salle made it Acansa on his map and Father Louis Hennepin, who was one of La Salle's exploring Jesuits, gave the region wide publicity in 1681 as Akansa. Hennepin gave the Arkansas region more publicity than any other explorer of his time with an extraordinary book by the extraordinary title of *Nouvelle Découverte d'un Tres-Grand Pays Situé dans l'Amérique entre le Nouveau Mexique et la Mer Glaciale,* which included his *Description de la Louisiane.*

Father Hennepin described astonishing flora and fauna and the strange habits of the natives of that wild land of "Akansa." Not the least astonishing thing about this astonishing description was the fact that Father Hennepin never was in Arkansas. At the time he said he was making his observations he actually was up in Minnesota discovering China. He knew Minnesota was China because he had noticed that the Minnesota Indians spoke Chinese.

Father Hennepin wanted to go down the Mississippi with La Salle to Louisiana, but La Salle ordered the imaginative priest back to Minnesota after a cargo of the best Minnesota tea. So Hennepin, miffed, went back across the Atlantic and turned his attention to literature.

The first time the name was spelled Arkansas, apparently, is on a map based on the journeys of Sieur Bernard La Harpe in 1718-1722, though even he termed the Indians living at the river's mouth as "Les Akansa."

Zebulon Pike (of Pikes Peak fame) was the first man to plot the river's course and in 1811 he spelled it

Arkansaw. It also was spelled Arkansaw ten times in the 1819 act of Congress creating the territory.

The first white man to lay eyes on the Arkansas River were Francisco Vasquez de Coronado and Hernando De Soto. Coronado, contrary to popular supposition, had the jump on De Soto, crossing the river near the Colorado line in western Kansas in the early summer of 1541. De Soto crossed it a thousand miles downstream the following year.

Neither of these Spanish adventurers was pleased with his discovery. Both were frankly annoyed, for they were looking for yellow gold instead of yellow water. They made no ceremony over their discoveries. They just crossed the stream the best way they could and continued their quests. Three hundred and thirty-odd years later plenty of gold was found on the Arkansas River. But not where Coronado and De Soto had been looking.

If Coronado had dropped a bottle with a message in the river, De Soto might have picked it up down in Arkansas and De Soto would have known that he and his countryman were getting their feet muddy on the same stream. As it was, both merely grumbled about the obstacle and went their way without showing proper appreciation for a stream which really is quite a river.

Up there in that high valley between Climax and Leadville, Colorado, the Arkansas is such a puny creek that the snowball-throwing small boy can stand with a foot on each bank and let the stream burble between his legs. It is very quiet up there except when the wind comes booming down from the peaks. The air is so thin and clear and crisp that you get the notion it has been carbonated. It tingles down in the bottom of your lungs, but it doesn't seem to have much substance. Walk briskly uphill for a quarter mile and you are panting like Shakespeare's furnace and those awesome ridges of rock on each side begin to shimmy slightly in the sunshine. Then it's time to sit down on a boulder and contemplate the Arkansas River.

Did you know, for instance, that the drainage basin of the Arkansas River is about 185,000 square miles—which is more than that of the upper Mississippi?

Consider this gentle mountain brook and then let me tell you what I have seen that brook do only 160 miles or so downstream. I have seen it pick up a passenger train like a bludgeon and bash out the brains of another passenger train. I have seen it cut a ghastly swath through the industrial city of Pueblo, washing away six or seven hundred buildings and drowning maybe five hundred people in an evening.

This little brook moves, once it gets going. Even at Leadville it has grown into a respectable creek. It drops about 5,000 feet in its first 125 miles.

About 70 miles south of the point where the boy may bridge the stream with his legs the Arkansas River bumbles sullenly through the Royal Gorge. Maybe the river had some volcanic assistance there once, but the record books chalk up the chasm on the Arkansas' credit side. For a young river, which was born only a couple of counties up the line, the Royal Gorge is a job. At one point the channel is a full half mile below the crest of the sheer granite cliffs.

This, you must remember, is entirely without benefit of husky tributaries coming in to help. The Royal Gorge was strictly a lone wolf job—just the Arkansas pounding away year after year. There isn't a tributary worthy of the name until the Arkansas reaches Pueblo, the oldest community in the state, and there the Fountain River joins up.

From Pueblo, the river pursues a general southeastern route for a matter of 70 miles before the Picketwire

River comes up from the south. This takes us into the flat eastern Colorado country which yields wonderful crops when the Arkansas water is taken for irrigation and yields wonderful black roller dust storms when it isn't.

The Picketwire River doesn't look like much of a tributary and, as far as water is concerned, it isn't much of a tributary. But the Picketwire has its points, nevertheless.

For instance, take its name, Picketwire. The French voyageurs named it the Purgatoire because the cañon to the south suggested Purgatory to their fertile imaginations. Purgatoire with a French pronunciation meant nothing to the English-speaking pioneers who followed the fur-seeking Gauls, so they spelled it Picketwire [1] and didn't bother about the meaning. One of the daily newspapers in Trinidad, Colorado, is the *Picketwire*.

The Picketwire, or Purgatoire, has other distinctions too. This cañon was once the habitat of a race of prehistoric artists who decorated its walls with rude murals of heroic size. Also, in the stream's bed are rocks with the gigantic footprints of antediluvian diplodocuses. Also, again, the headwaters of the Picketwire are in wild mountain country inhabited by a strange race of Penitente Indians, wild country where there are many caves in which a race of badmen from Billy the Kid to the modern machine-gun breed have found refuge.

On into Kansas flows the Arkansas, through a dry plateau so flat that the horizon meets the sky in a faraway lavender haze, through a country where the scenery is mostly clouds. Past Garden City it flows, and past

[1] The Spanish-speaking settlers did a better job of translating "Purgatoire." They called the stream, *El Rio de las Animas Perdidas en Purgatorio*, which means approximately, "The River of Souls Lost in Purgatory," and is quite a name for such a little river. The Spanish version lives now in the town of Las Animas, Colorado, at the mouth of the Picketwire.

Dodge City, which once was one of the toughest towns on earth, the shipping center of buffalo hunters, the terminus of the old Chisholm cattle trail where in the seventies Texas longhorns were driven to be shipped over the Santa Fe Railway to the eastern markets.

So, through the state of Kansas goes our river, without receiving a single important tributary. Well, that must be amended. The Arkansas *does* receive an important Kansas tributary, but the Neosho doesn't flow into the Arkansas until the Arkansas is well into Oklahoma.

The Neosho (or Grand, as it is sometimes called) is a respectable river in its own right and in turn the Neosho in Kansas receives a tributary which someone made immortal in verse. This tributary of the Neosho is the Cottonwood River. It oozes past Emporia, Kansas, so I suspect the versifier probably was William Allen White. If my memory does not fail me, the verse runs as follows:

> The grand, majestic Cottonwood
>   Is neither slow nor swift;
> Its banks are lined with rotten wood
>   And other kinds of drift.

In Oklahoma the Arkansas picks up the flood and silt of the Cimarron, passes Tulsa with its mammoth oil refineries, bisects the old Cherokee Strip, gathers in the Neosho and the Verdigris and then the Illinois, which drains down from the Missouri Ozarks. The river, now looking as large as the Mississippi at Davenport, Iowa, curves through a broad valley carved directly across the Ozark uplift, past Fort Smith, Arkansas, and beyond.

From the Oklahoma line to Little Rock the river winds past farms that grow cotton and more cotton. There are some fields of corn and wheat and oats, but cotton still is the principal crop of Arkansas. Lately they have been turning to soybeans as a profitable rotation crop.

Around Fort Smith and Van Buren the soil is mostly a red clay. By Russellville the red clay has changed to yellow clay with fine black loam in the bottom lands.

Because it has a definite channel bound by hills, the river can do little changing of course as midwestern and southern rivers love to do in January and June. The hills continue past Little Rock and begin to dwindle near Pine Bluff. From Pine Bluff on to the confluence of the White River and on to the Mississippi the country is made to order for a vengeful and rambunctious river.

The White River and its principal tributary, the Black River, coming down from the north, also have opportunities for spreading out and picking some planter's cottonfield for a new bed.

It is a flat, alluvial country, full of oxbow lakes or bayous where the river used to live, and full of swamps and cypress knees and water moccasins and buzzards and sharecroppers.

It also is a country rich in historical lore.

CHAPTER TWO

Elusive Golconda

NEITHER Coronado nor De Soto was interested in territory or rivers. What they wanted was gold and silver or nothing. They got nothing.

De Soto wasn't much impressed with the Mississippi River nor the Arkansas River. Coronado was the first white man to view the Grand Cañon of the Colorado, and that was a disappointment because the chasm wasn't inlaid with gold.

Neither of these grandees was cursed by a kind heart nor a conscience. Subjugating inferior races was their creed as well as their trade and consequently neither built up a tradition of graciousness for the white man among the aborigines.

De Soto, pendulous-lipped, bearded and sullen-eyed, was the first of this precious pair to set foot on North America proper. Before that he had been with a Christian crusader named Pizarro showing the Incas the way to heaven and starting them on their journey.

King Charles I of Spain recognized De Soto's valor in Peru by making the cutthroat governor of Florida and Cuba, so De Soto came back to America to look for the Fountain of Youth in Florida and for gold any place he could find it.

That was in 1539 and, as De Soto still was only forty, he was considerably more interested in gold than in the Fountain of Youth.

Immediately he set out on a march that was to last nearly three years and end only with his body being loaded into a bag of sand and sunk in the Mississippi. He traveled north into Georgia, back into Alabama, north again to sight the Mississippi River a little upstream from the upper mouth of the White River. There he crossed the broad Mississippi into Arkansas about the same time that Coronado's men were crossing the Arkansas River out on the plains. De Soto could have gone downstream a few miles and crossed the Arkansas at this time, thus running a dead heat with his fellow grandee, but he didn't know the Arkansas River was there and he wouldn't have been interested anyhow.

Instead, he pushed through the swamps up into the Arkansas Ozarks, still being led on by tales of gold. All along the route he buried Spanish soldiers, victims of swamp fever and Indian arrows. And all along the route he captured sturdy-looking Indians, thrashed them until they were willing to submit to slavery, and took them with him as beasts of burden. In pay for their labors De Soto told these Indians about Jesus Christ and showed them how to lash two sticks together in the form of a cross which they could pray before.

In the Ozark Mountains De Soto found no gold, but apparently he and his men did find the anopheles mosquito, for most of them became ill with chills and fever.

Some of the Ozark Indians, not knowing De Soto very well as yet, sympathized with his illness and told him about some "hot lakes" to the south that had the quality of healing people afflicted with all manner of maladies. So De Soto followed the route of State Highway 7 down, crossing the river at the site of Dardanelle, and took the baths at Hot Springs. There he met a lot of interesting Indians from up in Nebraska and Iowa and Kansas who had come down for the cure. Some of these chiefs bragged to De Soto about the fine fishing in their territory and invited him up for a vacation. But none of them would admit there were any gold mines where he lived and De Soto was not one to get excited about fishing. He could go fishing back home in Spain.

The baths helped De Soto, but failed to effect a cure, apparently because he didn't stay for the complete course of twenty-one baths. When he began to feel better he started off again looking for gold. He followed the Ouachita River down to its confluence with the Red River in Louisiana and he followed the Red River down to the Mississippi River, where his old aches and shakes caught up with him again. There, on May 21, 1542, Hernando De Soto passed to his reward and his followers stealthily sank him into the river at night so that his devoted slaves, the Indian beasts of burden, wouldn't learn of his demise.

De Soto had convinced the humble red man that he, De Soto, was immortal and could not die. His Spanish colleagues were fearful of the slaves' reaction once they discovered the fiction, so they disposed of the body and fled down the river to Mexico.

De Soto's contemporary, Coronado, had the same lovable nature and found no more gold. And *he* didn't get back to Spain with his life either.

Coronado was about the same age as De Soto. His wife was a favorite with the crown, so Francisco Vasquez de Coronado became governor of the province of New Galicia, which was conveniently far away from the court of Spain. Besides his executive duties in New Galicia, King Charles thought Coronado might pick up a shipload or so of gold, so, on February 23, 1540, the governor set sail from Spain with four Franciscans, 260

Spanish cavaliers, 70 Spanish footmen, six cannon, and about a thousand horses.

They traveled up from the Gulf of California, finding no gold, but picking up an Indian here and there in the good old Spanish grandee fashion until they had approximately a thousand slaves.

They spent that winter on the Rio Grande in New Mexico at one of the legendary "Seven Cities of Cibola," where gold was supposed to be but wasn't. This Cibolan city stood on the site of the present town of Bernalillo, a few miles north of Albuquerque, and the Spaniards employed the winter months in being objectionable to their Indian hosts.

With Coronado in the guest room for four or five months the chief learned a good deal about grandee nature and he discovered the one thing that would speed Coronado and his bullies on their way.

This chief appears to have had a native sense of diplomacy unsurpassed in the marble halls of Europe. He appears to have been a master at playing major cards in a casual fashion. One day at dinner the chief in an offhand manner dropped a remark about the town of Quivira.

I can picture the scene there in that low-ceilinged and dusky room—the imperious Coronado decked out in velvet and soft gleaming silver with the beady-eyed, poker-faced chief opposite him.

I can picture the conversation between them, the chief innocently laying the trap.

"Never was at Quivira myself," he said, "but my father took a trip up there once when he was buffalo hunting. Great place, they tell me."

Coronado tore off a chunk of venison in a courtly manner. "What's so cockeyed great about Quivira," he demanded. "No gold there, is there?"

The chief smiled in a patronizing way. "Gold?" he said. "They tell me gold is a pest at Quivira. So much of it laying around the corn fields they have to put the papooses to digging it out and piling it up. The boys throw chunks of gold at stray cats at Quivira. It's too common to build houses with, but they do build walls with hunks of gold to keep the cattle out of the corn-fields." The chief shook his head sadly. "You see, gold in chunks like that ain't much good. Take a slab the size of an adobe brick and it's all two men want to lift."

Coronado picked his teeth with a dagger in a courtly manner. "Can't be real gold laying around like that," he said loftily.

"Oh, there can't, eh," said the chief. "I've known a dozen men who've been in Quivira. I told you my own father was there, didn't I? You wouldn't call my father a liar, would you, Mr. Coronado?"

The chief could see his plan was beginning to work. Despite Coronado's efforts to keep his poise, there was a lustful glitter in his eyes.

"No," said Coronado, "I don't say your father was lying. It just seems incredible there could be that much gold anywhere. Just sounds too good to be true. But, after all, there must be loads of gold around here some-where from the amount Cortez found in Mexico. Must be a mother lode someplace."

"Well, wait a minute," said the chief. He sent an orderly out to call in a bright young man who perhaps was an officer in the chief's secret service, a young man from up north whom Coronado and his followers later called "the Turk."

"Listen, Joe," said the chief, winking slyly at the young brave, "you used to live up Quivira way. Tell Mr. Coronado about things up there."

The Turk shrugged his shoulders. "Not much to

tell, chief," he said. "Flat country. Thousands of buffalo. Lots of antelope. Good hunting. Pretty good farming land over to the east, but it ain't near as pretty or as healthy as this country. I like it better here, personally."

"No, Joe," said the chief, "I don't mean that. Tell Mr. Coronado about the streets in Quivira."

"Oh," said the Turk. "Well, you see it ain't so sandy there and the roads get pretty muddy, come the spring rains, so they paved the streets in town. Pretty good idea, too. They got scads of this gold stuff up there, so they smooth up chunks of it and put 'em down even, and then you can walk along without getting your feet muddy."

"Real gold?" Coronado demanded.

"Oh, sure."

"Like this?"

Coronado handed the Turk a nugget he'd got from Pizarro or Cortez or one of the other conquistadores.

The Turk tossed the nugget up and caught it. "That's right," he said. "Kind of heavy stuff to handle, but it's awful soft and you can cut it most any way you want."

Coronado's face was pale and his voice quivered. "Listen, you savages," he said, "maybe gold doesn't mean anything but cobblestones to you, but we're going to Quivira. How far is it?"

"Two moon's march—maybe moon and a half," said the Turk.

"Well, get your duffel bag. We're starting right away." He stuck his head out the pueblo door. "Hey, sentry," he yelled, "have the bugler blow assembly."

Of course, the chief knew there wasn't any gold at Quivira. He had rehearsed the play with the Turk and the Turk was instructed to take these Spaniards clear up into Kansas or even Nebraska and to lose them. Take them so far they couldn't possibly find their way back and then slip away from them some dark night.

It was a fine assignment for an ambitious young man like the Turk and he knew the least he'd get out of the job if he were successful would be a loving cup with three stars and a palm and an honorary doctor of laws degree.

So on April 21, 1541, the Turk led Coronado and his Franciscans and cavaliers and footmen and slaves off to the northeast. Their exact route is unknown, but if the Turk was well acquainted with the territory he probably took them over Raton Pass and then northeast along the Picketwire River. The party did pass through southeastern Colorado because dry-farmers, plowing up good grazing land to raise dust storms, have unearthed old Spanish breastplates and other relics bearing religious sentiments in the Castilian. They did come to the Arkansas River and crossed it, some say in eastern Colorado and some say near Dodge City, Kansas. And thirty-five days after they left the town that now is Bernalillo, New Mexico, they came to an Indian town approximately 650 miles from their winter quarters.

If they had traveled in a straight line directly northeast, the 650 miles would have taken them close to Beatrice, Nebraska. But no doubt the party wandered and no doubt the 650 was closer to being 400 as a ruler lies on a map.

At any rate the poor Indians of this Kansas town never had heard of the marvelous city of Quivira with its streets of gold and they lived almost entirely on the flesh of what Coronado described as "humpbacked cows."

The corn the Spaniards had brought from New Mexico was running low, so Coronado sent his army back toward Cibola and continued his dogged quest for Quivira with thirty picked horsemen and the Turk.

For forty-two more days they continued, finally reaching another Indian town, as Coronado wrote King Charles, at 40° north latitude. The 40th parallel now marks the Kansas-Nebraska boundary.

This town was a miserable collection of grass huts inhabited by Indians (probably Pawnees) who lived on corn and beans and catfish and buffalo meat.

Things hadn't been working out as the Turk had hoped and he must have been growing discouraged by the time they entered this town. He was afraid the main body of Coronado's men might find their way back to Bernalillo; and if so, what sort of reception would he get from the chief? Where would his loving cup with the stars and palm be? How about his longed-for honorary LL.D. degree?

The Turk was growing disgusted with prospects, and to make things worse Coronado had been growing more petulant day by day. The Turk decided to give his

grandee boss a real headache and the Turk's love of the dramatic ran away with his good Indian judgment. He and his chief had planned for him to slip away silently in the night, but the Turk couldn't resist giving Coronado the business.

"Well, Mr. Coronado," he said, "here we are."

"What you mean, here we are?" blurted Coronado.

"Well, Quivira. You know—Quivira."

"You don't call this dump Quivira?"

"Sure. This is the town you've been looking for—Quivira. Well, good-bye. I've got to go home now. Glad to met you, Mr. Coronado."

"Hey, wait-a-minute, you." An orderly grabbed the Turk's horse. "Where," demanded Coronado, "are those golden streets you were talking about? Where are those golden fences? Where is that tree with the tinkling golden bells? Where are those Indian brats chucking chunks of gold at stray cats?"

The Turk peered curiously at the mud streets. "Gosh," he said innocently, "they don't seem to be gold any more, do they? Well, I guess they didn't stand up very well. Guess they must have had to tear up the paving. Well, like I told you first, gold isn't worth so much. Too soft and heavy. Well, like I said, I'm glad to know you and I got to be going now."

So Coronado pulled the Turk off his horse and choked him unconscious. They stayed at Quivira twenty-five days and each day a new Spaniard choked the Turk unconscious.

They planned to stay there thirty-one days so each conquistador could have the pleasure of choking the Turk unconscious, with Coronado himself finishing him off on the last day. But on the twenty-fifth day an overly zealous private choked too hard and the Turk didn't come to. So the next day, with a couple of Quivira guides, Coronado and his party struck off southwest and finally reached Bernalillo, picked up his army and in disgust went back to Mexico.

These were the first gold seekers along the Arkansas River. Hundreds of millions of dollars in gold and silver were waiting for them on this river, but De Soto and Coronado didn't look in the right place. And a century and a third passed before another white man even glimpsed the river.

Between the time De Soto was sunk in the Mississippi and Coronado went sullenly back to New Spain from Quivira and the day when Father Jacques Marquette and Louis Joliet came down the Mississippi and made friends with the Indians at the swampy mouth of the Arkansas River, a period of time elapsed equal to that from the heyday of Napoleon Bonaparte to the present time.

When Coronado crossed the Arkansas on the plains

and De Soto was looking for gold in the Ozark Mountains, Henry VIII had just made himself supreme head of the Irish Church and deemed things so peaceful in Erin that he was sending Irishmen to fight in Scotland. Catherine Howard was being led to the block to make way for Catherine Parr while Henry was working over his church and building up a navy which would prove handy to Queen Elizabeth in a few years.

James V was sending his Scot army down to destruction at Solway Moss and he would die a few days before the birth of his daughter, Mary Stuart, leaving his uncomfortable crown to the baby girl.

Copernicus was at Frauenburg, writing his exposition which made him the father of modern astronomy.

Michelangelo had just completed his "Last Judgment" and would live for twenty-two years more to repaint his "Conversion of St. Paul," "The Martyrdom of St. Peter," and to work seventeen years on St. Peter's Dome.

Benvenuto Cellini, a refugee from St. Angelo prison after shooting Charles, the Duke of Bourbonnais, was making his first attempt at sculpture in Paris.

This is what was going on in 1542 in Europe. But before Joliet and Marquette became the next white men to see the Arkansas River, "Bloody Mary," the Tudor queen, had taken over the throne of her father, Henry VIII; had executed Lady Jane Grey; restored in part the Catholic Church to the British Isles; had burned three hundred or so heretics including the Archbishop of Canterbury, and died in 1558.

Mary Stuart was crowned Queen of Scotland when less than a year old, instigated a few murders, called Queen Elizabeth a bastard and went to the chopping block.

And Elizabeth, daughter of Henry VIII and of

Anne Boleyn, followed "Bloody Mary" to the throne, reigned forty years, ousted the Catholics again, defeated the Spanish Armada with the navy her father had built and with the assistance of a few sailors including Admirals Howard, Drake and Hawkins, and finally died in 1603—still seventy years before the third party of white men saw the Arkansas River.

And William Shakespeare was born and grew up and married Anne Hathaway and poached a deer and wrote the greatest plays ever penned, and died.

And Sir Francis Bacon was born, grew up, studied profoundly, worked his political intrigues, wrote his essays that convinced many he must have been author of Shakespeare's works, and died ten years after Shakespeare.

And John Milton was born and grew up and went blind and wrote *Paradise Lost* and sold it for £20 on the installment plan.

And over in the "Low Countries" Rembrandt was born, grew up in a mill, painted his "Night Watch," fifty portraits of himself, a great deal of other work, and died.

And Cervantes was born near Madrid, grew up, went to war, lost his left hand fighting for the Pope, spent five years in slavery in Algiers, wrote *Don Quixote,* and died.

And Oliver Cromwell was born, grew up, wrote his name large in England's military annals, became Lord Protector of the Commonwealth, signed the death warrant for King Charles I, and died.

And Ben Jonson was born, grew up, wrote his plays, and died.

And Catharine de' Medici was born in Florence, married Henry II, became regent of France and insti-

gated the murder of Gaspard de Coligny and the massacre of twenty to thirty thousand Huguenots in Paris.

And William Harvey was born in Kent, England,
became a physician, discovered the circulation of the
blood, and died.

Between De Soto and Joliet England burned more
than a hundred witches at the stake.

And the Council of Trent in the Austrian Tyrol
conducted sessions for eighteen solid years to decide that
John Calvin and Martin Luther weren't nice fellows
from its point of view.

And Virginia Dare was born in Virginia.

And Guy Fawkes plotted to blow up the English
Parliament with gunpowder.

And the slave trade was introduced to American
colonies.

And the Pilgrim Fathers landed at Plymouth Rock.

And John Bunyan was born, became a tinker, went
to prison as an heretic preacher and wrote *Pilgrim's
Progress*.

And the great plague swept London, killing 68,000
persons, followed by a fire which burned 13,200 houses
and 89 churches.

And Christopher Marlowe was born in Canterbury,
wrote his plays and poems that have convinced some that
he also wrote Shakespeare's plays and poems, and was
killed in a street brawl when twenty-nine years old.

And Isaac Newton was born in Lincolnshire, England, excelled in mathematics at Trinity College, Cam-
bridge, and had been working on his theory of gravita-
tion for eight years when Marquette and Joliet saw the
Arkansas River.

But even after all these 131 elapsed years since De
Soto and Coronado, Joliet and Marquette did not explore the river. They rested and ate roast dog and smoked

the pipe of peace with the Arkansas Indians for a few days.

They had hoped to go down the Mississippi River to China, but the Indians assured them, what De Soto's men had found out 131 years before, that the Mississippi ran into the Gulf of Mexico instead of the China Sea. The Indians also warned against fierce savages downriver and against supernatural terrors lurking to the south. So Marquette and Joliet told the Indians about Christ and the Virgin Mary and went back to Canada.

Lust for gold brought the first white men to the Arkansas River. If Coronado or De Soto had merely followed the river to its headwaters, the grandeur of Spain might not have waned. As it was, however, more than three hundred years elapsed before the Arkansas gave up its treasure.

CHAPTER THREE

The Pikes Peak Hoax

O<small>N</small> M<small>AY</small> 29, 1848, Walter Colton, American alcalde at Monterey, capital of the then Mexican state of California, wrote the following in his diary:

"Our town was startled out of its quiet dreams today by the announcement that gold had been discovered in the American Fork. The men wondered and talked and the women, too; but neither believed. The sibyls were less skeptical. They said the moon had, for several nights, appeared not more than a cable's length from the earth; that a white ram had been seen playing with an infant, and that an owl had rung the church bells."

This was the beginning of the great gold rush west.

From January 24th John A. Sutter and James W. Marshall had kept the secret that Marshall had discovered gold in Sutter's millrace. But finally Sutter sent an agent to Monterey to obtain a patent on the mining rights.

The next year 230 American vessels reached California ports jammed with gold seekers from the east and south of the United States. At least 35,000 persons traveled overland in 1849 seeking California gold.

Among these 35,000 overland argonauts were three Georgia brothers, Dr. Levi Russell, Oliver Russell, and William Green Russell.

William Green Russell was a fantastic buckskin dandy with waxed horizontal mustachios fully ten inches long and a beard braided neatly into two pigtails. Green Russell's wife was a Cherokee squaw and he was taking her and her relatives along to California.

The Russells took the Santa Fe Trail at first, but there was too much traffic to suit them so they continued to follow the Arkansas River after the trail swung down to Cimarron Springs in Kansas.

They were not the first white men to follow the Arkansas to the Colorado Rockies. Young Zebulon Pike had plotted the river's course to the mountains in 1806. General John Charles Frémont, led by Kit Carson, had explored the South Park region of Colorado in 1842. These were official explorations. But before Frémont and before Pike, French trappers and fur hunters had made various unofficial explorations of the Colorado mountains. They even had started several unofficial posts and settlements which might have endured if the silk hat hadn't been invented. Someone did invent the silk hat, however, and the bottom dropped out of the beaver fur market in about 1840 and the Rockies were returned to the Indians and solitude to be explored later by official explorers.

The Russell party, at least, was the first party of gold seekers to travel along the Arkansas River since Coronado. Following the river to the collection of adobe huts that became the city of Pueblo, the Georgians turned north on the old trappers' trail, intending to hook up with the Overland Trail in Wyoming.

They camped one night in the foothills north of Pikes Peak and Green Russell's Cherokee relatives struck up an acquaintanceship with some Arapahos who were camped near by. They told the Arapahos where they were going and why. They told the Arapahos they would find much gold in California, which would make them all persons of very high standing back in Georgia.

The Arapahos were contemptuous of such a crusade. "Why," they said, "you can find that stuff around here if you want it. Kind of pretty junk, but not much good except there's a rumor it'll keep off rheumatism if you wear a quill of it around your neck."

So the Cherokees told their brother-in-law and Green Russell was shown some quills of gold dust which the Arapaho squaws had picked out of creek sand when they hadn't anything else to do. A quillful of gold wasn't very much, but it was enough to make a mild impression on Green Russell.

The next night they camped at the confluence of a small creek with a north-flowing river. The banks of this creek were lined with wild chokecherry trees and here Green Russell got out his shovel and wash pan, tied his braided beard around his neck, and went to work.

He knew how to pan for gold, for there were placer workings near his Georgia home. He shoveled a dab of sand into the pan, filled the pan half full of water and, squatting on his haunches, he began to shake the pan slowly with a circular motion that mixed the water with the sand and then sent the muddied water sluicing over the rim until the water was gone and most of the light sand and mud was washed off with it. In the bottom of the pan was a collection of pebbles and coarse sand, too heavy to sluice away readily. And among this debris Green Russell found a few grains of glistening free gold.

Thus, on Cherry Creek, which now trickles between concrete retaining walls through the city of Denver, Green Russell of Auraria, Georgia, made history by finding "color." But it wasn't enough color to excite a man bound for the wondrous land of California where one could shovel up nuggets by the bucketful. The party went on north toward the Overland Trail and a few days later found color in the Cache la Poudre River. They noted these discoveries carefully as something worthy of investigating further—if by any strange chance they didn't get all the gold they wanted in California.

Eight years later the Russells were back in Auraria, Georgia. They hadn't dug a million dollars from the California mines after all, so they got to talking about the dust Green had washed out in the shadow of the Rocky Mountains. The California streams, it had turned out, were too crowded for a man to have a chance. The Russells didn't like crowds. Well, in Colorado there certainly were no crowds and where there was color to be found in the creeks along the plains, it was probable rich deposits were waiting higher up the streams.

The next spring the Russells with their Cherokee friends and nearly a hundred other adventurers again were making their way across the buffalo grass of western Kansas and eastern Colorado, all of which was known then as Kansas Territory.

Again they turned north and again they camped under the scraggly cottonwood trees and chokecherries of Cherry Creek and the South Platte River. There, while they prospected, they founded a settlement and they named it after their home town in Georgia.

Green Russell and his party prospected on up the South Platte. On one sand bar, with his braided beard tied around his neck in working position, Green Russell washed out a panful that showed gold in paying quantities. He loosed a yell and the Georgians and Cherokees came on the gallop.

"We've struck her rich!" shouted Green. "We're all rich as kings."

But the sand bar, when shoveled entirely away and washed out in the pans, totaled less than five ounces of gold. They moved on upstream, off the plains and into granite-walled Platte Cañon.

When winter came the Russell party had a total of about $800 in dust and they moved back out of the mountains to their shack town of Auraria.

There was a surprise awaiting the Georgians. When they reached Cherry Creek they found another town in the making. A party headed by a Lawrence, Kansas, man named John Easter had arrived to get their share of Rocky Mountain gold.

How did they suspect there was any gold there? Well, some Delaware Indians had passed through Lawrence and the Indians told of white men shoveling gold from the mountain streams as if it were common building sand.

This was the beginning of the great Pikes Peak gold rush.

What little gold the Georgians had found was not at Pikes Peak, but Pikes Peak was a good landmark which could be seen seventy miles to the south on a clear day. Just why the Delaware Indians spread such a rumor is unknown. It is possible they had a grievance against the Arapahos inhabiting the foothill country.

The 1857 depression still held industrial America. Thousands were jobless and starving, for there were no government relief agencies in those days. Businesses and factories were going bankrupt every day.

So fantastic stories of free gold by the wagonload in the Kansas mountains fell on eager ears. It was the old story of Quivira all over again, but magnified thousands of diameters. The outfitting stores encouraged the rumors wholeheartedly. Leavenworth, Kansas; St. Joseph, Missouri; Nebraska City and St. Louis began to boom as gold seekers bought supplies.

The press of Kansas printed little else but fabricated stories of the immense amount of gold in the "Shining

Mountains," as they sometimes were called. Each liar tried to outlie the last and succeeded notably.

During the spring and early summer of 1859, it is estimated that a hundred thousand persons started the trek across the plains for the untold riches to be picked up in the mountains. They traveled by oxcart, on horseback, by carriage, and they walked carrying packs on their backs. Hundreds walked, shoving small pushcarts ahead of them laden with their blankets, gold pans and picks and shovels. And hundreds of them left their bones on the virtual desert of western Kansas and Nebraska.

The material basis for this extraordinary, feverish migration was approximately $800 worth of dust dug along the South Platte River by Green Russell's party of seventy or eighty diggers. They had worked for four months at backbreaking labor to gain this—slightly more than eight cents a day for each man.

First blame for this tragedy of mass migration may lie on the Delaware Indians. But greater blame rests upon the avaricious outfittings stores and the sensation-mongering newspaper editors and the authors of several *Guidebooks to the Gold Fields.*

Green Russell himself was horrified as the excited thousands raced into the foothills. He took time out from his own gold hunting to travel to Lawrence, Kansas, and tell the truth in an attempt to stop the rush.

But the emigrants smiled knowingly and went on with their packing. They understood. Green Russell wanted all the gold for himself.

It wasn't long, however, before the migration reversed itself. The brave prairie schooners with "Pikes Peak or Bust" painted on their covers, now with the single word "Busted" on the canvas, creaked eastward with dished wheels.

The Kansas Territory gold excitement was de-

nounced as "the most stupendous humbug ever perpetrated upon the American people."

One miner, safely east of the Missouri River, said
he visited all the Colorado diggings and found no man
making more than twenty cents a day.

The settlement started at the juncture of Cherry
Creek and the South Platte River by Green Russell, now
was known as Denver City, combining the towns of
Auraria, Montana City, and St. Charles. It had been

named for James W. Denver, governor of Kansas Territory. For a few weeks it appeared that Denver would be
a major city before a year had passed. But now that the
bubble had burst, auctioneers were bellowing from
morning until night selling blankets, horses, wagons, firearms, mining tools, and even clothing for the desperate
who wished to raise a few cents toward financing their
long walk back to civilization before the blizzards swept
down from the snowy summit of Mt. Evans.

There was a good deal of talk about hanging the
Kansas editors whose lies had contributed to the rush,
but none actually was killed. D. C. Oakes, author of one

of the most popular "guidebooks," was badly beaten by a party of home-going argonauts and a mound was erected beside the Kansas trail with a tombstone bearing the epitaph:

> Here lies the body of D. C. Oakes,
> Lynched for aiding the Pikes Peak hoax.

But no one got around to putting Mr. Oakes under his gravestone.

Perhaps the dejected, returning gold seekers had no energy even for revenge with a 600-mile walk ahead of them—600 miles across sandy plains where the sun beats down with dizzying intensity, where clouds of gnats and flies chew one's ears to a swollen pulp, where the hot winds pound powder-fine sand into one's pores and where the scant water is charged with kidney-burning alkali.

All the gold seekers did not return home, however. There were some like Green Russell who still were convinced that large quantities of gold were to be found in the mountains. There were other optimists who could be stampeded forward but not back.

Among these was a man who by fate or luck was to play one of the leading roles in the story of Colorado and of the Arkansas River.

Horace Austin Warner Tabor in 1859 was twenty-nine years old. He was heavy-bodied, short-legged, slow of thought, and something of an oaf. His eyes were prominent and dull. His dark mustache was big enough to tack on a broomstick and use for a floor mop. He talked loudly and was a congenital backslapper.

Horace Tabor was born in Vermont, and learned the stonecutter's trade. He married his employer's daughter, Miss Augusta Pierce, a frail-bodied, bespectacled, circumspect New England girl with a stock of common sense, but with not enough force or charm to keep her husband in line.

Tabor and his wife lived with her father in Portland, Maine, for a year. But business was bad and the young stonecutter was restless.

At this time in Boston there was an abolitionist named Amos A. Lawrence who was putting in what he believed to be shrewd licks for the Free-Soilers. As head of the Emigrant Aid Society, Lawrence was financing penniless New Englanders to move to Kansas where they could work for abolition of slavery and perhaps hang a few Democrats and burn their houses. Lawrence issued literature depicting the joys of life on the Kansas prairies and of the wealth to be gained from scratching the rich Kansas soil.

This all sounded very nice to Horace Tabor, so he and Augusta sought out Lawrence in Boston and were sent to Kansas. They found an abandoned homestead near Fort Riley in the eastern part of the state and they settled in the abandoned shack.

The country around Manhattan, Kansas, is not New England, but it is a pretty farming country now—especially when compared to the flat lands farther west. But it didn't look like the promised land to Augusta Tabor, who was a woefully thin little woman well along in pregnancy. She confessed to her diary that she sat on the straw tick bed and cried for homesickness.

Tabor went to work plowing and planting. He normally was a lazy man, but he would work when necessity demanded. So he worked the farm now and got some stonecutting to do at Fort Riley and he found a couple of men boarders for Augusta to feed.

While Tabor was away working or meeting with the abolition societies, Augusta lived in terror of Indians and rattlesnakes. The Indians used to come around and peer into the shack. The rattlesnakes used to come around and shake their tails at Augusta. These were the days when the potency of prenatal influence never was doubted and Augusta worried about her baby. She was delighted when the boy was born without war paint on his face and without rattles.

A drought came and burned out the crops. Grasshoppers came and ate up even the baby's diapers hanging on the clothesline. It was dreadfully hot and the rattlesnakes multiplied and the Indians got more curious and Tabor's abolitionist friends never got an opportunity to hang even one Democrat.

So, when news roared in that slabs of pure gold could be hacked from the flanks of the Rocky Mountains with a sharp mattock, it was inevitable that the Tabors must yoke their oxen and set out for Pikes Peak.

Tabor never had seen any gold except in a jeweler's window and had no notion of mining. But in that he was no different than 99 per cent of the others who had been pushing by Fort Riley optimistically westward bound and doomed to disillusionment.

When the Tabors were ready to move to the mountains their boarders decided to go along. They were Nathaniel Maxcy and a man named Kellogg. Maxcy was an old friend of the Pierce family in Portland and the baby was named Maxcy in his honor. But by no means was he a sweetheart of Augusta's. Augusta was not the sort of wife to have sweethearts nor to attract would-be sweethearts.

The three men trudged along beside the wagon while Augusta rode with her teething baby, who was fretful and sickly.

It was May and sultry and hot. They narrowly missed one tornado and were frightened almost every afternoon by billowed thunderheads piling up on the horizon. Augusta also was uneasy about the Indians that followed them.

Each morning they were on the road by seven o'clock, sometimes in company with other parties bound, so they fondly hoped, for great wealth in the mountains. At noon Augusta would scurry around with the baby on her hip and cook dinner while the men took a nap in the shade of the wagon. Then they would travel until evening and camp amongst the wildflowers on the prairie.

In the course of time they plodded away from the country where trees grow. The grass became shorter and tougher and there was spiked yucca and prickly pear instead of bushes. The horizon stretched farther away in the clear air and the sun beat down more fiercely and the gnats and flies went to work on Augusta and the baby and the men and the oxen so voraciously that Tabor built smudge fires when they camped.

When they were past the point where wood was available, Augusta had another duty when they stopped. She must hustle around the prairie and gather dried buffalo chips in her apron with which to cook. In her diary Augusta hinted she didn't care for that.

Later, however, when great emotional unhappiness had come upon her, she looked back to the days of that journey across the plains with something like home-sickness. She was almost poetic in her nostalgia as she wrote: "I can almost see the approach of each night's camping ground. I can tell how, when and where and how many buffaloes my husband killed. I can see just how the Indians looked as they came on begging expeditions to our wagon. The antelope, the great herds of buffalo, the wild flowers I gathered, the prairie chickens, the bright mornings, the fragrant atmosphere. I was a girl then, filled with enthusiasm. I feared nothing."

In those later years Augusta had forgotten recording her many apprehensions in her diary.

On they went westward. And finally, mounting a rise, they sighted a strange white cloud on the far western horizon, which in a day or two resolved itself into Pikes Peak. Then they were only a hundred miles or so from their goal. A week or ten days later the wagon bumbled down to Denver City on the South Platte.

There had been no actual gold strike in Colorado when the Tabors left their squatters' shack in eastern Kansas. But there had been two real strikes when they arrived in Denver, and the town was blazing with excitement.

Tabor took this excitement as a matter of course. He had expected excitement. He had expected gold strikes. No matter how scant his evidence, he had become convinced that millions in gold were waiting to be dug from the Rocky Mountains and he wouldn't believe otherwise. He had laughed off the testimony of a considerable number of disgusted homeward-bound argonauts he met on the trail and declared them lacking in gumption.

Tabor was like that. His skull was more than ordinarily thick, but when an idea penetrated that skull it took giant powder to blast it out.

CHAPTER FOUR

"This here is California!"

Perhaps a short description of the Colorado gold country would be appropriate now.

The Front Range of the Rocky Mountains runs roughly north and south for about 200 miles. The northern terminus of this range is west and slightly north of Fort Collins, Colorado. The southern end is west and slightly south of Pueblo.

There are three particularly prominent mountains in this range. Pikes Peak, the most southern, is also the farthest east by some miles and thus may be seen farther out on the plains. Its elevation is 14,109 feet above sea level and it rises just above Colorado Springs. Next is Mt. Evans, about fifty miles due west of Denver and about seventy miles north of Pikes Peak. Its altitude is 14,260 feet. Approximately sixty miles farther north is Longs Peak, 14,255 feet.

Between these peaks is the jagged Continental Divide and behind them a welter of mountains including forty or fifty peaks rising more than 14,000 feet.

We have this Front Range of the Rockies extending south from just below the Wyoming line. Through breaks in the granite rampart numerous streams flow down to the plains. From north to south, some of the more important of these brawling torrents are the Cache la Poudre (named by early French trappers as the spot where they hid some ammunition); the Big Thompson

River, the Little Thompson, Clear Creek, Bear Creek, and Turkey Creek. All these are tributaries of the South Platte River.

Near Colorado Springs is the Fountain River and then the greatest of all eastern slope streams, the Arkansas River.

Clear Creek is a respectable watercourse which joins the South Platte north of Denver. It emerges from the mountains thirteen miles west of Denver and winds around the bases of some flat-topped buttes at the present town of Golden, seat of the Colorado School of Mines.

The source of Clear Creek is the high country around Grays and Torrey peaks and Berthoud Pass. It boils down over boulders between mountains once beautifully pine clad, and finally roars its way along the bed of a magnificent cañon.

When Green Russell of the braided beard got back to Colorado from his vain attempt to halt the abortive gold rush, he decided there was no gold in paying quantities up the Platte Cañon, so he and his Cherokees began to prospect Clear Creek.

He was not alone in this quest. Other prospectors had built a straggling settlement at the foot of the buttes near the cañon's mouth and had named it Arapaho after the original inhabitants of the region.

Digging in the Clear Creek sands and washing them in the creek water were Tom Golden, for whom Golden, Colorado, was named; John H. Gregory, one of Russell's Georgians; Wilkes Defrees from Indiana; George Jackson, a cousin of Kit Carson; and a strange shadowy individual known only as Black Hawk.

These all were hardy souls and mighty serious in their intention to find gold if there was any gold in the Rockies. While the weaker vessels either deserted Colorado and went back east or spent the winter in the Cherry Creek settlements playing cards and drinking whisky and fighting and talking about building a great city when they got around to it, these other men were exploring the small gulches running down to Clear Creek Cañon, floundering through deep snow, building fires to thaw the sand and melting ice to wash it out.

Jackson and Golden struck it rich on Chicago Creek. Gregory worked his way up Virginia Cañon and over the ridge and gave his name to a gulch near the present Central City where tons of pure gold were taken out. And Green Russell, the first white man to take gold from a Colorado stream, the leader of the first gold seekers to Colorado, after all these years founded Russell Gulch three miles from Gregory's and panned $35,000 worth of dust in a single week.

William Larimer, a Leavenworth, Kansas, general of militia and townsite promoter, who had gone to Colorado to build a city and sell lots, wrote back in pompous phrases that intimated he himself had put the gold in the mountains. "Colorado is richer in gold than California in its palmiest days," declared the general.

So, as it turned out, the writers of guidebooks and the sellers of outfitting supplies in St. Louis and Westport Landing and St. Joseph and Leavenworth were not lying after all, although their intentions were of the best.

And Tabor—thick-bodied, big-mustached, stupid Horace Tabor—and his ninety-pound wife and baby son were on hand just in time for the excitement.

They did not stay long in Denver after hearing news of the strikes at Russell Gulch and Gregory Gulch and Chicago Creek.

"Where at is Clear Creek?" H. A. W. Tabor demanded of a storekeeper. The merchant led Tabor to the door and pointed over to the purple, flat-topped buttes at the foot of the snow-capped range.

So the Vermont stonecutter bought a few supplies and pulled away from the collection of shacks and tents on the Platte and moved thirteen miles more westward. They camped on Clear Creek at the mouth of the cañon, making a tent of the canvas wagon cover.

The boarders still were with the Tabors—Maxcy and Kellogg. And the boarders went with Tabor up the cañon the next day, leaving the frail Augusta and the baby to keep up the camp.

They told her to "be good to yourself" and, with packs of blankets and provisions on their backs, struck up Clear Creek to find another Golconda. That was on the Fourth of July.

Deathly afraid of Indians and a whole catalogue of wild animals her imagination saw coming out of the mountains to devour her and the baby, Augusta stayed alone three weeks in the makeshift tent while her menfolk were prospecting. One animal did come into her camp, but Augusta wasn't afraid of it. The animal was a stray burro which she adopted. That was her sole adventure.

When Tabor came back he had found no gold, but his enthusiasm ran even higher. "You'll have so many diamonds we'll have to hire a nigger to carry 'em for you," he told Augusta and was hurt when she declared somewhat petulantly that she didn't care much for diamonds, that all she wanted was a comfortable home.

Tabor decided they would be better off camped in the mountains. So they yoked the oxen and started up the cañon. There was only a narrow trail up the gulch and theirs was the first wagon to attempt the trip. They had to work with pick and shovel, cutting away the bank, digging out boulders and filling holes. Sometimes they had to unload the wagon and help the oxen drag it over bad spots.

It took three weeks of hard labor to push and dig their way to Payne's Bar, which now is the town of Idaho Springs. Once there, Horace built a house for his family. At least he built something that could serve as a house until he had dug a few millions' worth of gold. The house was of logs piled about four feet high and the wagon canvas arched over this for a roof.

Tabor staked out his first claim on Chicago Creek where Jackson and Golden had struck it rich. He went to work energetically with his pan, but he found practically no gold. As a matter of fact, not one prospector in twenty-five was making what he would have considered a living wage back home.

So Augusta Tabor, with enterprise greater than her strength, started a business career she was to follow for

nearly twenty years in the mountains. Already she had the boarders, Maxcy and Kellogg, to cook for. Now she opened a bakery in her canvas-covered log shack, baking pies and bread for sale to the miners. It was a profitable undertaking. She had a market weeks in advance for everything she could bake.

Then Nathaniel Maxcy came down with mountain fever—a malady something akin to typhoid, probably caused by polluted water and aggravated by bad whisky and the high altitude. Augusta was the only woman in the camp and she acted as nurse and physician to the boarder while he lay near death in the wagon. Another miner suffering from a gunshot wound was brought to her to receive the care of a woman's gentle hand, so now she was practically running a hospital with her bakery and boardinghouse, to say nothing of the sickly baby needing almost constant care.

The Chicago Creek claim didn't pan out to suit Tabor, so he took another in the vicinity of Gregory Gulch where shacks already were strung out for five miles. There men were living in the utmost squalor, so excited over prospects that they couldn't take time to wash and wore the same clothing night and day until the flannel shirts and jeans fell off their bodies in rags. There was no time to dispose of garbage. The vitalizing mountain air reeked with refuse. Swarms of flies were everywhere and the miners died in droves from dysentery, pneumonia, typhoid, and other diseases. Had men been forced to work under such conditions in a prison camp it would have been a scandal the press of America would have relished spreading over their front pages. But these miners were prisoners only of their own greed for gold, and the press itself was so fascinated by the thought of millions in glittering yellow metal that the ghastly aspects of the camp were virtually overlooked.

One day a strange trio rode into Gregory Gulch on mules. There was Horace Greeley, representing his New York *Tribune;* Henry Villard from the Cincinnati *Commercial-Enquirer* and A. D. Richardson of the Boston *Journal.* They wanted to see for themselves what Colorado gold mining was like.

Greeley demanded in his squeaky voice, "Is there really gold in quantities here? The readers of the *Tribune* have a right to know."

So a group of miners with true chamber of commerce spirit set out to prove the worth of Gregory Gulch to the great editor. They loaded a shotgun with gold dust and shot it into a marked spot. Then they carefully showed Greeley how to pan it out.

Greeley was convinced. That night he made a speech to the assembled miners in the glare of pitch pine torches. "Gentlemen," he shouted, "I have washed with my own hands and seen with my own eyes, and the news of your rich discovery shall go forth over all the world as far as my newspaper can carry it."

So the gold rush started all over again. Presently there were thousands of prospectors all over the mountains, a few actually finding pay dirt, more growing discouraged and taking jobs at a dollar a day and board, digging in the mines of the more fortunate. Others went to work at trades. Half a dozen blacksmiths found financial independence by sharpening miners' picks at fifty cents apiece.

There was a young cobbler named W. L. Douglas who opened a shop below Gregory Gulch in a settlement named for the mystery man, "Black Hawk," and Douglas made enough pegging shoes to start a shoe factory back east and to become rich as a manufacturer. There was another young man named George Pullman who made a large enough stake in Gregory Gulch to allow him to perfect his invention of a sleeping car.

H. A. W. Tabor, however, did not have to go to work for others, although he had no stake. Although he found almost no gold, he did not have to set up a stone-cutting establishment in order to make a living. The demand for Augusta Tabor's pies and bread was growing, so Horace was able to devote all his energies to prospecting and to dreaming of the time when he would be a millionaire. He had one claim, but he wanted many others. He wanted to find a claim richer than those of Gregory and Russell, so he didn't waste much time at the arduous toil of shoveling sand and washing it. It was more exciting to roam through the gulches sampling the sand here and there, for one never knew what moment he might uncover a bonanza.

As autumn came on, a prospector who talked as if he knew his Rocky Mountains warned Tabor of the danger of snowslides and urged him to take his wife and child back to the plains for the winter. So Tabor took Augusta and the baby down to Denver and found a shack for them in live in. Then he returned to Payne's Bar and discovered the mountain-wise prospector had jumped his claim.

In disgust, Tabor went down the cañon to rejoin Augusta who was busily baking pies and bread in Denver. Augusta acquired a stock of provisions and other supplies and opened a general store in their shack. She also took in some more boarders while Horace put in the winter dreaming large daydreams, playing a little poker, and drinking a little liquor.

In the spring when the oxen again were yoked for the journey into the mountains, Tabor turned south, away from the Clear Creek settlements—away from

Gregory Gulch and Chicago Creek and Central City and Payne's Bar.

The surface gold was playing out in that district. The gold business had resolved itself into the slow toil of hacking out quartz by primitive methods. That was too tedious for H. A. W. Tabor and too slow also, for most of the prospectors and placer miners who made the initial Clear Creek discoveries.

Gregory sold his claim for $21,000, went back to Georgia, spent his money, and finally returned to Colorado to roam over the mountains looking vainly for more gold. Jackson went to the South Park district and was killed by a gunshot.

The Tabors went south and in the shadow of snow-crested Pikes Peak labored over Ute Pass and west across the green mountain valley of South Park. They traveled so slowly up the grade that at night Tabor frequently could see the smoke of his last campfire below him. Such almost criminal carelessness on the part of early gold seekers explains why so much of the mining country now is barren of trees.

Across the valley, they struggled upward again and over Trout Creek Pass and then down to the Arkansas River, rippling crystal clear in the sunshine near the present town of Buena Vista. They followed the Arkansas upstream until they came to a small creek at the site of the present hamlet of Granite, about twenty miles below Leadville. Here they pitched camp and here Tabor found better color than he ever had found before.

He made sluice boxes with riffle boards in the bottom and tried to wash out the gold. But the sand was peculiar. It was blackish and heavier than sand had any right to be. The sand would hang to the crease in the gold pan. It would stick to the cleats of the sluice boxes.

Tabor felt almost positive that this queer sand was

heavy because of its gold content and he wished he had some quicksilver to put along the sluice-box cleats. He took a spadeful of sand to the camp and Augusta sifted it with her fingers all day, examining each small dab with a magnifying glass. There was gold, lots of gold in that sand, but they couldn't pick it out grain by grain.

So the Tabors packed up and moved on to get away from the heavy sand. They left millions lying behind them there in Cache Creek.

They now were traveling through high country— about 10,000 feet above sea level—a valley with towering mountains on each side. Going north up the Arkansas, to the left was the sharp peak of Mt. Elbert, the highest mountain in Colorado, and just beyond was the astonishing bulk of Mt. Massive, only a few feet lower than Elbert.

At that time, before the repeated forest fires had devastated the slopes, the country was a paradise of timber for more than a thousand feet above the valley— timber line being about 11,500 feet there. The country was alive with game—elk, deer by herds, beaver in the creeks, mountain sheep in the rocks above the trees, and all manner of predatory beasts preying on them all.

The air was intoxicating. But a man could not swing a pick long at this altitude until he became acclimated.

Slowly, the Tabors moved on upstream. Because of occasional cliffs and shoulders of granite running into the river, they were forced to cross the swift current several times. Once as they crossed the wagon slipped from a rock ledge into a pool and the wagon bed floated off the running gear, bearing Augusta and the baby downstream. The wagon bed spun rapidly end for end and swept under some overhanging trees. Desperately, Augusta grabbed a branch and clung to it with one hand, holding the baby with the other, until Tabor could plunge in and rescue the pair of them. A few hundred yards downstream the wagon bed, now filled with water, ran aground and Tabor reclaimed it and his cargo of supplies.

All the next day they traveled, looking for a likely prospect creek. And as evening approached the Tabors heard shots ahead. The shots seemed to be signals of some sort, so Tabor fired his gun in reply. There were more shots and then the yells of men.

Deer and elk crashed through the brush and took to the hills. Then the Tabors sighted a column of smoke ahead and they began to wonder if there was a forest fire. They began to wonder if they had better turn back.

Presently a party of men appeared on the trail above them. They were whooping at the top of their voices and now and then firing pistols in the air. When the celebrants sighted the Tabor wagon they rushed up and told Horace and Augusta the news, shouted out drunkenly the whole story which they all were sworn to keep secret.

A few days earlier two groups of prospectors from over Georgetown and Gregory Gulch way had met along the Arkansas and camped together. One group, headed by William Jones, was from Iowa originally. The other group was composed of Georgians, veterans of Green Russell's gang, headed by a former Virginian named Abe Lee.

The country looked likely and they decided each gang should select a gulch and prospect it. Should one party find gold in paying quantities they should announce it to the other gang by building a fire and discharging firearms.

The Iowans took a small cañon now known as Big Evans Gulch. The Georgians went up the watercourse immediately to the south. Abe Lee's party camped a short way up this cañon and Lee himself decided to make a test at once. He shoveled some dirt into his pan and washed it. Then he pawed his finger in the debris and blinked his eyes. Lee was a veteran not only of Russell Gulch, but of the California gold rush of 1849, so he knew his pay dirt when he saw it. Abe Lee blinked his eyes at what he saw in his pan and then let out a war whoop. "By God, boys!" he yelled. "This here is California!"

Thus was California Gulch named. And in the next twenty years nearly $20,000,000 in placer gold was washed from this little cañon.

The Tabors joined in the celebration with a will— at least Horace did—and they moved into California Gulch with the Georgians and the Iowans, who had abandoned Evans Gulch without even making a test. Horace staked out a claim and put up a shanty of logs to shelter Augusta and the baby. So certain was he that they should find their fortune here, that their days of wandering were over, he sawed up the wagon lumber for furniture and butchered the work-worn oxen for food.

Augusta had a stock of dried apples with her supplies and now, having beef, she took in some more boarders and the Tabors were established as people of importance in the new community of Oro, as they named the settlement. Augusta was the only white woman within a hundred miles. Little Maxcy was the only child.

Tabor went to work with his pan and sluice boxes and by the end of the summer had $5,000 worth of gold cached in tin cans in the cabin. He, however, accumulated only a fraction of the amount some others washed out—either because their claims were richer or because they worked harder. Tabor had the only pair of scales in the camp and Augusta kept a record of the gold panned. She wrote down that one claim produced $80,000 that summer.

It was inevitable that news of the strike should reach the plains and inevitable that a great rush to the upper Arkansas should follow. More than ten thousand persons were camping in California Gulch and vicinity before frost. A Methodist church was there, dozens of saloons, gambling houses, brothels, and stores were scattered up the cañon before the summer of 1860 was well along.

The richest claim in the gulch was held by two mountain rats named Jack Ferguson and Pete Wells. Each day they washed out a buckskin pouch of gold. And each night Ferguson and Wells scattered what they had washed out—probably more than $1,000.

Jack Ferguson and Pete Wells were such distinguished citizens that a canny businessman built a combined saloon, gambling house, and brothel up the gulch on the edge of the Ferguson-Wells claim to save the boys the trouble of walking down the gulch for their nightly debauch. The boys were appreciative of this thoughtfulness. All the boys were appreciative of the luxuries brought to their door.

One prostitute known only as Red Stocking left the gulch that fall with $100,000 and an announced intention of reforming and settling down to enjoy the fruits of her summer's ordeal.

Meanwhile there were developments elsewhere in the territory. Denver was growing to the dignity of a regular, organized city and other towns were springing up.

Down at the east end of Ute Pass, where the Tabors had passed on their way to California Gulch, a settlement had sprung up around some hot springs. The settlement was called Colorado City because of the red rock in the vicinity.

Ambitious settlers of the mountain region, which still was a part of Kansas Territory, attempted as early as 1859 to form not a new territory, but a full-fledged state. They wrote a constitution for the State of Jefferson, but couldn't convince Congress that there should be a state in that mountain wilderness.

Colorado City, at the foot of Pikes Peak, then sent its own delegate or lobbyist to petition Congress to form a mountain territory and name it Colorado. This was a shrewd plot. It was suspected, if the new territory were called Colorado, that Colorado City, being virtually in the center of the region, would become the capital.

But besides Jefferson there were other names which had strong backing for the proposed territory. There were Columbus and Lafayette and Franklin and Colona and especially Idaho, which meant Mountain Jewel in the Indian language.

Finally, however, the Colorado City lobbyist won out. When Congress on February 26, 1861, passed the bill forming a new territory from parts of Kansas, Utah, New Mexico, and Nebraska, Colorado was selected for the name. The psychological plot of Colorado City was successful further, for, with selection of the territory's name, Colorado City became the capital.

William Gilpin of Missouri was appointed territorial governor and the territorial legislature was called for a session on July 7, 1862. The legislators, flannel-shirted and bearded and booted, went to the capital city mostly on horseback and when they arrived they discovered the civic spirit and enterprise of the Colorado City leaders had waned sadly once the capitol was obtained. There were no accommodations for the lawmakers; they were obliged to camp under the trees. They met in a log cabin where there were neither desks, paper, pens and ink, nor an adequate supply of whisky.

For two days the legislature met and grumbled there. Then they adopted a resolution to move the capitol to Denver where there were beds and writing material and enough liquor with which a legislative body could be operated. Colorado City complained bitterly that the legislature had exceeded its authority in moving the territorial capitol so summarily, but no one paid much attention and Denver thus became capital of Colorado.

When the winter of 1860-61 came most of the California Gulchers left Oro City, which almost overnight had become the most prominent mining camp in the state. Winter is bitter up there two miles above the sea and it is virtually impossible to do business with a placer mine when the thermometer is 20° to 30° below zero.

The Tabors were among those who left. It took them two weeks to reach Denver by stage, a journey one can make with an automobile in a few hours. There were five or six thousand dollars in the Tabor poke now, more money than Horace had ever seen. So Augusta took a trip back to visit her family in Maine and Horace stayed in Denver, making friends and playing poker and drinking.

Denver was a wild, wild town by then, overrun by brigands, swindlers, promoters, gamblers, come-on girls, and plain crib women. Gold dust was legal tender. The buyer would pour a pinch of dust on the bar and if the pinch looked sufficient to pay for the round, the bartender brushed it off into a dustpan. Usually it was a rule of the thumb matter but usually, also, the saloon got twice the value of the drinks—sometimes ten times the value if the patron was drunk enough.

In the saloon there would be poker tables and roulette and faro and red dog and along one side of the room a long bench presided over by the keno caller and his goose. Farther back was the dance hall with red-stockinged come-on gals. Upstairs were the bedrooms.

During this period Tabor became acquainted with a man named David H. Moffat who was running a stationery and book shop in Denver. And Moffat was to play a large part in the history of Colorado also, although not particularly around the valley of the Arkansas.

When Augusta returned to Denver from Maine she didn't fold her hands and wait for spring. She opened a boardinghouse again and made back at least as much money as she had spent on her trip. She convinced Tabor that they should open a store up in California Gulch and she bought supplies for it with their diminishing stock of dust.

The Civil War started that spring, but it caused little stir in California Gulch. The Georgians and the Iowans worked side by side during the day and got drunk side by side at night. At the other end of the Arkansas River passions were aflame and neighbor was arrayed against neighbor—as the fancy writers have it—but even Tabor had practically forgotten his enlistment in Boston with the Free-Soilers, had practically forgotten his meeting with old John Brown in Kansas and his alignment with the Jayhawkers. Why get excited about a war when there is gold to be dug?

But Augusta's store prospered more than Horace's mining claim in the summer of 1861. There was more of that heavy, dark sand which had clogged Tabor's sluice boxes on Cache Creek. And because he had taken his claim at the top of a waterfall, much of his gold washed downstream to be panned out by those lucky playboys, Ferguson and Wells.

Other claims began to play out and once the downturn started it progressed rapidly. Miners deserted California Gulch by ones and twos and presently by platoons. Finally Ferguson and Wells couldn't pan out enough in the day to put on more than a second-degree debauch at night, so, penniless, they struck out over the Mosquito Range. Sad days had come upon Oro City.

It wasn't long, however, before a report drifted over the ridge that the playboys had struck it rich again. They had found a bonanza near a settlement called Buckskin Joe.

Immediately the rush was on from California Gulch. The saloons were abandoned. The Tabors packed their store goods into their two new wagons and the migration over the Mosquito Range was on.

Miners leveled off the trail for the Tabors and they made shelters for Augusta and her little boy at night. They liked the lusty, backslapping Horace and they liked his thin little wife too. She had given them credit at the store when they needed it and she had nursed many of them, also, when they were ill or wounded.

So they built up the town of Buckskin Joe and the Tabors succeeded in getting the post office for their store. The saloons came and the gamblers and the prostitutes. And the Tabors stayed in Buckskin Joe six years.

In those six years Horace worked more than twenty claims, but little or no gold found its way into his pouch. It was Augusta's store that kept the family in bacon and beans.

Before the Buckskin Joe placer mines began to play out and the drift started back over the Mosquitoes, there were about six thousand persons in the town. By 1870 the place was entirely abandoned. The neighboring camp of Fairplay held on longer and it still is a town of about two hundred population.

When there no longer was need for a store and post office at Buckskin Joe, the Tabors were discouraged.

Nine years they had been in Colorado, undergoing great hardships, living always in hope of a great strike. Now they were broke once more and they had no real prospects of ever being otherwise.

CHAPTER FIVE

Lead Carbonates

IN THE dark days of Buckskin Joe's decline the Tabors recalled California Gulch. They knew there still were fifty or sixty miners around old Oro City rocking out a modicum of gold from the heavy sands. And they had heard of a new minor strike farther up the ravine. Suppose there was no chance of wealth at Oro City. Suppose Tabor at last must forget his glittering dreams and come down to earth. At least they might make a living in California Gulch with a store and post office.

So back over the rocky Mosquitoes they traveled, found a good-sized abandoned shack, and moved in with their store shelves and counters.

Tabor was digusted with mining. He was forty years old and it was becoming less fun to swing a pick all day than it had been ten years before. And Tabor never had been one to enjoy manual labor. He devoted himself to the post office, to waiting on the few customers who came into the store, and to playing poker with some luck and skill. Augusta, as usual, took in boarders.

In this manner the Tabors lived there in crumbling Oro City for ten long years more.

Day after day for ten years the sun came up over the Mosquitoes, swung its short course across the zenith and sank behind the Sawatch Range. And the winters came with their blizzards. And the springs came with their freshets and big mountain bluebirds. And the graying miners hacked and shoveled and washed by day and drank bad whisky and sang old songs by night.

It was a primitive life with no conveniences at all, but Augusta was fairly content. True, their businesses—the store, the post office, the boarders—brought them only a bare living, but at least there was none of the dangerous and disquieting hurly-burly of a boom camp.

Despite his delicate childhood, the boy Maxcy was growing into a sturdy youth. Augusta wanted to send the boy to school in Denver. Horace objected. The lad could be a lot of assistance around the store and incidentally could be learning business. Most school education was nonsense, anyhow.

"Pshaw," said Augusta, "maybe you're willing to let your son grow up an ignoramus, but I won't stand for it. I can do all the work Maxcy would do in my spare time."

So Maxcy went to school in Denver.

As the years went by Horace developed the rambling garrulousness of an old mountainman, talking long and often to customers about the many times he had come within a gnat's eyebrow of being a millionaire. The margin had been considerably larger than a gnat's eyebrow, but his auditors accepted his estimate and matched Tabor's tales with their own.

All this time there was talk about another boom coming to California Gulch and the upper Arkansas valley. Such talk was inevitable, but deep down no one really believed it.

The annual gold output of California Gulch had dwindled to about $20,000 a year instead of the millions produced in 1860 and 1861. The cabins and buildings of the old prosperous days were falling apart and two prospectors with an idea tore down the wreckage of an abandoned saloon to pan $2,000 from the dirt under the floor—dust that carelessly had been let fall through the cracks when times were good.

When the greatest boom of them all came to the upper Arkansas, Tabor and his cronies were living lazily in the past. Horace was nearly fifty and had put on a good deal of weight. He had quit dreaming of great wealth and power.

One of his friends was an old mountain rat like himself, a veteran of the Gregory Gulch days of 1859. His name was Stevens—Uncle Billy Stevens, he was called. A careful placer man, Uncle Billy was making his living panning out abandoned dumps of the flush days.

Stevens was a friendly man, in his cups or out, and when a stranger came one day to the gulch Stevens showed him all the hospitality in his power. This stranger's name was A. B. Wood. He was from the Lake Superior region and he knew his metals.

Uncle Billy Stevens took Wood into partnership and the two, moved by Wood's energy, built some new sluice boxes and essayed to make some money.

"Biggest trouble," said Uncle Billy to his new partner, "is this damn heavy sand. Clogs up the sluice boxes. Lots of times it's most ornery right where there's best pay dirt, too."

He gave Wood a demonstration.

"Hmm," said Wood, looking over a sample. "Got any idea what this stuff is?"

Stevens shook his head and pawed his whiskers. "No," he said, "only I reckon it's got lead in it. Heard tell of fellers melting it with a blowtorch to make bullets out of."

Wood took a sample of the heavy sand and sent it to Harrison's smelter in St. Louis for assay. And that was the beginning of real prosperity for the upper Arkansas region. The heavy sand proved to be lead carbonates, running at least $400 a ton in silver.

Up to that time about $50,000,000 in gold had been taken from the Colorado mountains. But ten times that in silver was destined to be mined from this region at the foot of Mt. Massive.

With the new rush business began to boom again at the Tabor store in California Gulch. The Harrison smelter people of St. Louis erected a branch near Oro City. The Wood-Stevens mine was producing wealth at a great rate and other mines were running in a month. Uncle Billy Stevens got drunk and sold his holdings for a few thousands. Wood sold out for $50,000, but could have made millions had he held to the property. Abe Lee came back to his original gold discovery and struck it rich in silver. Scores of teamsters, sawmill hands, and roustabouts became rich almost overnight.

Tabor, however, had lost his ambition. He did no prospecting. He no longer had faith in his luck and he was making a good profit from his store and his wife's boarders. And it was an easier life than digging silver ore with a pick and grinding it up to the surface with a windlass, locally known as an "armstrong."

The Tabors did move down the gulch, however, and opened a new store and four-room hotel in the new section of the revived Oro City, which with a population of about three hundred was renamed Leadville after the lead carbonates that brought the boom. The genial storekeeper, Horace Austin Warner Tabor, was elected mayor.

The mayor played a good deal of poker in his store. He played a good game, too, and many of the miners who came in to win a week's supply of groceries left without the groceries and without their pokes.

One day a couple of German cobblers named George Hook and August Rische came into the store followed by a lean and hungry dog. They were ragged and un-shorn and plaintive. They had come over the Mosquitoes from Fairplay and, they said, they had made a rich silver strike at some indefinite spot on the trail. They wanted Tabor to grubstake them for a third interest in their mine.

Tabor was playing poker and didn't want to be disturbed. They pleaded with him. "We already tried a lot of other fellers," Hook said. "Ed Harrison at the smelter, he kind of promised, but he got sick and we might starve to death waiting for him. Be an awful thing to starve to death when Gus and me has got a million dollar mine."

"I'll call that bet and raise you a blue," said Tabor.

"You mean you'll give us a stake?" asked Rische.

"Naw," said Tabor. "I was just talking to Fred here."

"I pass," said Fred. "Take the pot."

Tabor raked in the chips and started to shuffle the cards.

"We just thought," went on Hook, "that you being mayor and all, you might help us. We don't need much stake. Just a little bit of beans and sowbelly and meal, that's all. And you get a third of a million dollars."

The other poker players laughed.

"Oh, hell's afire," said Tabor, "quit bothering me when I'm busy. Go help yourselves and leave me a list on the counter."

So Hook and Rische helped themselves liberally from the shelves and bins and made out a careful list. Under the counter Rische spied some jugs of whisky. He lifted one out tentatively and glanced at Tabor. Horace A. W. was busy with his cards. So on the bottom of the list Rische scrawled, "Whisky, 1 jug," and with their arms full of provisions and the jug, the two cobblers stumped out the door.

"Much obliged to you, Mr. Tabor," they called.

"Don't forget," said Tabor. "I got a third interest in a million dollars."

The poker players laughed and Hook and Rische swore they wouldn't forget.

Up the trail went the two ragged prospectors, happy with their stake and with their jug of whisky. But the sun was blazing hot and their burdens made them pant as they climbed. They came to the brow of a hill and in the shade of a clump of pines they sat down to rest and to sample Tabor's whisky.

They drank to "Good Old Tabor" once, twice and

again, and they admired the view of Mt. Massive and of the pine-clad hills. Then they drank to Good Old Tabor once more and Rische remarked, "You know, George, this here under the trees is loads nicer than our damn old prospect hole."

"Hell of a lot nicer," agreed Hook. "No trees at our prospect hole."

"I like trees," observed Rische. "I love trees and I love good old Tabor. Let's have a drink to trees and good old Tabor."

So they had another drink and then Hook said, "I don't see no use going way up to our prospect hole. This looks awful nice here under the trees. Let's do our

mining right here and I bet we get millions, just millions right here."

The two cobblers staggered to their feet and with pick and shovel started digging in the shade of the beautiful trees.

And the hole the drunken Rische and Hook dug at random became the Little Pittsburgh mine. In a few weeks it was producing $20,000 worth of ore a week and Hook sold his share for $100,000, invested it in government bonds, bought a farm in eastern Colorado and increased his wealth. Rische hung on a little longer until he had made $145,000 from ore and sold his share of the mine for $265,000. Then he went to Denver and opened a saloon. For a while he prospered, but liquor and bad investments ruined him. Down and out, old friends finally got him a job as watchman at the state capitol.

Did the cobblers forget "Good Old Tabor" who grubstaked them with a few dollars' worth of groceries and a jug of whisky? They did not. Tabor got his third share as promised and he sold it to a couple of Denver bankers for $1,000,000 in cash. One of these bankers was David H. Moffat. He was the man, you remember, who was running the little stationery shop in Denver.

Tabor invested a couple of hundred thousand of his million in shares of the Little Pittsburgh mine and when that stock mounted from $5 to $30 in a month or so, he sold and made another million.

By this time there were fifteen thousand persons in Leadville. Harrison Avenue, which is the main street, and Chestnut Avenue, which *was* the main street, and State Street, the red-light thoroughfare, were roaring with activity, vice, and crime.

Tabor, now that he had become wealthy, suddenly lost his apathy. He was leading citizen as well as mayor and postmaster. He built a new brick building to house his store and post office. He bought some broadcloth clothing with Prince Albert coats. He bought stiff-bosomed shirts and plug hats and diamonds and, in his own estimation, he became the most important man in the West. His joyful course down Chestnut Avenue was one of wild arm waving and shouted greetings to acquaintances. The politician in Tabor blossomed into full flower.

There came to Leadville then a boomer by the name of Lovell, generally known over the mountains as Chicken Bill.

Chicken Bill Lovell had a prospect hole that showed nothing but rock of no value to anyone except a mason. Chicken Bill was disconsolate because good fortune didn't come to him as it had come to Tabor and others. He was a little jealous, too, of the ecstasy in Mayor Tabor's face as that dignitary loped over the mud puddles and unassorted garbage in Harrison Avenue. So Chicken Bill got an idea which has become legendary in the Rocky Mountain region.

In the dead of night Chicken Bill went over to the Little Pittsburgh and stole a few sacks of the rich carbonate ore. He took this ore to his own prospect hole and salted it liberally.

The next day Lovell went down to Harrison Avenue and waited until he saw Tabor galloping along, shouting his hullos to everyone in sight. The mayor darted into a saloon and Chicken Bill followed. Pretending to be well along in his cups, Bill began to talk loudly of his rich strike up there on Fryer Hill, by God.

Tabor cocked an ear.

"You," said Chicken Bill belligerently, "think that little old Little Pittsburgh's some mine, don't you?"

Good Old Tabor laughed uproariously. He enjoyed drunks. He slapped Chicken Bill on the back and Chicken

Bill, who didn't have enough money to buy a round of drinks, hiccupped convincingly. "Look it," he said, holding up a chunk of the Little Pittsburgh ore he had stolen the night before. "Little Pittsburgh never had as good ore as that, by God. That's the ore from my Chry—Chrysolite Mine."

Mayor Tabor squinted at the ore. He still didn't know a great deal about mining or he would have recognized the rock as from his own mine. But he did know enough to see it was very rich ore.

"Come with me," he said to Chicken Bill.

"Wait a minute," said Chicken Bill. "No hurry about anything. I'm rich and I want a drink."

"Give this man a drink," Good Old Tabor ordered in his baronial manner, and Chicken Bill tossed off four fingers of bourbon. Then in the mayor's shining new carriage the two rode the short mile out to Fryer Hill and inspected Chicken Bill's prospect hole. Tabor went down in the hole and got his new alligator skin boots muddy. He looked over the broken Little Pittsburgh ore that Chicken Bill had sprinkled around and he grew excited. He came up into the sunshine and slapped Bill on the back again.

"How much you want for that little hole?" Tabor demanded.

Chicken Bill named a figure, still feigning drunkenness, and Tabor immediately wrote a check.

I do not know the amount of that check. Accounts vary greatly. I have heard it was $1,000. I have heard it was $20,000. George F. Willison in *Here They Dug the Gold* says it was $40,000. Henry C. Butler, editor of the Leadville *Herald-Democrat,* believes it was only $900.

Anyhow Chicken Bill hurried to the bank, cashed his check, and left town. And Good Old Tabor hired a gang of miners to start immediate operations on his new

Chrysolite Mine. The men went out to Chicken Bill's prospect hole, took one look at the situation, and rolled on the ground with laughter. They all recognized the Little Pittsburgh rock at once. They saw the hole had been salted and that the joke was on Good Old Tabor.

So a delegation, attempting desperately to suppress hysteria, visited upon Tabor and told him the news. Tabor, the poker player, didn't change expression.

"I didn't hire you fellers," he said, "to make me a report on that there hole. I hired you to sink it. Now get the hell back and start digging."

So the gang went back to Chicken Bill's prospect hole and soberly started digging. They dug for three days, but with no enthusiasm, and they sunk the hole eight or ten feet more. And on the evening of the third day they struck a vein richer even than the ore Chicken Bill had stolen from the Little Pittsburgh.

For more than two years the Chrysolite paid Tabor more than $100,000 a month net. He incorporated the company at $10,000,000 and made a couple more fortunes when the stock rose from $5 to $45 a share.

Frank E. Vaughn, who was a sort of poet laureate of early Leadville, immortalized this incident in verse which was published by the Elks Lodge in a souvenir booklet issued for its 1907 state convention in Leadville.

I believe it would be fitting to reprint Mr. Vaughn's *Ballad of Chicken Bill*, which he characterizes as "Being a truthful recital of an episode on Fryer Hill."

Of course you have read of the wicked ways
Of Leadville town in the early days,
Of the killers and grafters who lived here when
The place was peopled by gambling men,
    When it cost a fortune to eat and sleep,

When life and morals both were cheap,
And one owned all one could get—and keep.

Men who had sifted the golden sands
From the mountain peaks of many lands;
Capitalist, criminal, tenderfoot, tramp,
All drifted into the silver camp.
  By luck, design, or by God's will,
  There lived in a shack on Fryer Hill
  A prospector known as Chicken Bill.

This was way back in 'seventy-nine,
When every claim was a paying mine,
When money and suckers both were thick,
And prospectors sold without stroke or pick.
  Then the boys and the camp were thoroughbred,
  One got drunk and painted the other red,
  And maybe wound up half filled with lead.

This Chicken Bill was a queer old cuss,
Who worked away without making a fuss,
Sinking a hole on Fryer Hill
With pick and shovel and iron will.
  But he had a mild and simple look
  With a face you could read like an open book
  And a handshake that couldn't be mistook.

Bill's shaft was down some seventy feet
In a wash formation hard to beat
With one man twisting an old armstrong,
His work was hard and his hours were long;
  When Hook and Rische and Tabor found
  The Pittsburgh bonanza lying around,
  With dollars almost on top of the ground.

Old Chicken Bill went down to look
At the prospect opened by Rische and Hook,
Chloride ore of the finest kind,
And every seam was "shamrock" lined.
  He looked it over and opened his eyes
  At sight of the dazzling silver prize,
  But he said nothing—for Bill was wise.

That night as he lay on his lonely bed
On the old hillside in the dirt-thatched shed
A brilliant thought flashed through his brain
Which he sifted over and over again.
  For Bill had learned in bygone days
  Sundry and various crooked ways,
  And he said, "Everything's right that pays."

Three shifts were working on the jump
Piling the ore on the Pittsburgh dump,
Thousands of dollars were lying there,
And millions more below to spare.
  Bill took a few sacks of the Pittsburgh ore,
  Just what he needed—not a bit more;
  It never was missed from the bountiful store.

Things were doing 'round his shaft that night
In the pallid glare of the old moon's light,
And when he had finished he softly laughed
There was lots of ore in old Bill's shaft—
  Ore in the dump and lying around,
  Ore like the Little Pittsburgh found,
  Ore on top and underground.

Next day when Tabor came on the hill
He went to see old Chicken Bill
He found him sitting on the dump
With a microscope on a dam' rich lump.

Now Tabor didn't know it all,
But it was a big bluff he wouldn't call,
So he bought out Chicken Bill—that's all.

Nine hundred dollars, so they say,
Was the price that Tabor had to pay
(I may be wrong, or I may be right)
For a quit-claim deed to the Chrysolite.
  Out of the country went Chicken Bill
  Leaving Tabor with a mighty good will—
  And the "wash" hole up on Fryer Hill.

Some stories have sequels, so they say,
And when Tabor went up the following day
He wasn't feeling so very fine,
For he found he had purchased a salted mine.
  Salted, as I have said before,
  From the Pittsburgh dump with Tabor's ore—
  'Twas enough to make a man feel sore.

But Tabor had money and Tabor had sand,
With a world of faith at his command,
He put that shaft down ten feet more,
And this time Tabor got the ore!
  Three million dollars was what he made,
  After the trick the smooth man played—
  And that was because he always STAYED!

Now just a word about Tabor's ways
From one who knew him in bygone days:
His heart and bank account were big,
He stood by his friends and didn't renege.
  He was the man who won renown
  By making a city of Denver town,
  Before the parasites threw him down.

Times have changed—hair turned gray,
And many old timers have passed away.
The bad man has gone to his final rest
From the silver camp of the Golden West.
    Exit Tabor and Chicken Bill,
    But over there is Fryer Hill
    Quietly producing millions still.

The price Tabor paid Chicken Bill for the " 'wash' hole up on Fryer Hill" probably was either $1,000 or $900, rather than the larger sums mentioned. A few weeks before this incident Marshall Field of Chicago, destined to become a "merchant prince," had heard of H. A. W. Tabor's good fortune and alleged acumen and Field wrote Tabor a friendly letter of congratulation. He enclosed a check for $500, asking Tabor to "cut him in" on a good mining proposition if he saw a chance. So Good Old Tabor cut Field in on the Chicken Bill purchase, supposedly for a half interest, and a year or so later Field sold his interest in the Chrysolite for $700,000.

Meanwhile Tabor bought the famous Matchless Mine for $117,000 and spent another $100,000 straightening up claims against it. Metallurgists advised Tabor against this, declaring the mine never would pay. But the Tabor luck was the despair of metallurgists and the Tabor luck ran true to form once more, for the Matchless proved to be one of the richest silver mines in the world.

Tabor bought a dozen or more other mines and interests in mines and the money rolled in so fast that neither Tabor nor Augusta could begin to keep track of it.

CHAPTER SIX

Lawless Leadville

AUGUSTA TABOR was worried. Horace, drunken with joy, was slipping out of her control. There was too much celebrating with champagne. And too often he would come home like a conquering hero and announce blandly that he had just bought this or that property for more thousands of dollars than thrifty Augusta ever hoped to own. Vehemently, she urged Tabor to go slow. Vehemently, she put her foot down, but Horace had the bit in his teeth and nothing could stop him kicking up his heels.

For the first time in her life Augusta had a "hired girl" to do her housework. For the first time since she came west she had no boarders to cook for. Tabor bought diamonds for her and silken gowns, but she detested gaudy display. She went to a few of Good Old Tabor's parties at first, but she deeply disapproved wanton waste and drunkenness, and when she couldn't exert a calming influence on her husband she simply quit attending his parties.

Augusta worried about his generosity. He might work sharp business deals, but he would give money to anyone who asked for it. He contributed huge sums to the state Republican party. He contributed to every charitable agency he heard about and, as his fame was spreading over the nation by the daily press, he received hundreds of begging letters.

The Reverend Thomas Uzzell rode up from Denver in a jam-packed stage that nearly went over a cliff, and he started a little Methodist church in the roaring silver camp. He needed money for numerous things, of course, especially for a chandelier which would permit evening services. So he went to Mayor Tabor for a contribution.

"How much you need?" demanded Tabor.

The pastor hesitated. He had had experience with businessmen before and he decided it would be sensible to make a large request and then be glad to come down to what he expected.

"Well, Mr. Tabor," said the Reverend Mr. Uzzell, "we really need a hundred dollars."

"Oh, no," said Good Old Tabor, "you can't get a bang-up chandelier for a hundred dollars. Leadville folks deserve the best that can be got. Here's five hundred dollars and you get a real good chandelier. And I want you to get the best damn chandelier player in the state to play on it, too."

The sprawling town of wooden buildings and shacks was in grave danger of a fire, so Tabor bought a fine red fire engine and uniforms for the firemen. The name "Tabor" was on the fire engine and on the chests of the fire laddies also.

With that, the empire-building mania really captured Tabor. Leadville needed a town hall, so Mayor Tabor couldn't be bothered with asking the Council for an appropriation and waiting for a bond issue and what not. He built the town hall himself. He built a three-story brick structure to house the Tabor Grand Opera House, the finest theater between Chicago and San Francisco. He built in his own mind, also, a paternalistic god whose name was Horace Tabor.

Meanwhile Leadville was growing in population

and wickedness. It is probable no community in America ever has seen at the same time such lavish, medieval orgies and such extremes of poverty and privation. There have been other tough towns in America, but certainly nowhere were viciousness and crime more uncontrolled.

Strange characters gathered there from every point of the compass in such numbers that a normally rational and circumspect man was almost strange by comparison.

There was an odd character named James Ellis, better known as "Broken Nose Scotty," who was not at all unusual in Leadville. In such a community it would be impossible to pick a typical citizen, but if Broken Nose Scotty were not typical of Leadville, he at least was far from being unique.

Scotty had a claim on Carbonate Hill, and when his claim began to show signs of richness Scotty celebrated by getting very drunk and waking up in jail broke. With no money to pay his fine, he was serving out his $20 assessment at a dollar a day behind bars.

The manager of one of the big mining companies

investigated Ellis's claim meanwhile, found it had good prospects. So the executive went to the town lockup and asked the jailer to see James Ellis.

"Got nobody by that name here," said the jailer.

"You must have. He's a little Scotsman with a crooked nose."

"Oh, you must mean Broken Nose Scotty," the jailer observed and brought Scotty out for inspection.

Scotty admitted his name was James Ellis and admitted he owned a claim on Carbonate Hill.

"I'll give you thirty thousand cash for your claim," the operator offered, "if you'll come with me right away to my lawyers and make out the papers."

"Price is good," said Scotty. "But the other conditions ain't so good—unless you pay up my fine and get me out of this hole."

So the operator paid the $16 or $17 yet remaining of the fine and Scotty signed the papers and got his $30,000.

With this young fortune in his pockets Scotty stalked from the lawyers' office back to the jail smoking a fifty-cent cigar.

"I want," he said arrogantly to the jailer, "to pay off the fines of every son of a bitch in jail. Call the judge right now."

That was agreeable to the judge and agreeable to the jailbirds too, so presently Scotty strutted into Harrison Avenue followed by twenty-odd ex-prisoners. First he led his platoon into the May Store and bought each man a new outfit of clothing from hat to shoes. Then he presented each with a $10 gold piece. And next they paraded into the Saddle Rock for dinner on Scotty—a dinner with champagne.

By midnight virtually all the celebrants were back in jail. But not Scotty. He had plenty of money to pay his fine for being drunk and disorderly. He paid it and then he said to Magistrate John R. Curley, "Judge, I want to pay the fines of all these other fellers too. I got 'em in this time and I'm going to get 'em out again."

Following this party Scotty left for his homeland to visit his Scotch mother. He left several thousand dollars with her and then came back to Leadville without a dime in his pockets. He died penniless while prospecting in Wyoming.

At this time there were forty thousand persons in Leadville and housing facilities for perhaps five thousand. Forty thousand had climbed over the mountains on foot and by stage and on horseback, hoping and counting on quick wealth. The main thing was to get to Leadville. After that things would be easy—they fondly believed.

Even these days of fine mountain roads, you know you've been someplace if you drive to Leadville in the winter. The snow lies heavy on the mountain passes and there are sudden blinding storms that can't be forecast.

In those days the way to Leadville was over narrow, rutty wagon roads that clung precariously to the edges of 1,000-foot cliffs, slippery with ice and snow for seven or eight months of the year and almost impassable with mud for two months.

These forty thousand adventurers had traveled a hundred miles through that sort of country and hundreds of them died at the end of their journey without earning a dollar.

In the bitter winter of 1878-79 thousands of men slept in tents, in half-built log cabins, in sheds, in privies, and jammed tightly together on the floors of saloons, gambling halls, and brothels.

There is a saying that pneumonia is the curse of the high altitudes and that saying originated in Leadville. Perhaps the altitude *did* have something to do with it, for

even now physicians frequently rush pneumonia patients
to a lower altitude from the high country. But, living as
these men did, hundreds would have died of pneumonia
even if their camp had been at the mouth of the Arkansas
instead of the source.

Exhausted from breaking through the mountain
passes, the men would hurry to the warmth and levity of
resorts along State Street and Harrison Avenue and drink
quantities of extremely bad whisky. There is another old
saying to the effect that high altitude increases the
potency of whisky about 30 per cent—and that saying is
not a superstition.

After taking on a cargo of liquor the newcomers
either went outside in temperatures 20° to 40° below
zero to sleep in a drafty shack colder than a snow igloo
or huddled together on the saloon floor breathing fetid
air that would gag a snake.

In the morning the saloon porters would clear the
floor of sleepers and each day there were several who
couldn't rise. Some of them would be too far gone with
pneumonia to get up. Some of them would be dead.

There were many men, however, who couldn't even
sleep on the floor of a comparatively warm saloon. Some
saloons charged a nominal fee for sleeping privileges.
Most of them required only that the bar be patronized.
But if a man had no money at all he couldn't patronize
the bar or pay for sleeping space either.

Strong-arm artists, sluggers, and gunmen were lurking in the shadows everywhere in Leadville. In some of
the worst houses of prostitution thugs were sold the concession of robbing those prosperous-looking strangers
who were not drunk enough to be "rolled" by the girls.

A holdup victim might complain to the so-called
police department, which was composed of some of the
worst characters ever to grace any law-enforcement

agency. If the victim was loud in his indignation, the police would throw him in jail as a material witness and hold him there until inactivity got on his nerves and he was glad to drop the case. But in jail he at least had a place to sleep. Otherwise, a man who had lost all his money to a gunman had to walk all night or find a shed

to crawl into. It was not at all uncommon for a Leadville householder to find a frozen man on his premises in the morning.

From nightfall until after midnight the high board sidewalks along Harrison Avenue and State Street were so crowded that a pedestrian with a destination usually took to the road. For years not a night passed without several shooting scrapes and dozens of robberies. No one, except ignorant newcomers and the foolhardy, ever ventured out at night unarmed. From dusk to dawn not an hour passed without the reverberating banging of pistols —usually in the spirit of celebration, but often enough in deadly earnest.

No one could estimate the number of murders committed in Leadville during those first silver boom years. It was not necessary to obtain a burial permit for interment of a body. It was not necessary for the coroner to return a verdict in the case of violent death. So in scores, and perhaps in hundreds, of cases the murder victim was casually buried by the murderers.

In 1880, even after things had begun to adjust themselves somewhat in the mold of civilization, in the one month of October, forty men were arrested on forty charges of homicide. Leadville was callous to bloodshed in those days.

There was, however, one murder case across the range in Hinsdale County which shocked even the blasé spirits of Leadville.

A party of six Hinsdale County men started to cross the divide in early winter and were caught in a blizzard. They camped on a plateau near where Lake City now is located and the snow piled to such heights that travel was impossible. Their food was exhausted after a few days and no game was obtainable because of the deep snow.

In this party was a man named Alfred Packer, a tall, wiry fellow with long black hair and an imperial beard. There also was a big, rugged Englishman named Bell and four others named Swan, Miller, Noon, and Humphreys.

The next spring Packer hiked into the town of Saguache, about thirty miles south of the Arkansas River. He was fatter than usual and his pockets were filled with money which he began to distribute freely about the Saguache saloons and resorts.

The six men had been reported lost in the Hinsdale County blizzard, so the Saguache marshal questioned Packer. "What became of those men you were with last fall?" he asked. "What became of Bell and Humphreys and those fellows?"

"Oh, those fellows," said Packer, looking at the marshal with drooping eyes. "Four of 'em went south, but that fellow Noon, he died when he was caught in the storm."

"Where'd you get all this money you're spending?"

Packer grinned. "Made it," he said. "I been working."

That answer seemed incredible, so a posse was sent out to visit Packer's old campsite on the plateau. They took Packer with them and they found what was left of the five men's bodies. They had not been eaten by wild animals. The flesh had been cut carefully by someone acquainted with butchery.

They accused Packer.

"That's right," he said calmly. "I naturally didn't want to tell you. But I'll tell you the whole story now. One day I went floundering out through the snow trying to get a shot at some game and I didn't see a thing. I came back to camp and there was the Englishman Bell alone and he was cooking some meat.

"I says to Bell, 'Where in hell you get that meat?' and he jumped up and rushed at me with a hatchet. We fought all around in the snow and it was either him or me and I finally killed him.

"Then I see the other four was dead and killed by Bell. He'd cut some meat off of Noon and that's what was cooking. There I was with five dead men and me starving and some meat already cooking on the fire. So I tried it and it wasn't so bad if you was hungry enough and kept your mind off it.

"I camped right there until spring, eating the best parts of Noon and Bell and Humphreys and Miller and Swan. Sure, I took their money. No use letting it lay out there, was there?"

They arrested Packer on a charge of murder, but he escaped. He was recaptured in 1883 in Wyoming and brought back to Gunnison for trial.

Feeling ran high against the broad-browed, saturnine Packer and lynching was narrowly averted. A jury found him guilty of murdering his five companions and Judge M. P. Gerry sentenced him to hang on April 14, 1883.

Judge Gerry had a poetic streak in his frontiersman's soul and his legendary words in sentencing Packer to death were reported as follows:

"Alfred Packer, in 1874 you in company with five companions passed through this beautiful mountain valley . . .

"You and your victims had a weary march and, when the shadows of the mountains fell upon your little party and night drew her sable curtain around you, your unsuspecting victims lay down on the ground and were soon lost in the sleep of the weary. And when thus sweetly unconscious of danger from any quarter, and particularly from you, their trusted companion, you cruelly and brutally slew them all.

"I shall pass lightly over the other sickening details of your crime. Enough to say, Alfred Packer, God damn your soul, you have eaten up the Democratic majority in Hinsdale County."

Packer's sentence was commuted to forty years in prison. He served seventeen years and then was released after a campaign in the Denver *Post*. The newspaper contended that Packer really was not convicted of murder, but only of cannibalism. And the extraordinary Fred G. Bonfils, editor of the *Post*, may have felt kindly toward anyone who would eat up a Democratic majority in any Colorado county.

The country north of Lake City where Packer and his companions camped to the nutrition of Packer now is marked on maps as "Cannibal Plateau."

More and more people rushed over the mountains to the stupendous city of Leadville where dollars were reported as free as water . . . more gamblers, more thieves, more pickpockets from eastern cities; more prostitutes, more preachers, more bunko men, more real estate men, more Jews to open stores and pawnshops, more reformers to snatch brands from the burning. All supplies had to be hauled over the Mosquitoes at heavy expense and the storekeepers added 100 per cent as their legitimate profit. Ground space in Leadville jumped from $10 a lot to $5,000 in two years. Store sites which rented for $500 a month in 1878 could have been obtained for nothing a few months previously.

So a new business started for the lawless—lot jumping. They even jumped the lot of the Presbyterian church and frightened the congregation into relinquishing it. They attempted to jump the Catholic church lot, but the priest gathered a hundred or so rough and tough Irish parishioners who put the thugs to flight.

When Marshal O'Connor was shot dead by another peace officer in a brawl, Mayor Tabor decided the town needed a really tough man in the office. So he appointed Martin Duggan, who already had seven notches in his gun. Duggan was tough enough. He shot it out with desperadoes and innocent citizens alike. He jailed Tabor's angel, Gus Rische, for drunkenness, and when the mayor attempted to go Rische's bail, Duggan manhandled Tabor and chased the astonished Midas of the Mountains away from the jail with drawn pistol.

While hundreds of newcomers were working in the established mine shafts as laborers and in the smelters which had sprung up at the south end of town and in the stores and saloons, the prime reason for every newcomer's presence in Leadville was to find a mine of his own. Therefore, most of the men were putting in their time pawing around the hills trying to discover new veins of lead carbonate. These hopefuls more often than not were penniless or soon would be penniless in the hands of grafters and robbers. So, stripped of their resources and starving, the victims of thieves and robbers themselves turned to thievery and to holding up pedestrians at the point of a gun.

This situation brought forth a novel plan from the Leadville *Chronicle*. The editor urged residents to leave their meal boxes open outside the house for the benefit of the destitute.

"Few of these fellows will beg," observed the *Chronicle*. "They have used their last nickel. They know they will have to go down but ten feet more to strike it rich. They do not like to give up or give away their competence for a few mouthfuls of bread."

There was a man named Jack Gallagher who attained distinction by holding up a holdup.

Coming home from his sweetheart's house one night, Gallagher had his girl's watch in his pocket. She had asked him to take it to a jeweler for repair.

Near Gallagher's own home he was held up by a gunman who took Gallagher's purse and his sweetheart's watch. Enraged, Gallagher ran into his house, got his revolver and went hunting. Presently he sighted the robber sauntering along a dark side street; Gallagher slipped around the corner, went down an alley on the run, and confronted the stickup man with drawn pistol.

"Reach for the stars!" commanded Gallagher.

The bandit reached. "Now wait a minute, pardner," he objected. "We ain't getting nowhere this way. Let's talk this thing over and you take one part of town and I'll take the other."

"Listen," said Gallagher, "you know how a cottonwood sluice box leaks?"

"Yes," said the bandit. "Cottonwood ain't at all practical for a sluice box. It warps."

"All right," said Gallagher, "if you don't shut up you're going to leak worse than any cottonwood sluice box you ever saw and it ain't going to be from warping, either."

With that he took his own purse from the bandit and his girl's watch. Then he took the bandit's purse and gun and watch. He traded the robber's watch to the jeweler for a new watch chain for his girl, and became something of a hero for his feat.

Carl Boeckleim, a mild little barber, also became a hero after an encounter with a pair of bandits. Armed with a little .22 revolver, Boeckleim opened fire on the two gunmen, killing one and wounding the other. The wounded man was hanged by vigilantes and citizens carried Boeckleim around town in his barber chair the next morning.

The vigilante committee was organized because of the singular apathy of the courts toward murder. If a slain man had been armed, that was considered sufficient defense for the slayer—and virtually every man in Leadville carried a pistol. So the vigilantes began to take the law in their own hands.

The original vigilantes were what might be called men of the better class. They began to show violent aversion to the gamblers and swindlers, which made night life in Leadville more complicated than ever, for the gamblers and swindlers immediately organized a vigilante committee of their own to wage war on the other vigilantes.

About then the *Chronicle* started a campaign for civic virtue. The campaign was not directed against the general lawlessness nor against the confusion of duplicate vigilante systems. It was against the promiscuous dumping of garbage and filth in the rear of homes and hotels, which, as the *Chronicle* declared, threatened to "depopulate the city." "Today," wrote the editor, "I saw ton after ton of decaying meats and swill in the rear of some of the hotels."

As a result of this campaign, the Council passed an ordinance requiring that manure and garbage be not allowed to lie more than a week. That ordinance caused citizens on the outskirts of the town to rise and form a third vigilante committee because scavengers were coming in the middle of the night and dumping the town offal in the suburbanite's front yards.

The hotel men laughed at the citizens' indignation and inquired what the stench from a little garbage amounted to compared to the sulphuric gases from the smelters and they asserted that, if these people didn't like Leadville, let them go back where they came from.

One of these hotel men was an Irishman named Thomas F. Walsh, who operated the Grand. The Grand and the Clarendon were the best hotels in Leadville.

Walsh finally struck it rich and his daughter Evalyn married Edward B. McLean, wealthy owner of the Washington *Post*, acquired the fabled Hope diamond, paid the arch swindler Gaston Means $105,000 in a vain hope that he could find the kidnaped Lindbergh baby, and wrote her autobiography.

CHAPTER SEVEN

Royal Gorge War

ALL this time the Leadville smelters were throwing flame from their stacks twenty-four hours a day. There were two twelve-hour shifts and the men working at top speed in the punishing heat sometimes fainted and fell into the slag pots. This occurrence was so common that it warranted no more than a two-line item in the newspapers.

And the smelters were melting the rich lead carbonate ore into huge pigs of lead and silver which must be hauled across the mountains and down to Denver to be refined. This transportation was terrible work for both men and mules. In the snowy months the passes often could not be crossed. In the spring and fall the heavy wagons frequently became bogged down. It was killing work and very expensive. Leadville had crying need for a railroad.

H. A. W. Tabor's march of fortune continued at an increased pace. He bought more mines—in Colorado and New Mexico and any place where mines were offered for sale. He bought a half interest in Moffat's bank. He contributed so many thousands of dollars to the support of the Republican party that the party decided it must do something to keep this popeyed cornucopia producing, and Tabor was nominated for lieutenant governor.

Leadville's mayor easily was the most popular man in the mining region, the most genial backslapper in the mountains, the easiest man for any sort of a money touch. He was popular with the miners. He was popular with the gamblers and saloonkeepers. He was popular with the entrepreneurs of prostitution. Because of his liberal donations, he even was popular with the churches.

So Tabor not only was elected lieutenant governor, but his candidacy helped his running mate, Frederick R. Pitkin, become the new state's second governor.

To keep order in Leadville while he was away at the capital, Tabor established a militia organization which he uniformed gorgeously and named the Tabor Light Cavalry. In Denver the lieutenant governor purchased a $40,000 residence and spent another $25,000 redecorating it. Then he brought Augusta down to her new home and was annoyed at her uneasiness in this house of gauds.

Horace took the business of being lieutenant governor very seriously and Governor Pitkin, good politician that he was, found it expedient to be absent from Denver at intervals to allow the lieutenant governor opportunity to decide such ticklish questions as pardoning good Republican criminals from the state penitentiary. Incidentally, during these periods of power, Tabor did initiate several penal reforms such as prison farms and an honor system among the convicts.

Despite all his official duties and all his wide-flung business interests and his social affairs and his new plan to build America's finest theater in Denver, Tabor found time to agitate for a railroad to Leadville.

It was necessary for him only to cultivate the soil, however, for the seeds had been planted long before. For years there had been plans in the minds of at least two gentlemen for a railroad along the Arkansas River up the Royal Gorge and over the mountains.

One of these men was General William J. Palmer, handsome and dapper and mustachioed, head of the little, locally financed Denver & Rio Grande Railroad, which ran from Denver south along the base of the Rockies, following the old Indian and trapper trails—the trail that Green Russell's party took north from the Arkansas when they found color at Cherry Creek.

The other man was William B. Strong, general manager of the Atchison, Topeka & Santa Fe, which had powerful eastern backing.

When the Civil War closed General Palmer became connected with the Kansas Pacific Railroad, which drove a line across the plains from Kansas City to Denver, following generally the course taken by the Tabors when they went west during the gold rush.

General Palmer had been in charge of a reconnaissance for a proposed railroad line following substantially the route taken later by the Santa Fe as far as Pueblo. And as a result of his surveys in 1866, Palmer knew that the Royal Gorge was the only plausible passage through the mountains, and he saw to it that the original federal charter for the Denver & Rio Grande called for construction up this Grand Cañon of the Arkansas. Because of this charter, he believed his westward route was secure. He believed he could take his time about building westward when and if he ever wanted a line through the mountains, so Palmer devoted himself to swinging his road southward toward the Rio Grande.

The general graded his line down to El Moro, near the New Mexico line and surveyed Raton Pass across the mountains that lie along the Colorado border.

Raton Pass, however, was the Atchison, Topeka & Santa Fe's only entrance into New Mexico from Colorado, economically speaking, the only route by which the Sante Fe line could reach Santa Fe.

Strong demanded that the Denver & Rio Grande relinquish Raton Pass, threatening to extend a branch line north and drain off all the Rio Grande's traffic unless he was given uncontested right to Raton Pass.

When General Palmer ignored Strong's threats, the Santa Fe general manager sent out his chief engineer, A. A. Robinson, with a brigade of armed men. On February 25, 1868, Robinson sighted Palmer and a work gang heading south on a Rio Grande train. Robinson rushed ahead and at dawn assembled five hundred riflemen at El Moro, commanding Raton Pass.

Palmer looked over the Santa Fe breastworks. He was good enough soldier to know he couldn't hope to take that position without artillery—at least not without heavy loss of life. So he conceded victory and Raton Pass to the Santa Fe, gave up his plans to run his railroad to the Rio Grande and began to devote his thoughts to a western line which would run up the Royal Gorge, cross the Continental Divide at snowy Tennessee Pass and continue to Salt Lake City.

In April of 1869 General Palmer sent surveyors and pioneers into the cañon to reconnoiter.

Their report was discouraging. Such a railroad would be a stupendous undertaking—perhaps impossible. The rock walls rose a sheer two thousand feet and at some points the walls were only thirty feet apart with the boiling, leaping, roaring Arkansas taking up practically the whole floor at high-water stage. It was a dark place where the sun touched only a few minutes a day. It was an echoing, sinister place—a virtual cavern, except that a narrow slit of bright blue sky shone high overhead.

Despite this pessimistic report, Palmer sent engineers and a gang of a hundred men to start pioneer work in the Royal Gorge. The Santa Fe's espionage system, which had served William B. Strong so well at Raton Pass, still was working. And at word of Palmer's activities in the Royal Gorge, Strong sent a surveyor named William R. Morely speeding from La Junta in an attempt to beat Palmer to Cañon City, about two miles east of the gorge's mouth.

Morely reached Pueblo on the Santa Fe locomotive early on the morning of April 19th. He blandly went to the Rio Grande roundhouse and asked to hire a locomotive to take him to Cañon City. Someone at the roundhouse knew Morely's connections, however, and the surveyor was profanely told to go his way.

Morely went his way. He hired a fast horse and whipped him for forty-five miles westward until the horse fell dead. Then Morely ran the last several miles on foot, arriving in Cañon City in time to assemble an armed gang of Santa Fe sympathizers and move to the mouth of the cañon half an hour before Palmer's party arrived from Denver to find their way blocked.

There is a strange and rather contradictory angle concerning these Santa Fe sympathizers in Cañon City. The townspeople were bitter because General Palmer had constructed his line to Cañon City and then deserted this project to move south to El Moro before building a railroad through the gorge and over the mountains. Cañon City felt in a way like a jilted woman. The odd angle is Cañon City's friendship toward the Santa Fe, which also had gone to Raton Pass instead of Cañon City.

The Rio Grande party arrived at the Royal Gorge to find its mouth blocked by Cañon City men and Santa Fe rifles. So the Rio Grande party marched north and then west and then south to the brink of the chasm.

At that time no man had ever descended those fearsome granite walls. But Palmer's party went down and they built a rock fort at the bottom, blocking the Santa Fe crew from moving construction up the cañon. Then the Rio Grande gang went to work, blasting and leveling the cañon floor above the river. Where rock was over-hanging and dangerous, men were lowered on ropes from the top of the gorge to split and hack away the walls.

The Santa Fe rushed in reinforcements—hundreds of men known for their fighting ability and marksman-ship—and camped them at the mouth of the gorge. The Rio Grande also hired hundreds of fighting men and low-ered them by ropes to their fort.

Each day parties of snipers from the Santa Fe camp went up the cañon to fire on Rio Grande workmen and the strange multiple echoes of the gorge would make one shot sound like drumfire from a platoon. The Rio Grande riflemen would fire back and the Santa Fe crew would retire. There were few casualties from this business, but apparently it was Strong's idea of harassing the Rio Grande men.

Meanwhile General Palmer went to the state court and got an injunction restraining the Santa Fe from interfering with his construction work. He had a good argument in gaining this injunction—the fact his fed-eral charter called for a Rio Grande line up the gorge.

This all was eighteen years before the Interstate Commerce Commission was established by an act of Con-gress. There was no certainty in the minds of railroad men about the jurisdiction of railroad affairs, especially in a case like this where a railroad's operations were limited to one state.

A fortnight after Palmer got his restraining order he began worrying about this ambiguity in the laws con-cerning common carriers and wondered how strong his state court injunction might prove. So he took his cause to federal court for a transfer.

Strong was on hand fighting all the way against a federal injunction. The federal judge listened to both sets of arguments and then made a ruling, which to him

doubtless seemed as calm and considered as a decree of
Moses. He gave permission to *both* railroads to go ahead
and build their lines up the Royal Gorge, "neither to
obstruct the other" in any way.

On the face of it, this ruling was very just. But despite the majesty of the United States law, there still
wasn't room at the bottom of the Royal Gorge for the
Arkansas River and *one* railroad, without a tremendous
amount of work being done. It was a physical impos-
sibility for two sets of rails to be laid in the cañon, unless
one was laid on top of the other.

This ruling was a terrible blow to General Palmer.
His opponent, the Santa Fe, already was a rich railroad,
having earned $4,000,000 net the year before. The Rio
Grande was hard up and Palmer was being pressed dras-
tically by bondholders.

Palmer appealed to the United States Supreme Court
for a reversal. But meanwhile he had to do something. He
bowed to Strong's offer for arbitration, and in the end
he postponed his construction up the Royal Gorge and
leased the Rio Grande's whole line to the Santa Fe for a
period of thirty years. There was a definite understanding in this lease that the Santa Fe must not make any
discriminations against the city of Denver on freight
rates and that the track and rolling stock must be kept
in tiptop condition. This was in 1878.

General Palmer was guilty of bad judgment in making that lease. Or at least he played in bad luck. For no
sooner had the lease been signed than the great silver
boom started in Leadville.

Leadville silver mining developed incredibly fast.
Within a year the camp was a city. Within a year the
smelters were roaring full blast and twelve thousand
teams were freighting over the Mosquito Range and
down to Colorado Springs, hauling from fifty to a hun-

dred thousand pounds of silver-lead pigs a day. The freight charges to Colorado Springs were $18 a ton.

Much larger shipping was in prospect and Tabor and his Leadville chorus were clamoring for a railroad to bring them cheaper supplies and to carry away the bullion faster and cheaper.

General Palmer then repented the lease he had given the Santa Fe. He determined to do something about it, for the Santa Fe had left him plenty of opportunity for action.

Palmer went to New York to attempt a little financing. It was not a new experience for him. He had tried financing the Rio Grande before and it had taken a year of hard work and fancy salesmanship to float a million-dollar loan.

Now, however, the situation was different. With the tremendous publicity Leadville and Tabor and the other carbonate kings had received in the East, everyone with money was eager to make more money in the romantic gold- and silver-inlaid West.

Palmer decided to be brazen about it. He went into Wall Street and asked for $5,000,000 to extend the Rio Grande to Leadville and beyond. He felt he could squeeze along on $2,000,000, but he believed he knew how to handle financiers. If you need $3,000,000, ask them for $5,000,000 and perhaps you can raise $2,000,000 if you have what they called a "gilt-edged proposition" in those days.

But General Palmer didn't reckon on the Leadville publicity. In three days $10,000,000 had been subscribed. The dumbfounded Palmer took $7,000,000 and went back to Colorado to see how he could pry that lease away from the Santa Fe.

It was a complex situation. There was proof on hand that Strong had been discriminating against Denver on freight rates south. There was every business reason why the Santa Fe should do this, for Denver was on no main line. Kansas City was the Santa Fe's gateway to the West. It was reasonable and proper, from a railroad viewpoint, to discriminate against Denver and favor Kansas City. But legally that action was a violation of the terms of the Rio Grande lease.

Palmer, with the $7,000,000 in his jeans, went to court to break the lease. He charged not only discrimination against Denver, but that the Santa Fe was attempting to ruin the Rio Grande by permitting its tracks and rolling stock to deteriorate.

The court dallied and the legal talent of both sides sparred and feinted with writs and motions. And the Santa Fe casually went to work grading a right of way to build a railroad to Leadville up the Royal Gorge.

About this time General Palmer noticed among his men a young surveyor named James R. De Remer—a heavy-shouldered, square-jawed fighter.

A Pennsylvanian, De Remer had gone in the Union army at fifteen and had fought with distinction in several battles. After the war he had attended college at Poughkeepsie and then gone into railroad construction work. He had been a division superintendent of the Fox River Railroad. In 1866 he had been working with the Atlantic and Pacific Railroad laying out new towns. In 1867 he went west, working with the Kansas Pacific and for the last nine years was with the Rio Grande as rodman and engineer.

General Palmer liked the way De Remer went about his business and made him assistant chief engineer of the road. And in April, 1879, De Remer was sent with a gang to do something about Santa Fe construction in the Royal Gorge.

De Remer couldn't gain entrance to the cañon because the Santa Fe was in complete control at Cañon City. So he followed the system of his predecessors, moving west and then down the walls of the gorge—a half mile nearly straight down. They went down the cliffs and swam the turbulent stream near the bracket bridge site. They repaired the old stone fort of the Rio Grande and then went to work grading a right of way upstream behind their barricade.

Santa Fe officials came up the cañon and ordered De Remer out of the gorge, but the Rio Grande engineer, backed by a row of Winchesters, thumbed his nose at them.

The Santa Fe, controlling everything at Cañon City, had twenty deputy sheriffs sent up with orders to bring in De Remer, dead or alive. The deputies went up as far as the fort.

"De Remer," they called, "we got a warrant for your arrest."

"Come on over and arrest me, then," called the engineer, and some of his men began to knock off nodules of granite from the cliff walls with 45-70 rifle bullets. The fragments of granite showered down on the deputies, so they went back to Cañon City.

With that, the Santa Fe offered $10,000 for De Remer or his body, and even that respectable reward was not enough to bring him in.

Between the original stone fort and a point designated as Twenty Mile Post, De Remer built eleven more forts. At Twenty Mile Post the gorge widens enough to allow at least two tracks and the Rio Grande men made this point their Maginot Line. De Remer made no concerted effort to hold his outposts.

As a matter of fact, he was not sure of his legal position below Twenty Mile Post, for in the previous few years citizens of Cañon City had built a wagon road up the gorge to that point and the Santa Fe had obtained a lease on that wagon road.

At one time the Santa Fe had an army of twelve hundred men in the cañon who might have stormed De Remer's two hundred successfully, but there were no pitched battles. There was constant sniping with many casualties, but De Remer's method of harrying his enemy was as effective as it was primitive.

Rio Grande men would prowl the brink of the chasm until they spied a Santa Fe working party and then begin to roll boulders over the edge. When a fifty-pound rock comes bounding down an 80° slope for two thousand feet or so it makes a very frightening racket in an echoing gorge. It also lands with such emphasis that chunks of disintegrated granite whiz around with the hum of bluebottle flies. The Santa Fe workmen found this situation nerve shattering. True, no one was killed by these boulders because the men could hear the bumble, crash, whack, and boom of an approaching rock in time to run for safety. But this Rio Grande stone-rolling project didn't serve to make contented Santa Fe workmen.

The sheriff of Fremont County was a Santa Fe man, of course, and he had plenty of money at his disposal. He went to work hiring all the able-bodied men he could find as guards. He paid $5 a day and food. So the Rio Grande followed suit, paying the same wages to men who would parade up and down with Winchesters on their shoulders.

This all was very fine for the cowboys who were tired of riding range and the miners who were tired of prospecting or digging in someone else's tunnel. Many of them, it developed later, made a good thing of the situation by working for both parties simultaneously. As a matter of fact, De Remer sent some of his trusted men to act as Santa Fe guards and to draw Santa Fe pay while they kept him supplied with information about the enemy's activities.

For supplies it was necessary for one of the De Remer men to climb the cliffs and walk to Cañon City, cart the groceries back to the cañon rim and then, dangerously and laboriously, pack them down the precipitous walls.

One day a Rio Grande man was sent on this journey for mail and provisions. In Cañon City he was recognized as a Rio Grande employee and arrested.

When the messenger failed to return, De Remer sensed what had happened and went to Cañon City himself. Discovering at the grocery that his suspicions were correct, the engineer slipped over to court to go bail for his man.

A court attaché, dizzy with thoughts of a $10,000 reward, ran to Sheriff Ben Shaffer and told him De Remer was on hand and easy to pick as a ripe peach. Shaffer leaped on his horse, galloped to the courthouse, tied his horse, and stalked in with jangling spurs.

De Remer, however, wasn't quite ready for picking yet. At the sheriff's approach he leaped out the open window, slashed the reins of the sheriff's horse with his hunting knife, swung into the saddle and headed for the gorge, pursued in true western movie style by a yelling, shooting squad of officers and Santa Fe men.

At the brink of the cañon De Remer turned the horse loose and was safe again amongst his crags.

Gradually, however, the Rio Grande men were being pushed back toward their stronghold at Twenty Mile Post.

One day De Remer and a party were working near Stone Wall Point when he discovered a Santa Fe working party flanking around them on the other side of the gorge. He saw that unless the Santa Fe crew was headed off immediately they would gain a position upstream, cutting the Rio Grande men off from their stronghold. There was only one apparent means to stop the Santa Fe gang and that would be by dashing across the river and getting above them.

De Remer called his party around him and rapidly pointed out the situation. "I'll give," he said, "twenty dollars to every man who swims the river with me."

The men looked at the boiling, leaping white water. They shook their heads. "No man would have a chance in the river here," they said. "Look at it. It'd smash you into the rocks, bash your brains out in a second."

"All right," said De Remer, "I'll go alone."

He darted down the cañon wall and plunged into the river. As his men predicted, he was swept violently downstream. He was hurled into rocks. Half the time he was out of sight with the spume and billows passing over his head.

But De Remer reached the other side, clung to a rock a moment and then pulled himself out of the water and up the seamed granite like a frightened otter. He worked his way rapidly upward and downstream until he was above the Santa Fe working party.

The Santa Fe men sighted him and began to shoot. De Remer's gang across the cañon could see the white flicks as bullets banged into the rocks around their chief. But the Santa Fe men didn't shoot for long. In a moment boulders began to bound down the cliff in a cloud of rock smoke, booming with terrific impact into their right of way. The Santa Fe men fled back down the gorge and temporary victory was De Remer's at Stone Wall Point.

The siege kept up for months until at last the Rio Grande brigade was driven back to their main bulwark at Twenty Mile Post.

In 1905 De Remer described the situation to a reporter.

"Past the Twenty Mile Post," he said, "there was room in the cañon for a railroad on both sides of the river, and past that point there was nothing to hinder them from going on up. We determined they should not pass. We took a tie and marked it 'Dead Line' and placed it in the center of the grade where they could see it."

Behind this marker and behind their last stone fort the Rio Grande men toiled and starved on half rations, grading a right of way in the upper gorge, firmly declaring that this should be their Thermopylae.

But on came the Santa Fe, not only grading right of way, but actually laying track. They laid track until they came within sight of the Rio Grande rampart. De Remer called his men in to make ready for their last desperate defense and his gang lined up behind the stone wall, each man with a rifle in his hands and a revolver in his belt.

And on came the Santa Fe tracklayers, rail by rail, until they were within one foot of the Rio Grande tie marked "Dead Line."

Let De Remer tell of the incident that followed:

"One of the laborers picked up another tie and started across the dead line. I called to him, 'Don't you cross that line!'

"The foreman of the Santa Fe gang said, 'Oh, go on. He's got no authority to boss you. Go on and lay that tie.'

"The man started and I shouted, 'Don't you cross that line or you'll get hurt.'

"The laborer looked at the stone fort and at the Winchesters sticking over the parapet. Then the laborer turned back to his foreman and he said, 'Listen, if you want that tie across, go ahead and do it yourself. I don't want to.'

"The foreman stood there trying to get up his nerve, perhaps, and I suppose trying to convince himself that nobody would dare shoot him after all, and then one of the Santa Fe lawyers came running up and he shouted, 'By what authority do you stop the United States mails?'

"I said, 'What do you mean, stopping the United States mails? I'm not stopping the United States mails because the Santa Fe Railroad isn't hauling mails through this gorge. Not yet it isn't.'

"Then he said, 'By what authority do you try to stop construction of this railroad?'

"I said, 'By authority of the United States Supreme Court.' He looked at me and he didn't know whether I had authority of the United States Supreme Court or not, and he thought maybe I had. So he called the men away and that was all there was to it. The Santa Fe never got past Twenty Mile Post."

The battle then moved to another sector, starting with the state court in Alamosa, Colorado. General Palmer found there a court friendly to the Rio Grande cause in a Judge Bowen, who granted an injunction enjoining the Santa Fe from using Rio Grande tracks.

William Teller, attorney for the Santa Fe, stormed at this injunction, demanding a change of venue on a claim that Judge Bowen was prejudiced. At that the judge not only refused the motion, but tightened the injunction, forbidding any Santa Fe employee even to touch any Rio Grande material.

Teller stalked from the court and down to the railroad where he commanded a Rio Grande conductor to "hitch up a train" and drive him to Denver as fast as he could go. Teller intended to get immediate action from a Denver court, which he hoped would supersede the Alamosa decision, and get it in effect before anyone knew about Judge Bowen's ruling.

Authority to give such a command to the Rio Grande conductor was Teller's, for technically the Santa Fe's lease still was good. So the conductor "hitched up a train" and started for Denver. But first he stuck a copy of the Alamosa court writ in his boot.

Contemporary accounts of this incident are a little vague. The old Denver *Republican* failed even to give the conductor's name. It failed to say whether the engine crew were Santa Fe men, but at least it indicated the engineer and firemen were not in the confidence of the conductor.

The train reached Palmer Lake, which is on the crest of the Arkansas divide between Colorado Springs and Denver. Palmer Lake is fifty-two miles from Denver and more than two thousand feet higher.

It was night and the conductor ordered Teller's special to a siding to allow a hypothetical train past. And while the special waited, this conductor slipped up beside the locomotive and deftly unscrewed the nuts of a drive wheel's connecting rod and threw the rod into Palmer Lake.

Then this resourceful and loyal Rio Grande conductor obtained a push car, which was a hand car without the pump handles, and started coasting down the grade toward Denver.

According to the Denver *Republican* account, this conductor and his push car had a following wind, so he spread his raincoat like a spinnaker and sailed into Denver in better time than passenger train schedule. Meanwhile Attorney Teller paced back and forth in his special at the Palmer Lake siding, gnawing his fingernails and demanding that the engineer take him to Denver, connecting rod or no connecting rod.

Anyhow, the Denver & Rio Grande conductor was in Denver early in the morning and the Santa Fe attorney was not, and the Rio Grande triumphed in a Denver court decision abrogating the Santa Fe's lease.

The Santa Fe, however, was not disposed to relinquish the Rio Grande property, court order or no court order. Therefore, General Palmer, always the military man, mobilized an army in East Denver and marched over to the general offices of the railroad in West Denver. The Santa Fe workers had just enough time to lock the office doors before the Rio Grande army arrived.

Locking those doors was a pitifully futile gesture. Armed with a telegraph pole as a battering ram, the Palmer boys banged open the doors and chased all the Santa Fe workers home—those they didn't send to hospitals with cracked crowns.

Though this coup d'état left the northern terminus in Rio Grande hands, there were 118 miles of Rio Grande track between Denver and Pueblo still held by the Santa Fe.

Palmer made up a train, loaded his army aboard and moved southward. At each way station this train stopped. And at each way station the Santa Fe agent was taken prisoner aboard the train, a Rio Grande agent was deposited and the train puffed on south.

At Colorado Springs, however, the sheriff of El Paso County had taken possession of the railroad property to avert bloodshed and state cavalry was patrolling the yards. That was all right with General Palmer. He had a couple of court orders in his pocket to prove that he was representing the state and law and order himself.

The train steamed on down toward Pueblo and at Cucharas the Rio Grande army was faced with the necessity of killing a couple of Santa Fe men in the interest of law and order.

In anticipation of any concerted direct action on the part of Palmer men, the Santa Fe had converted the old Pueblo roundhouse into a fort. The doors were heavily barricaded with bridge timbers. There was a Gatling gun or two on hand and Bat Masterson, notorious as a gunman and killer, had been hired as captain over an army of riflemen to defend this citadel.

The Rio Grande military train steamed up within striking distance of this brick Gibraltar and the army lined up outside the cars and loaded their guns. There came the breathless pause before a desperate battle.

At this moment Robert F. Weitbrec, treasurer of the Rio Grande, stepped into the picture. Weitbrec was not a soldier. He was not a man of violence. Essentially his business was handling money and consequently he had great faith in the power of gold.

Weitbrec walked up to Palmer. "General," he said, "perhaps I can arbitrate this business to assure our success. It is possible you can storm this fort and capture it. But it is possible you may be repulsed. In any event there will be bloodshed if you resort to violence and perhaps heavy loss of life. Before you attack, let me try to arbitrate."

Then Treasurer Weitbrec outlined his plan. No doubt, these mercenaries of the Santa Fe were ready to fight because fighting was their business. But after all, they were not fighting for a principle. They were fighting because the Santa Fe was paying them money to fight. If they would fight for money, perhaps they would *not* fight for money. And the Rio Grande had a large part of Wall Street's $7,000,000 left.

This all sounded logical to General Palmer, so Weitbrec tied a white handkerchief on a stick as a flag of truce and walked confidently to the roundhouse. Bat Masterson himself opened the door.

For almost an hour Weitbrec was inside the roundhouse and Palmer began to wonder if his treasurer had been murdered.

Then the big door swung open and Weitbrec came out. With him, bearing flags of surrender, came the Santa Fe army. Wall Street gold had averted a battle.

The Rio Grande army then moved upon the dispatcher's office, but Weitbrec's strategy was useless in this instance. The beleaguered Santa Fe men in the dispatcher's office were no mercenary soldiers. They were railroaders loyal to their own line and they began to shoot as soon as the Rio Grande army came in sight. Several were wounded in this skirmish before the door was bat-tered in. Some clerks were captured, but the Santa Fe officials made their escape on a locomotive with bullets zinging around their ears.

General Manager Strong of the Santa Fe, beaten now by force, went to court, charging illegality of state injunctions in railroad matters and got the case transferred to federal court. And while Palmer had the edge in Colorado courts, Strong and his men had reached the representatives of United States law and equity first.

In two weeks the federal court declared the Rio Grande's injunctions invalid and the Rio Grande was ordered to hand back all captured property and right of way to the Santa Fe.

But meanwhile the Rio Grande had taken possession of the Royal Gorge and was so heavily barricaded that the court decision would have needed a full division of troops to back it up there.

So the two railroads decided to arbitrate once and for all. In February, 1880, officials of both lines met in Boston and signed a treaty of peace.

The Rio Grande agreed not to build to St. Louis or Kansas City or to El Paso, Texas. The Santa Fe agreed not to build to Denver or Leadville. And the Rio Grande paid the Santa Fe $1,400,000 for the track the latter had laid in the Royal Gorge.

Immediately General Palmer started construction to tap the rich freight bonanza at Leadville.

The first train to reach the headwaters of the Arkansas bore not only General Palmer, but General U. S. Grant, just returning from his tour of the world.

Thirty thousand people jammed the streets of Leadville—thirty thousand roaring, drinking, singing, cheering miners and their parasites. And foremost in the reception committee, in a four-horse open barouche with silver and gold trimmings, was Lieutenant Governor

Horace Austin Warner Tabor, face and silk hat glowing
and his fifty-caliber diamonds glittering in the mountain
sunshine.

Tabor whacked former President Grant affection-
ately on the back and told the general he should by all

means locate in Colorado where he could easily become
almost as rich as his host. And when the carriage drew
up in front of the Clarendon Hotel, a group of miners
(at Tabor's instigation) stepped ceremoniously forward
and sprinkled gold dust on the backs of the black stal-
lions that drew the barouche.

CHAPTER EIGHT

Love and Ruin

WITH the coming of the Denver & Rio Grande to Leadville, prices of commodities naturally were reduced in the stores. Groceries were cheaper. Meat was cheaper. Jeans and boots and flannel shirts were cheaper. Even whisky was cheaper because the railroad was bringing in greater quantities at a fraction of the stage freight charges.

And the railroad also was bringing in more men, fortune hunters who were glad to work in other men's mines for a stake so they could go out and find mines of their own. The railroad was bringing in hundreds of these jobless men who stood in line before mine offices asking for employment.

This situation gave the mineowners a grand idea. Already they had an association designed for mutual protection and to keep other mineowners and operators out of the district. These Leadville operators had established what amounted to a closed corporation and they —Tabor, Moffat, and the rest—met one day in the Clarendon Hotel and decided to reduce wages to $2.75 a day. Before that the average pay of a miner ranged between $3.50 and $8, but, as the operators agreed, he didn't need that much money now because the cost of living had been reduced.

Of course, the cost of mine operation also had been

reduced and the price of silver was up to $1.29 an ounce, but nothing was said about that item at this meeting.

Already there had been some labor trouble in Leadville with a man named Mike Mooney organizing the workers, demanding some safety devices in the mines and smelters and declaring, of all things, that twelve hours were too long for a man to work daily under prevailing conditions.

The operators decided it was time to teach these fellows a lesson. They had been growing altogether too cocky of late and there were plenty of jobless men in Leadville who would be happy to work for $2.75 a day if the unionized miners didn't want it.

Wages were reduced and a strike was called. It was the first real labor strike in Colorado's black strike history.

The mine operators called out Tabor's gaily caparisoned cavalry and called out also the Wolfe Tone Guards to "keep order." However, the Wolfe Tone Guards, which was sort of an irregular adjunct to the Leadville police department, turned out to be made up either of striking miners or their sympathizers. And to the consternation of the operators, the Wolfe Tone Guards lined up to protect the strikers from the Tabor Cavalry and to assist the miners in frightening strikebreakers.

Concerted rifle fire echoed up the Leadville gulches while Lieutenant Governor Tabor scuttled down to the capital to call out the National Guard. As Governor Pitkin was expediently absent, Tabor could mobilize the militia without argument. He immediately dispatched a trainload or two of troops to Leadville to do the operators' bidding and consequently the strike was short-lived.

Horace Austin Warner Tabor, however, definitely had torn his pants with the workingman of Colorado.

No longer was he Good Old Tabor, the friend of the common people. Instead, he became a somewhat ludicrous ogre. And, as his popularity ebbed away, so did his fantastic luck.

Several months before the strike, romance had come into the life of blunt-fingered, graying Horace Tabor. Augusta was not constituted physically or psychically to become a peahen. Even in the fine Denver mansion she insisted on wearing plain cotton house dresses and she refused to go to the grand drinking parties sponsored by the lieutenant governor.

Thus Tabor was ready when Elizabeth McCourt Doe came along. The beauteous, voluptuous blond wife of a Central City mine laborer baited her hook for Tabor and the Leadville Midas leaped hungrily to be snagged through the gills.

Tabor's political influence engineered a divorce for "Baby Doe," as the sentimental and admiring hard-rock men of Central City called her. And Baby Doe lived in luxury provided by the lieutenant governor for a long time—until Tabor got up nerve to walk out on Augusta and demand that she get a divorce.

Brokenhearted Augusta, who had followed her pop-eyed hero from Maine, who had crossed the scorched prairies with him and endured storms in shacks and tents and lived on scant rations and kept boarders to support him while he was prospecting and who had operated his store while Tabor was trying to mine; Augusta, the mother of his son and faithful partner in all his misadventures for thirty years, was put aside for the cooing voice and peach-bloom complexion of a wealth-bedazzled girl of twenty-two. Tabor settled about $350,000 on Augusta in payment for her loyalty and Augusta lived sadly alone for a while in her Capitol Hill mansion. Then she went out to Southern California and died.

Ambition and Indian summer romance now joined hands to drive Tabor to his doom. He bought millions of acres of so-called mahogany land in Honduras and he bought alleged silver mines in Mexico. He estimated his wealth at $100,000,000 and he set his goal at the presidency of the United States.

Lavishing money on the Republican party of Colorado, he made a bid for the United States Senate as the first step toward the White House. It was a delicate situation for the politicians. If they offended Tabor, they might cut off their private gold mine. But they certainly could not afford to make him senator, what with the scandal hanging over him because of his desertion of Augusta and his affair with Baby Doe. Also, from being easily the most popular man in the mountains, thanks to his strike coup he had become probably the most unpopular.

Tabor was either unconscious of all this or supremely unconcerned. He put up the finest office building in Denver, calling it the Tabor Block. He started construction of a theater which was to be one of the finest and certainly the most rococo in America. He sent to Europe for carpets and tapestries and to Japan for cherry timbers to be carved ornately into pillars and gingerbread gewgaws.

Eugene Field, then working on the Denver *Tribune,* enjoyed H. A. W. Tabor immensely. Field termed the Tabor Grand Opera House's architecture, "Modified Egyptian Moresque," which was all right for a generalization, but there also was a good deal of Florentine-Ulysses S. Grant and Ming Dynasty Gothic and more mansard roof, iron-stag-on-the-lawn, Rutherford B. Hayes-for-President American.

There is a story about the Tabor Grand which always must be told.

Tabor came into the building once as workmen were putting on the finishing gauds and he noted the colored portrait of some stranger high above on the proscenium arch. It was a high-foreheaded stranger with long curling hair and a short, pointed beard.

The lieutenant governor stared at the picture, "Who's that gent up there?" he demanded.

"Why, governor," said the contractor, "that's Shakespeare—the greatest playwright in history."

"Shakespeare, shake hell," blurted Tabor. "What'd *he* ever do for Denver? Paint him out and put me up there."

So for the grand opening Lieutenant Governor Tabor's flat-topped head and enormous mustaches graced the proscenium arch.

This opening of Tabor's opera house was something for Denver to talk about for years. Full dress was mandatory for admittance to see Emma Abbott enact the mad scene from *Lucia di Lammermoor* as a prelude to the opera *Maritana*. It was estimated the audience wore approximately sixty-eight pounds of diamonds.

The Tabor box, trimmed in gold and silver, was filled with flowers, but was otherwise vacant. Augusta Tabor was sitting bitterly alone in her $40,000 mansion. In the orchestra section, however, was a voluptuous blonde who thrilled at the thought her name soon would be Tabor—if everything went as she planned.

Tabor's chance to sit in the United States Senate came when President Chester A. Arthur appointed Colorado Senator Henry Teller secretary of the interior.

There was a real battle in the Colorado legislature over Teller's successor. Tabor was in there swinging every minute and scattering gold to the four winds, but the legislators were afraid of him. Legislators have to remember the labor vote and, in those days particularly, they had to remember scandals.

They ended the debate by appointing Tom Bowen to the Senate. Bowen had several millions himself, won at gold mining, and was a liberal contributor to the principles of the Republican party. He had made his start at the other end of the Arkansas River. A carpetbagger following the Civil War, Bowen was an Arkansas State Supreme Court justice until the original Ku-Klux Klan started burning too many fiery crosses in his neighborhood. Then Bowen moved west to gain fortune and political distinction.

To salve Tabor, the legislature appointed him to fill out Senator Teller's unexpired term, which had only a month to run. That honor not only salved Tabor, but delighted him. He sent each member of both houses a case of imported champagne.

The new senator-elect traveled to Washington in a private train, but the gorgeous Baby Doe was left behind in her gorgeous suite in Denver's new and gorgeous Windsor Hotel. Horace would wire her to come on after he had made arrangements in Washington for a wedding that would make social history.

At the Capital Tabor rented a suite of ten rooms in the Willard Hotel. Then he set out to conquer Washington society in the brief period before his wedding.

On his very first day on the floor of the Senate Tabor was a sensation. When he took his seat and preened the ends of his huge mustache with a two-handed gesture, the rest of the Upper House blinked its eyes before the fire of diamond rings huger than most of the senators had ever seen. And that wasn't all. Tabor wore his cuffs long to display his cuff links—inch-square checkerboards of diamonds and onyx.

The silver king was a lot of fun for the press gallery, but more fun for Eugene Field back in Denver. Daily, Field wrote a column recounting fictitious addresses delivered by the Colorado senator from the floor.

Typical was one in which Tabor was supposed to be defending himself from newspaper attacks and assailing a journal for terming him an "anomaly."

Eugene Field quoted Tabor as saying he had determined to pay no heed to utterances of his enemies. "But here," the silver king was supposed to have said, "is an instance where the libel is so unprovoked, so wanton, the slander so malicious and the charge so appalling that I feel compelled to notice it. How and at what time did I commit this offense? Who was my accessory to the deed? Honorable senators will observe there are absolutely no specifications. Why have my slanderers neglected to draw up a bill of particulars? I will tell the senators why—the charge is unqualifiedly and ignominiously false (applause)."

As a matter of fact, Tabor was present in the Senate only fourteen days of his thirty-day term. The rest of the time he was too busy arranging for his wedding to bother with affairs of state.

Eugene Field, however, gave Tabor many busy days and nights in Washington and New York society. He reported Tabor as the guest of Roscoe Conkling and quoted Conkling regarding a supposed passage between William Henry Vanderbilt and the Coloradan.

"Vanderbilt, who is something of a wag," the story read, "was inclined to banter Tabor for cracking nuts with his teeth instead of using the silver implements provided for that purpose. 'What have become of your crackers, Horace?' said he.

"Quick as a flash Tabor retorted, 'I ate 'em in my soup an hour ago.' "

For his beautiful young bride Tabor wished to obtain the finest, the most famous jewels in the world. He put a good deal of thought on this subject and finally racked an inspiration from his busy brain. From his scant schooling in childhood Horace recalled what he deemed to be the world's most notable historical fact concerning jewelry.

Queen Isabella of Spain had pawned her jewels to finance Columbus's voyage to America. Tabor slapped his hands in a decision. If money could make it possible, Baby Doe would wear those most famous of all gems when she knelt before the altar with Tabor.

The senator called a precious pair who were supposed to be jewelry experts. "Listen," said Tabor, "I don't care a damn what they cost, but I want to buy them jewels Queen Isabella hocked to send Columbus to America."

The precious pair gasped.

"That's right. I want you two to go to Spain right away. Want you to start tonight because we ain't got much time. And I want you to go through every hockshop in the place until you find the right jewels. Then you buy 'em. Get 'em cheap as you can, but buy 'em irregardless."

So the men went to New York and bought a pearl necklace and an antique brooch and a few other pretties, made out an elaborate expense account, came back to Washington and told the gullible Tabor their efforts in Europe had been crowned with spectacular success.

At the wedding Baby Doe wore the "Queen Isabella jewels," but disappointed the bridegroom by declining to twine a $90,000 diamond necklace in with the pearls.

The wedding really was quite a party. President Arthur was there and several Cabinet officers, as well as a sprinkling of senators and representatives. Washington society reporters took the event seriously and unleashed their best society reporter adjectives in their descriptions.

The bride was described as a "blue-eyed and golden-haired blonde of rare personal attractions, with a full, fine figure and of charming manner, with vivacious and entertaining conversational powers."

The ceremony was performed "amid a fairyland of flowers" by the Reverend Father P. L. Chappelle of St. Matthew's, who by some strange oversight had not been informed that both parties to the marriage had been divorced. When he learned of this fact—most important to a clergyman of the Catholic faith—he indignantly returned the $200 Tabor had given him and wrote a letter of explanation to his bishop.

But the wedding party itself was bubbling with joy and Baby Doe coyly pinned a posy from her wedding bouquet on President Arthur's lapel while H. A. W. slapped the President on the back and demanded to know if there had ever been a sweller party.

Particularly proud was Tabor of one item of his personal trousseau. This was a nightshirt of silk and lace with flounces and rose point insertion. Its buttons were of solid gold and the garment was reported to have cost him variously between $250 and $1,000.

The next day was Tabor's last in the Senate and Baby Doe sat in the gallery. She wore a brown silk dress and the $90,000 diamond necklace. She also wore fourteen-carat earrings, a bracelet that cracked the spectrum and scattered it all over the Chamber, and a girdle about her waist made of diamonds, rubies and emeralds in the shape of a serpent.

Tabor's valedictory, as could be expected, occasioned more fun for Eugene Field.

"Early in the day," he wrote, "the streets were alive with people hurrying to the Capitol. Flags were hung at half mast. . . . When Senator Tabor entered the room bearing a new patent leather grip sack and wearing a superb trousseau of broadcloth and diamonds, the vast crowd was hushed as the grave.

"The lobbies of the Senate were ornamented with such mottoes as 'The Nation Mourns,' 'He was the Noblest Roman,' 'Gone, but Not Forgotten,' etc. etc. Senator Tabor's chair was one mass of tuberoses and smilax and numerous floral designs were piled upon his desk. . . . It was generally remarked as the Senator passed down the aisle, looking pale and calm, and bowing modestly to the right and left, that his appearance bore a striking resemblance to the popular steel engraving of Mary, Queen of Scots, going to execution. He proceeded at once to his own place, from which he had thundered out those utterances which shook the world and will live in all history as the grandest monuments of his genius.

" . . . Senator Sherman submitted a series of resolutions lamenting Tabor's departure and eulogizing him as the first and foremost man among the peoples of our glorious land. . . . The resolutions were unanimously adopted; Senator Tabor maintaining his characteristic modesty to the last and refraining from voting. . . .

"The Senator rose to speak. . . . As he proceeded to recount . . . his love of country and devotion to the public weal, the men groaned and sobbed in speechless agony, and whole platoons of police were kept busy carrying insensible ladies out of the galleries. . . .

"The Senate stood up as Tabor passed from the midst of them and as he vanished through the storm doors of the Chamber, his late colleagues fell upon each other's necks and cried as if their hearts would break. At night there was a torchlight procession in Ex-Senator Tabor's honor. It was an imposing affair, numbering 12,000 persons in line and the entire American navy on wheels and gorgeously illuminated."

But everyone didn't take the Colorado Croesus so lightly. For instance, there was the Bayonne (N. J.) *Statesman* which started a move to put H. A. W. in the White House. It characterized him as "Silver King of the Pacific Slope; Colorado's honest citizen, banker and Senator of sterling talent and purpose of character. An independent statesman upholding the Constitution and the Union. A foe to monopoly and centralization of the money powers endangering liberty. Favors a gold and silver currency and protection to the manufacturing of the country. Champion of the working man. A new light from the ranks of the people."

Back in Denver and dreaming of the day when he would be President of the United States, Horace Tabor began planning the palace he should build his bride. He boasted that he'd bring mahogany from his Honduran empire and that all the woodwork, even to hidden timbers, would be of that beautiful and enduring wood.

"By God," said Tabor, "I'm even going to build the privy out of solid mahogany."

He bought a few hundred thousand acres in Texas. He bought alleged mining land in Arizona. He paid a million for a quarter interest in a New York hotel. He paid several hundreds of thousands for a hole suspected of being a gold mine near Boulder, Colorado.

At that time Tabor felt certain he was worth at least $200,000,000. He believed he would swell this to a round billion within a few years, that he was destined to become the richest man in the world—and the most powerful. Yet five years before Horace Tabor had been a poor, middle-aged storekeeper in a decaying mining camp, a man from whom energy, ambition, and hope apparently had departed.

He continued to pour money—actually millions of dollars—into the war chest of the Republican party in the hope that he should be rewarded with the governorship of Colorado or perhaps even a full term in the United States Senate. But the party leaders were afraid to have the bizarre Tabor too much in the limelight. They couldn't go that far, even for his money. But they did make him state chairman.

Despite his frustrated longing for greater political glory, Tabor continued his ecstatic way. He bought a solid block in Denver, tore down the buildings and constructed his palace of love—vaguely on the architectural lines of an Italian villa. The lawn was furnished magnificently with iron stags and hounds and a score or more of live peacocks. He owned one of the most regally gorgeous carriages ever to roll in America and six jet-black thoroughbreds to draw it. Denverites must indeed have turned to gape when the silk-hatted Tabor and the bediamonded Baby Doe went for a ride with two crimson-liveried Negroes perched with folded arms on the footmen's seat.

Tabor gave all evidence of being extremely happy in those days. But there is some doubt about Baby Doe. Denver women did not receive her. They remembered gray-haired Augusta Tabor living the sad life of a recluse.

Two daughters were born to Baby Doe. The first was named Elizabeth for the mother. Tabor himself named the second daughter and he named her with his usual flair for the spectacular. The child's full name was Rose Mary Echo Silver Dollar Tabor, though she usually was known simply as Silver Dollar.

Elizabeth's christening robe was of fine point lace and cost more than $1,000. For some strange reason Tabor did not raise the ante for Silver Dollar. Her christening robe cost only $800.

Perhaps that reduction of $200 in christening robes showed that Tabor was worrying just a little about a slump in his earnings from the fabulous Leadville silver mines. But he couldn't have been worrying much. He bought still more mines and spent hundreds of thousands of dollars developing them. He felt assured that his other investments were sound.

But Tabor lost a million trying to corner the wheat market. He lost another half million when a Lake Michigan dock project folded up. A couple of insurance companies in which he was heavily interested failed. His Honduras mahogany land proved to be without value. One after another, a dozen similar reverses struck at the Tabor treasury.

Still Horace wasn't much worried—even when he found himself incredibly pressed for ready money. The Matchless Mine at Leadville still was a rich producer, so he mortgaged it.

Then came the panic of 1893 and strikes and a whole catalogue of other economic trouble. Congress repealed the Sherman Silver Act, calling for purchase of silver bullion for coinage and abruptly the price of silver dropped from $1.29 an ounce to 50 cents.

Tabor mortgaged his Denver property to weather the storm. He even mortgaged the Tabor Grand Opera House. He mortgaged Baby Doe's Italian villa. He mortgaged everything.

And, before he knew how or what had happened, Tabor had lost everything he possessed except a doubtful title to the Matchless Mine.

Baby Doe's jewels were pawned—even to the pearl necklace Horace fondly believed had been pawned once before by Queen Isabella of Spain. The marble and mahogany and mother-of-pearl Italian villa was gone and the Tabor family moved to a little red brick $30-a-month rented cottage while Tabor scurried around desperately trying to salvage something from his fabled fortune.

Horace Tabor was not alone in his plight. The carbonate kings of Leadville were going broke right and left. Only a few had the acumen to see what was coming in time to protect themselves.

Among the few was a white-haired, stoop-shouldered little Jew named Meyer Guggenheim. Guggenheim had come to Leadville late, when the day of opportunity was far past its meridian. He came to Leadville from Philadelphia, where he had failed in a mercantile venture, and he was playing a long chance with the few hundred dollars he had left. Buying a couple of third-rate claims, Guggenheim and his partner, R. B. Graham, sank a shaft through the lead carbonate vein and hit the lower vein which had been rumored but never proved up to that time. As a result, Guggenheim took out several millions, the foundation of the great Guggenheim money empire.

From Leadville, Guggenheim went to Pueblo and opened a smelter. Then he branched out to Mexico and Alaska. But he did not buy blindly as Tabor had bought. When Meyer Guggenheim made an investment he knew what he was buying.

When the price of silver kept to its low level despite the oratory of William Jennings Bryan, there was no profit in the expensive operation of following Guggenheim's example and sinking deeper shafts after the sulphide deposits. Miners deserted Leadville almost as rapidly as they had rushed to the boom town.

So, if silver was not to be profitable any more, some of the mine operators turned again to the search for gold. They found it, too. They found it in quantities large enough to bring even another rush to the valley of the Arkansas over the Denver & Rio Grande and over the narrow-gauge South Park Railroad, which David Moffat and his associates had wound up over the Mosquitoes.

Among those who struck it rich in this gold rush was an elderly man named John F. Campion, a practical and hardheaded Canadian who went very deep in the Little Jonny Mine and found an exceptionally rich vein of gold. Campion made millions, but he was not one to lose his head over good fortune.

Yet Campion did have one ambition which he had nurtured from boyhood. He wanted to go to Europe. Particularly, he wanted to see Paris. He wanted to *do* Paris.

So, when his millions had stacked up and his business affairs were in good shape, John F. Campion gave way to his dream. He packed up and went to Europe. He went to Paris. And the most colorful thing I know about John F. Campion is the cablegram he sent back to a friend.

The cablegram read, "Arrived in Paris this morning —forty years too late."

When Tabor's fortune was swept away, the former carbonate king was a pitiable figure. Money had been his god and when his money departed, so did his spirit. No doubt, many of his old friends would have helped him regain his feet if they had realized his condition was so desperate, but the old pride made him avoid his former associates. As a matter of fact, the Tabor family was practically destitute.

Because he had been unable to borrow a cent on his "gold mine" on South Boulder Creek, Tabor still retained that dubious property. Alone, Horace slipped out of Denver with a pick and shovel and went to Boulder in a desperate effort to recoup his fortune.

He was an old man now, and in poor health, but he drilled and shoveled for several weeks, living in a shack as he sank a shaft.

Finally he was convinced there wasn't even a trace of gold in the workings and was forced to give up. He started to walk the thirty-odd miles back to Denver. When the old man was staggering with exhaustion a teamster picked him up and gave him a ride to the city on his wagon.

That night in a saloon the teamster told a story of a crazy old man he'd picked up on the road, a crazy old man who claimed to be Senator Tabor. It was very funny, but somebody ought to tell Senator Tabor about it. Things like that wouldn't do the senator any good. Some folks might believe the crazy old man.

The story spread around and Republican leaders in Denver suddenly realized they hadn't seen Senator Tabor in many weeks. Could it be? No, that was impossible, but still everyone knew the senator had been hit very hard.

So they investigated and they finally found the Tabor family practically starving. The party leaders were appalled as they thought of the millions Tabor had poured into the party coffers and an urgent appeal was telegraphed back to President McKinley.

So Horace Tabor, who a few short years before had aspired to the presidency himself and who thought he soon would be the richest man in the world, again became a postmaster—as he had been at Buckskin Joe and California Gulch. He was made postmaster of Denver to "rescue him from penury."

The Tabor family moved to one room in the Windsor Hotel to save Baby Doe the necessity of housekeeping. Horace lived only one more year, dying in 1899 either from a perforated stomach ulcer or from appendicitis.

Diagnosis of such things wasn't far advanced in those days.

Tabor's last words to Baby Doe were "Don't give up the Matchless." To his last breath he was convinced this mine was far from worked out. He was convinced that silver would come back.

No matter what judgment may be imposed on Baby Doe for deserting her young husband Harvey Doe for the middle-aged Midas of the Mountains, she apparently came to love Tabor deeply. She was still young and exceptionally attractive when the crash came, but she did not desert Tabor. And she took his wish concerning the Matchless Mine as a command from her deity.

When Elizabeth, the older daughter, married and went away, Baby Doe moved Silver Dollar and herself to a shack next to the Matchless and lived there.

Silver Dollar grew up in this shack from a child of ten, grew into a strange wild girl with aspirations beyond her talents.

She wrote two or three songs—very bad songs—which she published. One was about Theodore Roosevelt going bear hunting in Colorado and she dedicated this one to the memory of her father. Silver Dollar went down to Denver and tried to be a newspaper reporter, but the girl was virtually illiterate and without a semblance of self-discipline.

Those who knew her say she had a strange sort of wild beauty, which is not borne out by her photographs. After writing a lurid short novel called, *Star of Blood*, Silver Dollar went to Chicago to become an actress. For a period she traveled with a cheap burlesque show. She lived with dozens of men. She became a dipsomaniac and apparently also was addicted to the use of drugs.

All this time Baby Doe believed her youngest daughter was in a convent back east. She kept her vigil at the Matchless Mine with a shotgun. Wearing overalls and boots, she worked day after day in the shaft—labor that would tax the strength of a man—trying to uncover newer and richer veins of silver, or perhaps of gold. Horace Tabor had told her the Matchless Mine would bring back the Tabor fortunes, and that was enough for Baby Doe.

Several times she was evicted by law, but Baby Doe would not stay evicted. When anyone approached her dilapidated, unpainted, one-room shack she was out with her shotgun warning him away.

She did come to Denver several times to consult with lawyers. I remember one of these times. She was wearing a man's tattered coat, much too large for her, and patched overalls and rubber boots. And this woman, whose jewels once startled the United States Senate, was carrying a burlap bag. Her once voluptuous mouth was sunken and thin and harshly straight. Her large and wide-set blue eyes looked upon the world with fear and suspicion.

Baby Doe Tabor lived in her shack on Fryer Hill for more than thirty years. One day the storekeeper where Baby Doe bought her stale bread and other scanty provisions recalled he hadn't seen Mrs. Tabor in some time. He investigated and found Baby Doe dead in her shack.

Silver Dollar died in mysterious circumstances after a debauch in a Chicago tenement. Baby Doe's estranged brother, Peter McCourt, sent $300 to Chicago to save his niece from a pauper's grave.

Improved methods of smelting gave several spurts to silver mining in Leadville, but the population dropped from 40,000 to 30,000 and then down to about 10,000 in 1910. In 1920 there were about 5,000 residents. At present there are no more than 3,000.

State Street, which once was one of the wildest and most boisterous streets America has ever seen, now is a ruin of shacks.

So that is the story of Leadville—the first town on the Arkansas River. That is the story of the greatest mining camp in Colorado's history. And it is the story of the most striking citizen of that wild, wild camp.

That is the story of Leadville, but it is not the whole story. It would take several volumes the size of this one to tell even the parts of Leadville's story which are available at this time; to tell the story of the great ice palace and of the saloon with the huge family Bible open on a handy shelf, but chained down so it wouldn't be stolen, the Bible which, the Reverend Mr. Uzzell believed, was read more than any other Bible in Leadville.

And there was the preacher who preached long and fervently about the wrath of God and then went up on the mountainside to pray and was struck down by lightning. And many a chapter could be written about the famous figures who came to Tabor's Leadville theater —including Oscar Wilde who came in knee breeches and with a sunflower in his lapel to lecture an audience of bewildered and incredulous miners on "The Practical Application of the Aesthetic Theory to Exterior and Interior House Decoration, With Observations on Dress and Personal Adornment." Probably less than one per cent of the audience was unarmed that night. They were largely uncouth men who lived lives of violence. But they showed Wilde more courtesy than did some of the more cultured communities in the East.

Several chapters could be devoted to the molybdenum business above Leadville now—the greatest deposit of this steel alloy in the world.

Several times in Leadville's strange history there have been periods when the town was practically dead and abandoned. But always there came new strikes and new prosperity.

People of Leadville are calmly awaiting the next boom—calmly and confidently. Leadville has always come back, bigger and better than ever, they say. There's nothing to worry about. It'll be along any day now.

Well, there is plenty of silver in the low-lying sulphide streaks under Leadville.

If the price of silver should go up—

CHAPTER NINE

Cripple Creek

THE great Cripple Creek gold field came in op-
portunely just when the first Leadville silver boom was
waning.

There are a number of strange things about the
Cripple Creek district, which became one of the greatest
—if not *the* greatest—gold camps in the history of
United States proper.

It is situated on the eastern edge of the South Park
District in Colorado and in the shadow of Pikes Peak,
which rears its head to the northeast.

You remember that the original Colorado gold
rushes were supposedly to Pikes Peak. "Pikes Peak or
Bust" was painted on the prairie schooners. But those
argonauts actually were bound for Cherry Creek and
Clear Creek and Gregory Gulch and Russell Gulch, all
of which were seventy to a hundred miles from the great
white-headed landmark.

In the light of future events, this all was strange,
because more than thirty years later the richest gold deposits ever found in the Rocky Mountains were uncovered on the flanks of Pikes Peak.

Prospectors did travel all over the grassy uplands of
the Cripple Creek region for most of those thirty years.
But they didn't bother to look for gold there. It wasn't
the right kind of country for gold.

During the rushes to Leadville, literally thousands

of gold seekers crossed the mountains in the vicinity of Cripple Creek to hurry west and north to California Gulch and Leadville. It probably never occurred to any of these early prospectors to bring out a shovel and pan and investigate the Cripple Creek region.

So this naturally rich pasture land, 9,000 feet above sea level, became a cattle country.

In 1884, however, a promoter in the district got an idea. He decided to provide some excitement and perhaps some real profit for himself.

He loaded a shotgun with some California Gulch gold, dug a prospect hole in a declivity of Mt. Pisgah and blasted the free gold into the rocks. Then he went to Colorado Springs with simulated excitement and announced he had made a gold strike.

The result was a great rush over the mountains and in a few days there were at least two thousand persons camped around the salted mine. The promoter sold his claims and vanished. Then the fraud was discovered and the 2,000 wended their sad way back down the mountains to Colorado Springs, and the Cripple Creek country continued to support beef steers.

Among the cowboys in this region was a fellow named Bob Womack, and Bob Womack had the gold fever. He didn't know much about minerals or he wouldn't have developed a habit of getting off his horse now and then to pick up a piece of float. If he had known much about gold, he'd have known there couldn't be any pay dirt in that sort of formation.

Once Bob Womack gathered up a hatful of float that he felt sure was full of gold. That was silly and the other cowboys laughed at him, but at the first opportunity Womack took this float down to Colorado Springs. An assay showed Womack was right. There was gold, all right, but no bonanza. It was doubtful if there was enough gold in the samples to be mined profitably.

Womack went to several capitalists with his samples and assay report. He wanted someone to finance a mine on the Cripple Creek plateau. But no capitalist could be interested. These Colorado Springs money men knew their mountain district. Hadn't they been up to Mt. Pisgah during the hoax rush? Didn't they know the geological formation of Cripple Creek proved there could not be gold there in substantial quantities?

So Womack went back to his cowpunching. But in his spare time he built a shack up Poverty Gulch and when the other cowpunchers were playing poker Womack would lope up to his shack and put in an hour or so with pick and shovel.

The cowboys regarded Bob Womack as a little touched in the head—which probably was correct. They made jokes at him. They would make up long, rambling stories that had to do with Womack cherishing a nugget he had found in the horses' stable, so old Bob took to sleeping in his shack to get away from his tormentors.

One windy day in January of 1891, Womack was riding herd and the snow had been blown clear from a rock outcropping near his shack. He got off his horse and examined a piece of float with his magnifying glass. It looked much better than anything he had found before, so he sent it to an assayer in Colorado Springs. The report came back that this float assayed $250 a ton in gold.

Womack said nothing but went to digging, and in a few days he had uncovered a vein of glittering sylvanite —a gold telluride.

Old Bob didn't bother to ask leave from the ranch. He rode right down to Colorado Springs and he stopped at the first barroom to celebrate. In an hour he was gal-

loping drunkenly down Pikes Peak Avenue shouting that he'd found the richest gold mine in all history.

Someone lured Womack back into a saloon and, from his almost incoherent howlings, finally got his whole story and a sample of his sylvanite. They offered him $500 for his claim and Womack accepted it. Why not? He needed pocket money, and couldn't he find another claim even better in a few days?

With the $500 in his pocket, Bob Womack stayed drunk for several days. His discovery became the El Paso lode of the Gold King Company—one of the richest gold mines ever found in Colorado, producing many millions of dollars.

Bob Womack, however, never found another mine. He died destitute a few years later.

This was in January. In April and May about forty Colorado Springs men located claims along Cripple Creek —so named because of its treacherous banks where cattle frequently crippled themselves falling into the stream.

But still there was no concerted rush. Everyone remembered Mt. Pisgah and didn't intend to be taken in again. Colorado's most famous gold camp was slow in starting, but a wonder when it finally was under way.

As Horace Austin Warner Tabor was to Leadville, so a mild-appearing, slim-shouldered, patient-eyed man named Winfield Scott Stratton was to Cripple Creek.

Born in Indiana in 1848, Stratton learned the carpenter trade as a boy and went to Colorado shortly before he was twenty-one. That would have been in 1868.

He went prospecting, like thousands of others, and like thousands of others he had no real knowledge of mineralogy or geology. At first he probably wouldn't have known it if he had stumbled over a bonanza.

Soft-spoken Winfield Stratton was different from most of the others in one respect, however. He realized he was ill-equipped to make a strike, so he went to work in an assay office for the purpose of learning something about ores.

From then on he alternated between working at his carpentering, working in assay offices, and going out prospecting.

I have read that Tabor grubstaked Stratton on several prospecting jaunts after Stratton had done some carpentry work for the senator. That is possible, for Tabor would grubstake anyone who asked for it. But Tabor didn't get around Colorado Springs very much and there is a question whether the shy Stratton would have braved the flamboyant Tabor to ask a grubstake.

Anyhow, Stratton was in Colorado for more than twenty years before he found anything. He was credu-

lous enough to believe there might be something to Bob
Womack's bonanza, even if most of Colorado Springs
was laughing and saying, "Another Mt. Pisgah. Well,
any man can get stung once, but it takes a damn fool
to get stung twice in the same place."

Maybe Stratton hadn't learned enough in the assay
offices. Maybe he learned more than his teachers taught
him. Anyhow, he didn't believe it impossible for gold to
be found in paying quantities in that ancient lava bed
above Colorado Springs.

Womack made his discovery in January. In May,
when winter had broken in those high altitudes and the
wildflowers were blooming where the sun had melted the
snow and the magpies were showing increased interest in
life, Winfield Scott Stratton packed his bedding roll and
meal and bacon and beans on his burro and struck out
over a trail that approximated the route of a later railroad called the Cripple Creek Short Line and which still
later became State Highway 122.

Stratton prospected around the district until July
3rd and was becoming discouraged. On the night of
July 3rd he camped near where the town of Victor now
stands and he sat there in the mountain stillness beside
his campfire and thought about the Fourth of July coming on the morrow and of the celebrations he had seen,
boy and man. Stratton was a very patriotic man. He also
was considerable of a mystic, believing in signs and
portents.

When he finally rolled up in his blankets with his
burro picketed near by, Winfield Scott Stratton had a
dream. He dreamed of a mine, a gold mine of fabulous
wealth under the boulders on the north slope of Battle
Mountain.

It was a very realistic dream. Stratton identified
Battle Mountain plainly in the dream. He was certain

he knew the very seam on the north slope where the gold lay.

He awoke early and was yanking a diamond hitch on his burro while the sun was only pinking the sky over the eastern mountain ridge. He hurried to Battle Mountain. He located the seam he had seen in the dream.

Methodically, Winfield Scott Stratton went to work with pick and shovel. And before the sun went down on Independence Day, 1891, the sad-eyed Indiana carpenter had uncovered the vein which made the Independence and Martha Washington mines. From the former mine he took between three and four millions and then sold the mine to a British syndicate for $10,000,000.

Stratton was the antithesis of Tabor in most ways. Shy and retiring, he kept away from public life, although he did hold political weight because of his contributions to the party. He never was extravagant in his tastes, either in clothing or in his mode of life. He preferred plain whisky to champagne and, while he could hold his share of rye in any company, he permitted neither his money nor liquor to go to his head.

While not a scholar, Stratton loved to read. That was his idea of a good time—comfortable clothing, a big soft chair, a bottle, and a book.

He built no gaudy theaters nor bought any Queen Isabella pearls. But once Stratton had seen flames sweep an eastern firetrap of a building, so he went to work constructing some office buildings as nearly fireproof as possible.

He had many charities, but he derived his greatest pleasure from personal charities, which sometimes took quaint form.

For instance: This was the day of the bicycle's first great popularity and Stratton thought bicycles were wonderful. One day he saw a group of urchins standing in open-mouthed admiration before a bicycle shop window, gazing in at a display of shiny new wheels.

Stratton pulled on his drooping white mustache and stepped timidly up to the boys.

"How," he asked, "would you fellers like to own one of them bicycles apiece?"

One of the boys ventured that, if he thought he could get a bicycle in heaven, he'd start being so good that he'd stink.

So Stratton led the group of boys into the bicycle shop and bought each a new wheel, complete with bell and tool case. Bicycles in those days cost more than $100 in Colorado Springs.

One warm evening Stratton saw a party of laundry girls leaving work to walk wearily home. He passed the laundry and felt the hot breath of the place as he went by the door. He felt very sorry that these girls had a long walk home after working all day in such a place, so he went into the office and inquired how many girls were employed there. Then he went to all the other laundries in Colorado Springs and got the total number of girl laundry workers in the city. Then he bought bicycles for them all. He tried to do this anonymously, but he couldn't keep it secret long.

When he placed the order, the bewildered proprietor of the bicycle shop said to him, "Say, you must be working for Winfield Scott Stratton."

"What makes you say that?" Stratton inquired mildly.

"Because," said the bicycle man, "there's only one big enough damn fool in Colorado to do anything like this."

"I expect you're right," Stratton agreed.

Stratton's dream discovery on Battle Mountain started a rush to Cripple Creek in earnest. By October there was a sprawling settlement of shacks and tents with town lots selling at $25. A mining district had been formed and the settlement named for the creek.

By the next spring Cripple Creek really was booming. People no longer raised their eyebrows and referred to Mt. Pisgah. They knew now that, geology or no geology, there was something to those grassy uplands besides cow pasture.

A huge hotel was built in Cripple Creek and business blocks were going up. There was a newspaper and electric lights and many, many saloons.

No one strolled along the streets of Cripple Creek. No matter what an altitude of 9,300 feet might do to the heart, the men traveled at a trot. Casual conversations were conducted in excited shouts. Everyone was making millions—or hoped to be. Trading was going on at a feverish rate on the board sidewalks. In a single day, for instance, stock in the Buena Vista Mine jumped from $1.25 to $5.

Each day new mines were being opened, and many of these mines were destined to become famous as producers of millions. There was the Portland and the Blue Bell and the Hub and the Ironclad and the Marguerite and the Princess and the Star of the West and the Tam o' Shanter and many others.

The production of gold by Colorado mines jumped from $5,000,000 to $28,000,000 in 1892 as a result of the Cripple Creek field. The population of the town grew to ten thousand and it was as wild, almost, as Leadville had been in its day. By 1900, more than a hundred gold mines were operating profitably in the district, which took in the near-by town of Victor, and scores of millionaires were made, including Verner Z. Reed, who became known for his philanthropies, and Foster M. Symes.

Before Cripple Creek waned, the mines had given up more than $350,000,000 in gold.

Stories of the great strike brought James F. Burns and James Doyle all the way from Portland, Maine, in search of their fortune. However, the young men were late getting on the scene and by the time they reached the high plateau virtually all available claims had been taken up.

Pretty discouraged over prospects, Doyle still went nosing around and finally did find a small triangle of land which unaccountably had not been filed upon. The tract was surrounded by the property of established mines, so the Maine boys kept their activities secret after filing. In a few days they had uncovered a vein of rich ore.

Doyle and Burns were dreadfully afraid the adjoining property owners might have some claim on their little triangle, so they mined as silently as possible by day and then carried sacks of ore on their backs down to their wagon at night.

In this manner the Maine boys accumulated sufficient money to buy those dangerous adjoining claims, which weren't producing anyhow. Then they went to mining in earnest. They named their mine the Portland and it produced more than $40,000,000.

Myers Avenue in Cripple Creek corresponded with State Street in Leadville, lined with prostitutes' cribs and "parlor houses" and gambling palaces. The day started in Myers Avenue when the sun went down and closed only when the sun was rising again.

But, as is the case with all mining camps, production finally began to wane. There still is some mining in Cripple Creek, but the town has shrunk from a lusty and growing ten thousand to fourteen hundred.

The town had run down considerably even in 1914

when Julian Street made a tour of the nation to write an original and interesting book called *Abroad at Home.*

Mr. Street journeyed by the Cripple Creek Short Line to the mining camp. And Cripple Creek shocked Julian Street.

He wrote, "The depressing houses run from shabbiness to downright ruin."

He elaborated on that theme and then said: "The outlying districts . . . are a horror of smokestacks, ore dumps, shaft houses, reducing plants, gallows frames and squalid shanties situated in the mud. It seemed to me that Cripple Creek must be the most awful looking little city in the world."

In Cripple Creek someone gave Mr. Street a curious piece of misinformation. He wrote with all seriousness that the altitude—9,300 feet—was too high for domestic cats to live, that if a house cat was taken to Cripple Creek it sickened and died within a few days.

This is not at all true. Leadville and Cripple Creek and all of the high towns of Colorado seem to have as many house cats per capita as any place at sea level.

The larger part of Julian Street's chapter on Cripple Creek, however, was devoted to a description of a jaunt down Myers Avenue and an interview with an ancient harlot who went under the name of "Leo, the Lion—Mother of Prostitutes."

Mr. Street plainly was deeply horrified by this woman. But his horror was nothing to that of the Cripple Creek citizens when they read his description of their home town. You see, local pride can be just as strong in a mining town as in a textile manufacturing city or farming community or any other place.

The late James E. Hanley was mayor of Cripple Creek when Julian Street's article appeared in *Collier's.* Mr. Hanley read the article aloud at the next meeting of the Common Council and if Mr. Street had been available he might have suffered physical violence. Someone wanted to send a delegation back to New York with a barrel of tar and a feather bed, but Mayor Hanley stood up and protested.

"No," he said, "that would cost a lot of money and probably raise a big stink there in New York City and maybe give Cripple Creek a worse name back there than this fellow already has given it. I've got an idea how to get even with this Julian Street permanently. It seems like Julian Street was more interested in our red-light district than any other part of town. All right, I make a motion to change the name of Myers Avenue to Julian Street."

The motion was carried unanimously and so Mr. Street has achieved a sort of immortality with a folk who probably never read any of his very fine books.

CHAPTER TEN

Colorado Civil Wars

CRIPPLE CREEK, throughout its hectic history, achieved notoriety as the scene of bloody mine strikes.

In 1894 the first strike came and developed practically into a civil war. The Western Federation of Miners was organized the year before and on the first of the year forty gold mines in the district were working on an eight-hour schedule for a $3 a day minimum wage.

On January 17th the Pharmacist Mine posted a notice that hereafter the miners would work a ten-hour day and eat lunch on their own time. The proclamation was followed the next day by similar notices at the mines controlled by David H. Moffat, J. J. Hagerman, and Eben Smith.

These mines were the largest producers in the Cripple Creek region and employed at least one-third of all the working miners. The reason given for the increase in working hours at no increase of pay was that production did not warrant the wages paid. However, the last quarterly statement of all mines involved showed large dividends and no decrease.

There is evidence to show that David Moffat was a leading spirit in this motion, although he kept well in the background. Moffat, you may remember, was an operator at Leadville when Lieutenant Governor Tabor sent the militia up and quelled the strike to the great satisfaction of the operators.

The situation at Cripple Creek in 1894 was somewhat different from that in Leadville fourteen years
earlier. The miners were better organized, for one thing.
And H. A. W. Tabor no longer was lieutenant governor.

On February 2nd the miners held a huge mass meeting at Anaconda and demanded adherence to the union
rules. Then they declared a strike in effect and began
picketing mines which held for a ten-hour day.

Strikebreakers were brought in and the strikebreakers were beaten and chased out of town by the union
men.

The mine operators had six deputy sheriffs sent up
from Colorado Springs to preserve order and the strikers
shot one, manhandled the others, and took them all under
"arrest" to the near-by village of Altman where a union
miner was magistrate. This magistrate found the deputies guilty of carrying concealed weapons and put them
in jail.

With that, M. F. Bowers, sheriff of El Paso County,
angrily swore in fifty more deputies and wired Governor
Davis H. Waite that an insurrection was in effect in
Cripple Creek. "Rush troops at once," Sheriff Bowers
urged.

Governor Waite was a Populist in politics and
strongly in sympathy with the cause of the workingman.
So was his adjutant general, T. J. Tarsney. But of course
Governor Waite's first duty was to put down an insur-
rection—if such existed. He dispatched a trainload of
National Guard troops under General Tarsney and Gen-
eral E. J. Brooks, and his militia marched into Cripple
Creek on March 18th.

They were met by a delegation of operators who
demanded that the troops be used to protect strikebreakers working in the mines.

"No," said Tarsney, "that isn't the purpose of state

troops. If there's an insurrection here, we'll put it down. But we're not strikebreakers."

So General Tarsney went over to the town of Altman and talked with the magistrate there.

"Pshaw," said the mine union magistrate, "there's no real trouble up here. Never was a mining camp where you couldn't find a fight if you was looking for it. These strikers have got everything under control. Nothing to worry about at all."

Adjutant General Tarsney was satisfied. He loaded his troops back on the train and coasted down the hill back to Denver.

Sheriff Bowers, however, was no man to submit weakly to reverses. He began recruiting gunmen and swearing them in as deputies. He brought gunmen from Wyoming and New Mexico and Oklahoma and Texas until he had an army of twelve hundred, who were on the pay roll of the mine operators and each of whom wore the badge of El Paso County on his shirt.

Imperiled by these shock troops, the miners armed themselves, dug trenches on Bull Hill, and waited for an attack. The days stretched into weeks and the strikers got tired of waiting for the army of deputies to attempt storming their stronghold. They waited until May 24th and then a party of the strikers marched down Bull Hill, captured a squad of deputies, seized the Strong Mine and dynamited the shaft house. Then they went back up Bull Hill again.

The next day three hundred strikers made another attack with guns blazing on both sides. Herman Crawley, a strike leader, and Frank Robideau, a deputy, were killed.

Governor Waite was sympathetic with the strikers all right, but he considered this going too far—especially when he got word of miners holding mass meetings all

over the state and sending delegations of fighters to
Cripple Creek. In southwestern Colorado, for instance,
a hundred strike sympathizers had seized a freight train
and ordered the crew to take them to Cripple Creek
where they were going to "Show Sheriff Bowers's Hes-
sians a thing or two."

The governor went to Cripple Creek himself and on
June 4th held a formal meeting with the mine operators.
Earlier he had talked the situation over with representatives of the miners and he knew what the strikers wanted.
He may have been a prejudiced mediator, but the operators signed an agreement for an eight-hour day and a $3
minimum wage—exactly the status before the mineowners made their proclamation.

So the strike was over and the union men went wild
with joy. The town was decorated with flags and bunt-
ing. There was parade after parade until the bandmen's
swollen lips couldn't toot another note.

But before the day was over Governor Waite had
telegraphed Denver an urgent call for the entire Colorado National Guard to be sent to Cripple Creek immediately.

Perhaps the mine operators were willing to capitu-
late, but Sheriff Bowers wasn't licked yet. He had come
up from Colorado Springs and at the head of his army
of twelve hundred gunmen deputies was marching on
Bull Hill.

While the state troops were being mobilized in
Denver and Pueblo, one of those June cloudbursts peculiar to Colorado roared down, washing out the Cripple
Creek Short Line track, and it was not until three days
later that the militia began to arrive at the scene of
insurrection.

Strikers and Sheriff Bowers's army of deputies were
engaging in what amounted to trench warfare by the

time the soldiers came in. It was civil war certainly, but the identity of the rebels depended upon your own perspective.

Sheriff Bowers declared he was the chief of law enforcement in El Paso County and that those who opposed him were lawbreakers. That included Populist Governor Davis Waite and Adjutant General Tarsney.

The governor, on the other hand, had declared military law and technically had superseded the sheriff's authority.

On June 8th General Brooks, at the head of a skeleton brigade, marched out toward Bull Hill and issued a command for both strikers and deputies to disperse. The strikers (who already had won their point) obeyed without opposition. The deputies made no official reply to the general's command, but retired down Squaw Gulch. The soldiers camped outside of town.

On the following day the army of deputies circled the troops and marched through Cripple Creek. Many of them had been drinking and they frightened women and children off the streets by firing their rifles and revolvers in the air. Men who failed to flee from the streets were caught and clubbed and kicked and thrown into jail.

General Tarsney went into a conference with the mineowners, who agreed after this demonstration that maybe they could get along without their private army. The following day the troops drove the deputies down to Colorado Springs where Sheriff Bowers paid them off— with operators' money—and discharged them.

Thirty-seven of the strikers were indicted, charged with various offenses, but all of these were discharged except three. Two of the three were convicted of blowing up the Strong Mine shaft house and sentenced to seven years in the state penitentiary. They were pardoned, however, before they had served long.

Adjutant General Tarsney—if he hadn't done so before—revealed his sympathies during the trial by acting as attorney for the defendants. For a politician, this was indiscreet, to say the least. The sentiment in Colorado Springs was strongly opposed to the mine union. It was more strongly opposed to the Populist administration of Governor Waite. But it was practically rabid in its opposition to General Tarsney.

One midnight during the trial a gang of masked men entered the Alamo Hotel where Tarsney was staying, dragged the adjutant general from bed, hit him on the head with a revolver butt, and spirited him out on the prairie. There they stripped him of clothing and covered his body with hot tar and sprinkled the hot tar liberally with feathers. The perpetrators of this attack were never discovered. Or at least they never were arrested and convicted.

This strike ended in victory for the union. But another strike in 1904 ended the reign of the Western Federation of Miners in the Cripple Creek district.

In the late spring of 1904 there had been a strike in the Findley and Deadwood mines and strikebreakers were working fairly successfully.

At two o'clock in the morning of June 6th there were twenty-seven nonunion men from the night shifts of these mines assembled at the Independence station waiting for a suburban train which would take them back to Cripple Creek. The train was due at 2:15 A.M.

It was a warm night for Cripple Creek and most of the men were standing on the station platform when the approaching train whistled. Immediately following the whistle came a terrific explosion, which men experienced in explosives estimated as from about two hundred pounds of dynamite. Thirteen men were killed outright. The rest of the strikebreakers were injured.

The blast patently was from a gigantic bomb, for about a hundred yards of electric wire was found leading from the wrecked station to a kitchen chair placed in a shadowy spot where a man might watch the station and not be seen.

At once the whole Cripple Creek region was seething with excitement and armed men were running from their homes to congregate on the streets.

Sheriff Robertson was on hand before dawn and ordered all saloons in Cripple Creek, Victor, and Goldfield closed for the period of emergency. But that was the sheriff's last official act. It was freely rumored that this sheriff had strong leanings in favor of the mine union. A group of mine operators gathered and decided they must take matters in their own hands.

Sheriff Robertson was abducted by the mineowners, taken out to a tree, and a rope was thrown around his neck.

"Now, Robertson, you can have your choice," he was told. "You can resign your badge or hang."

Robertson saw these men meant exactly what they said. He resigned his badge.

The next move of the mine operators was to appoint Edward Bell sheriff—Edward Bell being a member of the Mine Owners' Association.

Sheriff Bell fired the entire staff of Robertson's deputies and appointed a hundred new ones—men handy with guns whom he knew he could trust. With his deputies he marched through the streets of Cripple Creek. Marching beside him was C. C. Hamlin, secretary of the Mine Owners' Association.

At the corner of Fourth and Victor streets a crowd of more than a thousand had congregated listening to a miner shout out an appeal for solidarity. In the crowd were many women and children.

"Out with your guns, men," Sheriff Bell ordered his deputies.

"Wait a minute," said Secretary Hamlin, "I want to talk to them myself."

Hamlin climbed into a wagon. With quivering voice he addressed the crowd. "I want to tell you men," he said, "that the badge of the Western Federation of Miners is a badge of murder and everyone who is responsible for the outrage at Independence should be driven from the district."

At that someone threw a brick and in an instant fighting was general between the new deputies and the crowd. At least two hundred shots were fired, but, strangely enough, only two were killed and five wounded. However, 175 union sympathizers were arrested and put in a stockade. Among them was George E. Kyner, editor of the Victor *Record*.

On the 7th of June twenty-eight union men were deported. Seven deputies accompanied the miners, who were herded into a boxcar. By then the National Guard was on hand, but this time the sympathies of the state administration were with the operators. Possession of a union card was sufficient grounds for arrest, in the opinion of then Adjutant General Sherman M. Bell.

Colonel Leo W. Kennedy was ordered by General Bell to get a list of seventy-three union men and deport them from the state.

"It is a military necessity," said General Bell. "They are men against whom crimes cannot be specified, but their presence in Cripple Creek is regarded as dangerous to law and order."

Colonel Kennedy got seventy-seven men. All had been working in the Cripple Creek mines. A majority of them were married and had families living in Cripple Creek. But they were herded in front of bayonets into boxcars and, with the soldiers packed on top of the cars, the train left Cripple Creek at 2 P. M. on June 10th.

At five o'clock the next morning the train stopped at a point a half mile from the Kansas border on the Santa Fe line. Colonel Kennedy ordered the conductor to proceed into Kansas.

"I'll do nothing of the kind," said the conductor. "You have no jurisdiction in Kansas and I'm in command of this train."

So Colonel Kennedy ordered his militia down and the deportees out of the cars.

"Now march east," Kennedy commanded.

The miners started walking east with the Colorado troops at their backs. As they approached the border the Guardsmen fired a volley over the miners' heads to speed them on their way.

"Don't any of you ever dare set foot in Colorado again!" shouted Colonel Kennedy.

But the miners were not out of Colorado yet . . .

Lined up on the border stood several hundred armed deputies of Hamilton County, Kansas, with Sheriff John Brady in charge.

"You men can't come into Kansas," called Sheriff Brady.

"You fellows will be shot on sight if you come back into Colorado," said Colonel Kennedy. Whereupon he and his soldiers climbed aboard the train and steamed back west.

The region along the Arkansas River at the Kansas-Colorado line is no garden spot now. In 1904 it was a virtual desert. The exiled miners were without food or water or money. They couldn't stay in Colorado and they couldn't enter Kansas. If they tried to march the hundred miles or so down to the first town in Oklahoma most of them would perish.

Half a dozen of the deportees pleaded with Sheriff Brady that they were native Kansans and they were permitted to cross the line. The seventy-one others walked wearily back seven miles to the plains town of Holly, Colorado.

There were only a few hundred residents in Holly, but when the tired and discouraged miners plodded into their village the citizens organized immediately and fed them and told them they could camp there until they could find refuge elsewhere.

Later that day funds were telegraphed the exiled strikers by the union and they left Holly after holding a meeting in the street thanking the citizens for saving their lives.

Thirty-three more union men were deported on June 14th and the Western Federation was practically routed from the Cripple Creek district. As a matter of fact, it became impossible for a known union man to obtain employment in that region.

While on the subject of strikes, the Ludlow affair must at least be touched.

This strike occurred on September 23, 1913, in the southern Colorado coal fields—on the Picketwire River, incidentally.

The miners were asking recognition of their union, an increase of 10 per cent in wages, an eight-hour day, a check weighman to assure honest weight, and the privilege to trade or board in other than company institutions, if they saw fit.

The mines employed guards to protect strikebreakers and fighting started. There were battles at Berwind camp, on Seventh Street in Walsenburg and at La Veta and finally at the town of Ludlow, which is about eighteen miles north of Trinidad.

In all these coal camps the company maintained boardinghouses for the single men and rows of identical, squalid shacks which were rented to the family men. It was mandatory that all employed miners live in these places.

However, when it appeared that the miners were in earnest about the strike, the companies executed mass evictions from their shacks.

With winter upon them, the strikers formed tent and shanty colonies. The largest of these colonies was at Ludlow where nine hundred men, women, and children lived through the winter until spring. For warmth, these people burrowed into the earth, making their tents serve only as roofs.

When rioting started between strikers and strike-breakers, state troops were sent to southern Colorado to maintain order. The militia was under command of Colonel Patrick Hamrock.

All winter there was sniping along the coal front, from Trinidad to Walsenburg, but particularly in the vicinity of Ludlow.

Finally, on April 20th, the order was given to "clean out" the Ludlow tent colony.

The attack by the militia was not entirely unprovoked as has been claimed. For weeks, strikers and strike sympathizers had been sniping at the military camp with deer rifles and Springfields stolen from the troops in night forays. And as the militia prepared to attack the camp, bullets began to zip around them from the colony and from the hillsides.

Someone in the militia command then lost his head and gave orders to set up machine guns and open fire on the colony.

An undetermined number were killed by the machine-gun barrage while the women, children, and other noncombatants crawled down into their warrens to escape the National Guard bullets. Consequently, they still were underground when the troops charged, driving the battling miners into the hills. And consequently the noncombatants still were there when the militia set the tent city ablaze. Scores of old men, women, and children either were burned to death or suffocated in the fire.

At news of the massacre, hundreds of outraged union men rushed to southern Colorado from all points of the compass seeking revenge on the National Guard. Federal troops were required to halt the civil war.

I have touched only on the mining business in the Arkansas River region of Colorado. I have attempted only to give a quick picture of that wild and exciting period and of some of the leading actors of the gold and silver drama.

I do not mean to give the impression that all the gold in the Colorado Rockies has been mined. There are many mines operating profitably now. There still are scores of optimistic prospectors roaming over the mountains hoping against hope to uncover another Cripple Creek or California Gulch, but the known bonanzas were pretty well stripped years ago.

There is a saying in Colorado, which no doubt is very true, that more money has been spent on Colorado mining than ever was taken from the mines. That is not supposed to take into account all the money lost investing in fake mining stock before blue-sky laws put a damper on that sort of enterprise.

The name of David H. Moffat has appeared in the annals of both Leadville and Cripple Creek. You may remember Moffat as the proprietor of a little stationery and book shop in Denver, a friend of Tabor before the carbonate king went to California Gulch.

Moffat became associated with Tabor in silver mines. He became associated with the senator in a bank that failed. He built the narrow-gauge South Park Railroad into Leadville to compete with the Denver & Rio Grande. He made millions more in Cripple Creek gold.

Moffat, like Tabor, acquired the empire builder bug, but Moffat's taste ran to railroads instead of to gaudy buildings.

He decided that what Colorado—and particularly Denver—needed was to be on the main line of a main railroad. So he started to build the Denver & Salt Lake, popularly known as the Moffat Road. It was a standard-gauge railway and ran west from Denver as directly as possible toward Salt Lake City.

In the first sixty miles there were about thirty tunnels before the line reached Tolland at the foot of James Peak, at an altitude of around nine thousand feet. Moffat's dream was to drive a tunnel right through the peak, but lacking the cash, he wound his track back and forth up the ridge of the Rockies, crossing the Continental Divide at Corona, well over twelve thousand feet—the highest point ever reached by a standard-gauge railroad.

For some reason Edward H. Harriman and his railroad group suddenly developed a craving for the Gore Cañon of the Colorado River on the western slope. But if Harriman wanted the cañon, Moffat needed it—if his road was to run farther west than the Continental Divide. Moffat put up a desperate battle against the powerful Harriman and Moffat won, although the fight ate up most of his capital. As a result, when his tracks reached the hamlet of Craig, in northwestern Colorado, Moffat was broke.

At first Moffat was not worried about his lack of

ready money. He felt his railroad already was a success in opening up the rich resources of Routt and Moffat counties, then almost an unexplored wilderness. He knew the soil there was deep and very rich. He knew there were vast outcroppings of good coal and he suspected the presence of other mineral wealth. He believed it would be a comparatively easy matter to tap these resources and make enough money to continue his construction to Salt Lake City.

However, the cost of hauling freight over the Divide at Corona proved almost prohibitive. The grades were so steep two big locomotives were required to haul even a short passenger train over the hump in good weather. And for at least half the year the arctic storms that sweep that high altitude were capable of blocking the railroad for weeks at a time.

When these things became apparent, Moffat devoted himself to an attempt at financing a tunnel through James Peak, which would do away with the necessity of climbing the Divide. It is possible he might have succeeded in this attempt, but Moffat had incurred the undying enmity of Wall Street in his fight with Harriman and the financiers vehemently rejected his plan. Moffat just didn't belong.

At last he lost his railroad. He lost everything. David H. Moffat, down to his last dollar, committed suicide in a New York hotel.

But the people of Colorado at least were convinced that Moffat's railroad and the proposed tunnel would bring prosperity to the state.

The thing was talked over for so long that virtually everybody accepted the need of a tunnel through James Peak as a prime necessity. It became an unquestioned fact. The sun and spring showers make the flowers grow.

The Moffat Tunnel would bring prosperity to Colorado. In the minds of most Coloradans it was as simple as that.

Finally the state appointed a Tunnel Commission, formed a tunnel district, which supposedly would benefit most from the project and which should be taxed to pay interest on the obligation, and tunnel bonds were issued. Engineers estimated the 6¼-mile railroad tunnel could be built for $6,000,000.

In October of 1923 they started to dig from the east and the west simultaneously. The uninitiated in engineering work worried a little lest the east and west tunnels fail to meet, but that was the very least of the builders' troubles. Inside the mountain they struck a soft rock condition that defied all the then known methods of tunnel construction. The mountain seemed to breathe and to force the soft, mulchy rock into lateral movements as well as up and down. I was in the bore several times during construction work and saw great timbers, 12 x 12 and larger, twisted and broken like wet toothpicks.

Finally the late George Lewis, chief engineer, devised an apparatus he called the Lewis Girder, which in effect was a steel frame that could be shoved along to support the walls and roof while the tunnel was being dug.

At last the tunnel was completed on March 1, 1928, and it was a great day in Colorado. That was a date to go down in history. Plans were made to hold an annual celebration on March 1st to commemorate the magnificent project which brought lasting prosperity to the state. True, the cost of the tunnel had reached $17,500,-000 instead of the estimated $6,000,000, but that was a small matter compared to the gigantic benefits to be obtained.

I don't suppose anyone ever questioned the tremendous value of the project. If they did question it, they kept pretty silent in their questioning.

It was assumed there would be a mad rush between western railroads and other private interests to gain use of the tunnel, to take over the Moffat Road and extend it immediately to Salt Lake City. The Tunnel Commission sat back and braced themselves for the clamor. They were determined to be hardheaded and make the applicants really fight for this opportunity.

Strangely, however, there was no clamor whatever. Slightly disconcerted, the Tunnel Commission sent out a hint to the railroads. Maybe they had failed to notice the newspapers, but the Moffat Tunnel was completed and ready for operation.

The Union Pacific congratulated the commission on its great engineering achievement, but really they had no need for a tunnel through the Rocky Mountains. They were quite fond of their own westward route that followed the old Overland Trail across the low hills of Wyoming, where Sherman Pass is not so high as the portals of the Moffat Tunnel. The Chicago, Burlington & Quincy didn't believe the James Peak tunnel fitted their present needs. They were sorry. Rejection of a tunnel should not be interpreted as a reflection on the engineering feat, but only that the tunnel did not fit into the Burlington's program. The Chicago, Rock Island & Pacific said they weren't interested. If, sometime in the future, they decided to build a road to San Francisco, they would talk it over. The Atchison, Topeka & Santa Fe said they were sorry, but under provisions of the treaty of Boston in 1880, they couldn't expand operations from Denver. The Denver & Rio Grande Western said they were sorry too, but they were thinking of laying off some tunnels themselves.

The Tunnel Commission and all of Colorado were

aghast. The Moffat Tunnel was completed and no one seemed to want it. The immutable laws of nature were overthrown. The sunshine and spring showers no longer made the flowers grow. There was the Moffat Tunnel—$17,500,000 worth of it—which was to make every Coloradan rich and happy, and it wasn't being used except for the dinky little trains of the Moffat Line puffing once a day out to Steamboat Springs and Craig. And it takes a lot of money to keep up a 6¼-mile tunnel—just to keep it from falling in.

Finally the desperate Tunnel Commission made an agreement with the apathetic Denver & Rio Grande Western. There was a point on the Rio Grande line where the track wound up to the town of Orestod, about thirty miles as the magpie flies from the town of Dotsero on the Moffat Line west of the tunnel. The Rio Grande would build a cutoff from Orestod to Dotsero and would run certain trains through the tunnel to Denver, saving a matter of 176 miles and the long drag over Tennessee Pass, Leadville, the Royal Gorge and Pueblo. They would pay the state of Colorado $345,900 a year for rental of the tunnel.

Of course, that rental would not pay half the interest on the tunnel bonds and this plan would leave Moffat's rich western Colorado empire still lying lonesome and untouched. But the Tunnel Commission had to do something and they accepted the bid.

At present, however, a practical purpose is being made of the pioneer bore of the Moffat Tunnel—that is, the small tunnel which was driven first so workmen could dig simultaneously in many spots from crosscuts on the big tunnel. The pioneer bore is being utilized to bring western-slope water over to the eastern slope where irrigation water has not been too plentiful.

CHAPTER ELEVEN

Meat on Friday, Melons and Dust

Now to leave the Rocky Mountains as the Arkansas booms out of the Royal Gorge and pursues its usually peaceful way east and south. The history of the river from now on is vastly different than it was in the mountains.

Just eight miles from Cañon City is the city of Florence, which is the center of a fruit district where apples are raised unsurpassed for flavor and firmness. For tasty apples you need warm days and cool, crisp nights. That is where Colorado has an edge on the great apple regions of Oregon and Washington.

Thirty-five miles more and you come to Pueblo, the second largest city in the state. Because of the steel plants and other manufactories and the pall of smoke hanging over it, they sometimes call Pueblo the Pittsburgh of the West. It is the oldest community in Colorado, situated at the mouth of the Fountain River, which runs down from the north.

Early in the nineteenth century—and probably before—French fur trappers used to winter at Pueblo and they named the Arkansas tributary "Fontaine qui Bouille," or Boiling Fountain.

Thomas J. Farnham visited the Indian settlement in 1839 and William Bent and his brothers built an adobe fort there while they experimented a little with farming. To Bent goes the credit not only of raising the first crop in Colorado, but for being the first man to employ irrigation in the state.

In July of 1843 the scout Kit Carson led General John C. Frémont to a camp of friendly Arapahos at the mouth of the Fountain. Frémont wrote: "A short distance above our encampment is a pueblo, as the Mexicans call their civilized Indian villages." He recorded that there were several white men in the pueblo, married to Indian women and engaging in farming and Indian trade. "There is a fine stock of cattle," Frémont added.

In theory, Frémont was exploring new territory. But not only had the ubiquitous and nameless French fur traders been there long before, but a party of Utah-bound Mormons had rested in Pueblo some months before Frémont.

The attempt at agriculture must have been abandoned in the four years following Frémont's visit. In 1847 Frederick Ruxton came along and, describing the village as a "small, square fort of adobe," he wrote that the Indians "live entirely on game and, the greater part of the year, without even bread, since but little maize is cultivated."

There is a curious religious fact connected with Pueblo, Colorado, which probably does not obtain in any other city in the world.

The Arkansas River bisects Pueblo, running approximately east and west. North of the river on Thursday evening and Friday the markets do a thriving business in fish—as is true any place where the Roman Catholic Church is substantially represented. South of the river, however, the markets sell no more fish on Thursday evening and Friday than any other period of the week. Yet the large majority of Pueblo Catholics live south of the river.

It happens frequently, also, that Catholics living

north of the river in Pueblo are seized by an appetite for a big steak on Friday and they blithely cross a bridge to a restaurant south of the Arkansas where they eat broiled sirloin without the slightest worry about purgatory.

The fact is that Catholics—especially Catholics of Spanish descent—do not observe the Friday fast south of the Arkansas River in Colorado. The situation holds also in the state of New Mexico and to some extent in Arizona, although there aren't so many Spanish in the latter state.

The indulgence is perfectly legal under church law. It is by no less authority than the Vatican itself.

Ask a southern Colorado Mexican (he'd much prefer being called a Spanish-American) the reason for this special privilege and he'll say in words to this effect, "Oh, in the early days around here you couldn't get many fish and the pope, he said it would be all right for us to eat meat on Friday."

The real reason for the indult is more complicated than that, however, and it goes back a deal further. It dates back to Pope Pius V, 1504-1572, who was canonized in 1712.

Pius V succeded Pius IV in 1566 and at once began prosecuting the cause of Christianity with great vigor, expelling the Jews from states of the church and burning heretics right and left.

At this time the Turks were growing rapidly in military power and threatening to gain control of the whole Mediterranean. Pope Pius V engaged the Turks in war and the Turks were joined by African corsairs and infidel Moors, imperiling Christianity so seriously that the pope formed a holy alliance between Austria, Spain, and Venice.

On October 7, 1571, came the great Battle of Le-

panto, in which a private soldier named Miguel de Cervantes lost his left hand while fighting with the forces of
King Philip II of Spain. The battle was fought in the
Gulf of Corinth and so shattered the Turkish fleet that
the Ottomans never again gained great naval strength.

Pope Pius was delighted with the fervor of King
Philip's attack on the Turks. As a reward to Philip he
issued a *bulla cruciabilis* giving the Spanish monarch
the privilege of eating meat on Friday. And the more the
pontiff thought about the Spanish valor at Lepanto, the
more delighted he became. In a day or two he extended
King Philip's indult to include all the subjects of Philip
in Spain. They weren't mentioned specifically, but all the
Spanish colonies took the rescript to mean them too.

Technically, then, Spanish colonies in North America which were free from restrictions of a Friday fast
comprised those territories gained later by the United
States in the Spanish cession of 1819, the Texas annexation of 1845, the first Mexican cession of 1848, the Texas
cession of 1850, and the Gadsden Purchase of 1852.

People of Spanish descent did not settle largely
in any of these regions, however, except Texas, New
Mexico, California, southern Arizona, and southern
Colorado.

In Colorado the Arkansas River marks the boundary
between the old Spanish territory and the old province of
Louisiana. So south of the river in Colorado and in New
Mexico and to some extent in Arizona, Catholics still enjoy the indulgence conferred upon King Philip II of
Spain by the pope in 1571. Under church practice, if
any such usage continues as long as a hundred years it
automatically is classed as an immemorial custom and
is not at all likely to be changed.

The early padres in California never took advantage
of King Philip's indult. Maybe their parishioners were

too pious. Maybe they merely wanted to help out the Monterey fish business.

A few years ago, however, some Spanish Catholics of California, jealous that their Golden State should be discriminated against when southern Colorado, New Mexico, and even the hated Arizona were taking advantage of this indult, went to Rome with a petition. If other former Spanish colonies could eat meat on Friday, why, in the name of all that's holy, couldn't Californians eat meat on Friday?

The pope considered the petition. Then he said he thought the Californians could eat enough meat six days a week.

While the available supply of fuel and fluxing material has made Pueblo a steel city, with all that term implies, the surrounding country is primarily agricultural—that is, the country bordering the Arkansas River. A few miles either side of the river and the land is better suited for grazing.

The father of the rich Arkansas Valley farming business was a bearded pioneer named George Washington Swink.

Swink went west in 1874 along with numerous other adventurers who were bent on becoming millionaires by digging gold out of the Rocky Mountains. Swink, however, was an amazingly levelheaded man. Maybe he was gifted with second sight. Or maybe he merely preferred farming to mining.

At any rate, George Washington Swink did not go on to the Rocky Mountains to pan gold. The rich soil along the Arkansas took his eye and by the time he had reached the present location of Rocky Ford, fifty miles or so below Pueblo, he wanted to go no farther. He unloaded his wagon and went to digging irrigation ditches through the rich, sandy loam.

Two years later he platted the town of Rocky Ford and set out hundreds of trees, cutting small ditches through the town's side streets through which he turned the life-giving Arkansas water.

Rocky Ford now is known across the continent for the quality of its melons. Swink is responsible for that too.

He planted sixty acres of melons himself and so successful was this venture that fifty carloads of melons were shipped from Rocky Ford twelve years after Swink yelled "whoa" to his team and started unloading his wagon.

In 1887 the *Rocky Mountain News* in Denver published a long description of affairs on the lower Arkansas valley of Colorado, characterizing Rocky Ford as an oasis in the desert with thrifty trees and rich fields of alfalfa stretching for miles on either side.

While few of the gold seekers found riches in the mountains, farmer Swink actually founded an empire and made a fortune with his plow and ditching spade.

More wealth by far has been produced by the Colorado sugar beet than ever was dug in precious metals from the Colorado mountains. William M. Byers, editor of the *Rocky Mountain News* in 1866, was partially responsible for that.

On November 3rd of that year Byers wrote an editorial declaring the rich soil of Colorado had "no superior for sugar beets," and urging ranchers to make their fortunes with that crop.

I don't know whether Byers knew what he was writing about or not. Perhaps he was an expert on sugar beets and sugar-beet soil. Perhaps he only had read something about the sugar-beet industry in Germany and jumped at a conclusion. Perhaps he needed an editorial to fill a space and sugar beets were the first thing that popped into his mind. Editorial writers are sometimes like that.

At any rate, the editorial was read by a beetle-browed Scandinavian pioneer named Peter Magnes and Magnes was convinced that he should try raising sugar beets. He brought the seed from Illinois and started an industry that now produces approximately two million tons of sugar beets annually.

Agricultural settlement of eastern Colorado came slowly. Before the invention of dry farming, it was not deemed possible to raise a crop without irrigation in a region where the annual precipitation was less than twenty inches. Arid prairie land with its buffalo grass was regarded as good grazing land, but entirely unfitted for agricultural purposes. And if they had continued to regard this land of eastern Colorado and western Oklahoma and western Kansas in that light they would have saved themselves and Uncle Sam no end of trouble.

A good example of what has happened is shown by a test tract in Baca County of southeastern Colorado, which has been under study by the Land Utilization Division of the United States Department of Agriculture.

In this tract of sixteen sections—10,240 acres, or sixteen square miles—only one 160-acre homestead had been filed on in 1888. Twenty-seven years later that same situation held—one 160-acre homestead surrounded by good grazing land.

The twenty-seven years, however, takes us to January 1, 1915, when the first World War was getting into its stride. The wheat market had broken records and was still climbing. Europe was calling for bread.

About this time someone discovered that in favorable years wheat could be grown on dry land by the expedient of plowing the soil in the fall to utilize the winter snows. With the tremendous demand for wheat, farmers were encouraged to go west and make their fortunes on dry land.

Homesteaders began to file on this Baca County land in February, 1915. By June all of these sixteen square miles had been entered on except three sections, and those were homesteaded in a year or two.

In 1909 an act had been passed, granting a homesteader the right to file on 320 acres of semiarid land instead of the traditional 160, so these sixteen square miles of old grazing land soon were fenced into 320-acre farms, each one with a nominal house and each one plowed up for wheat and wheat alone. The tough old buffalo grass was all plowed out.

It so happened that these first few years were in a "wet cycle." Sufficient rain fell to make good wheat crops and before long, attracted by the quick and easy money, most of the land surrounding our Baca County test tract was being homesteaded and plowed. The test tract is typical of that entire region.

Gasoline tractors were perfected and the land holders went in for cash crops. Although they technically are farmers and are regarded as farmers by Congress, these wheat raisers are not farmers. You might call them wheat miners.

A midwestern farmer or an eastern farmer or a Pacific coast farmer, if he is any good at all, rotates his cash crops to spare his land from depletion. He also raises hogs and chickens and some cows and horses and garden truck. He sells a certain amount of milk and he gets along even if his cash crops should be burned out in a drought or washed out in a flood.

The dry farmer of eastern Colorado, on the other

hand, plants nothing but wheat. He leases a lot of land, tractors it in the fall, puts in his seed, and then sits around praying for a lot of snow or rain. He buys his supplies at the town grocery and eats from tin cans. If he gets his snow and rain and the hail doesn't come and ruin his crop and the price of wheat isn't depressed too much, he celebrates by buying a new car and a new tractor and he leases more land for the next year.

If the crop fails, the dry farmer calls for farm relief and lives off the government until time for another gamble when the government, likely as not, buys his seed for him.

The traditional farmer works from dawn to sunset. The wheat miner stands around the streets of the nearest town all day, declaring something has got to be done about the New York Yankees before they ruin baseball, arguing whether a V-8 is superior to a Straight-8, squinting at the sky between cigarettes and wishing to God it would rain.

This is the Dust Bowl country. This is the country that never should have been plowed—the birthplace of the Black Rollers.

This is the land of the suitcase farmer, who doesn't even live on a farm. He is a city man and a gambler. He leases a dozen or so sections of land, puts a gang plow and tractor or so in a truck, goes out to his territory, and plows in a crop. He lives at a hotel in the nearest town and hires tractor operators to work for him. If he gets a crop he makes plenty of money. If he doesn't get a crop he hasn't lost much anyhow.

A good proportion of the resident farmers have become discouraged in recent years and have left the Dust Bowl. The Land Utilization Division has been buying this submarginal land to rescue the owners from starvation and to spare the beaten soil from further plowings. Eventually this land will grass over and the dust storms will be beaten.

It was the plowing that brought the dust storms— not the droughts. Droughts are almost the normal thing in eastern Colorado. The altitude ranges from 2,500 feet above sea level to about 5,000 feet and in the dry, clear air the sun beats down unmercifully. And how the wind does boom!

In the old days there were no real dust storms for the simple reason that the tough grass roots held the soil down. Now, with the land plowed, the sun and the wind pulverize it powder-fine and it rides the breeze as easily as smoke.

The now famous Black Rollers are spectacular and terrifying things. Everyone knows about them. But, as a matter of fact, the awesome Black Rollers don't do the real damage to the Dust Bowl area.

Take a bright spring day when the wind comes along in breezy gusts and it whips the soil along a foot or two above the ground. The dust drifts into the fence rows. It piles in hummocks about the sage and bunch grass. And it acts exactly like a sandblast to everything that lies in its way, cutting off the new grass and wheat close to the ground.

The submarginal land—the real Dust Bowl land which the government has been buying for some years—is being retired from cultivation. It will take a long time to get it well grassed again—from five to fifty years, it is estimated, according to how badly the soil is eroded. When it is grassed over again, the land once more will be good for cattle grazing.

From Rocky Ford it is just ten miles downstream to La Junta, which also owes its being to the foresight and industry of bearded George Swink, but its growth to the fact that the Santa Fe Railroad made this spot a junction point.

Twenty miles farther on and there is the town of Las Animas with the mouth of the Picketwire River and Fort Lyon where Kit Carson died and from whence rode the gigantic Reverend John C. Chivington one November day in 1864 at the head of the Third Colorado Cavalry. The Reverend Mr. Chivington was to commit a massacre on a village of Cheyenne and Arapahoe Indians forty miles to the north on the banks of Big Sandy Creek. Or, if you take the viewpoint of Colonel Chivington's partisans, he was to do battle with a force of savages, superior in numbers and equipment, and win a glorious victory.

However, a few days before Chivington's attack the Indians had appealed to the commandant at Fort Lyon for friendly relations. The attack was launched on the village without warning at dawn.

Massacre or glorious victory, the Reverend Mr. Chivington's own sworn statement was that five or six hundred Indians were killed, including women and children. This statement, made at the official investigation of the Battle of Sand Creek,[1] said the white cavalry lost seven killed, forty-seven wounded, and one missing.

Chivington's statement said further: "I do not know that any Indians were wounded that were not killed; if there were any wounded, I do not think they could have been made prisoner without endangering the lives of the soldiers; Indians usually fight as long as they have strength to resist."

Irving Howbert, later a financier and Republican politician in Colorado Springs, was a corporal in Colonel Chivington's command. Years after the battle, in writing a defense of Chivington, Howbert said: "Not once did I see anyone shoot at a squaw or child, nor did I see anyone take a scalp, although it is true that in some instances this was done, for, as I returned to camp, I saw a number of dead Indians whose scalps had been taken, among them a few squaws."

As a result of the affair on Big Sandy, Chivington gave up both military and clerical careers. He went back to Ohio and entered politics with indifferent success.

Now we have followed the Arkansas down to Lamar, Colorado, and the Kansas border where Coronado and his silver-plated Spaniards once went the wrong way in search for precious metals. It is a land which does not look friendly or even interesting to Easterners, but it is a land with a history.

Even in recent times, this country was the home of the Fleagle brothers, as brazen and heartless bandits as

[1] While this affair is known as the Battle of Sand Creek, it really occurred on the banks of Big Sandy Creek.

ever drew a gun. They were the boys who, after the Lamar bank robbery, took one of the tellers along as a shield from the posse's bullets. When they were through with the teller, they calmly killed him. One of their party was wounded and needed medical attention. The Fleagles went to town and kidnaped a physician. Held prisoner, the doctor was forced to treat the bandit's wound until he was recovering and then the Fleagles led the doctor out to an arroyo and shot him in the back.

Before we cross with the river into Kansas, just a word as to the origin of Colorado. Most states came from some single definite source. New York, for instance, was one of the thirteen original colonies. Missouri came from the Louisiana Purchase of 1803. Nevada was ceded by Mexico in 1848.

It took three such actions to bring Colorado into being—and then they overlooked part of it.

The eastern end of Colorado, north of the Arkansas River and east of the Colorado River, came into the United States by way of the Louisiana Purchase.

The land south of the Arkansas and a straight, narrow strip up through the state into Wyoming came in when Texas was annexed in 1845. The western part of Colorado was ceded by Mexico in 1848.

Strangely enough, no one ever stopped to consider until recently that there was a region comprising about two thousand square miles in Summit and Grand counties which lay between the Colorado River and the strip annexed along with Texas.

Those two thousand square miles never had been ceded by anyone or purchased from anyone or captured from anyone. It was a buffer state with nothing to buff. It had no official antecedents whatever, because officially it didn't exist.

When the people of Grand and Summit counties

became cognizant of this curious fact they began to worry. Maybe they weren't even American citizens although born right there in the center of Colorado. Maybe one of these days France or Spain or somebody would suddenly discover they owned a colony in the middle of continental United States and call on these good Colorado people to send fiefs across the sea.

So the women's clubs and civic leaders of Breckenridge, Dillon, Kremmling, and other towns of this orphan district got together to conduct a conquest for territory. On August 8, 1936, they marched into Breckenridge and captured the town without bloodshed, although there was considerable gunfire with blank cartridges. The American flag was raised and, while it is possible there may have been some inarticulate opposition from disorganized minorities, Summit and Grand counties, Colorado, were declared henceforth and forever to be part of the United States of America.

CHAPTER TWELVE

Western Kansas

Leaving Colorado, the Arkansas flows into southwestern Kansas—a high, spectacularly level plateau, ranging from two thousand feet above sea level to well over four thousand feet.

The scenery is mostly cloud scenery—great cumulus clouds heaped up into gigantic terraces and turrets. I know no place where one is more conscious of sky than in western Kansas. There is twice as much sky to look at as there is at sea. This is because you can see twice as far in the clear, dry air.

The first community you come to following the river is Syracuse. That is, Syracuse is the first community large enough to be called a town. Syracuse is twenty-two miles from the Colorado border and there are a couple of filling stations called Coolidge and Medway in between.

Syracuse has about fifteen hundred inhabitants now and it has the regulation stores and shops and movie theater. It has a history, too, but the thing I remember particularly about Syracuse, Kansas, has little to do with the history of Syracuse, Kansas.

It was in the early days of commercial flying and I was on a newspaper mission in a chartered plane. We flew southeast down from Denver over a country which seemed mostly desolate and uninhabited from the air, until we struck the irrigated greenery along the Arkansas. The pilot never had been over this country before.

I never had seen it from the air before. And our map was one of the primitive road maps they put out about twenty years ago.

So, while we knew we were on our course and we could follow the Arkansas River and the Santa Fe Railroad eastward to our destination, we didn't know whether we still were over Colorado or whether we might be as far east as Dodge City.

Finally, at about three thousand feet, we sighted a railroad station below and the pilot quieted the motor and said, "I'll nose her down and you read the sign on the depot."

He nosed her down with engine howling and the little brown Santa Fe station came rushing up at us. Far to the east across the dun and lavender plains we could see an approaching train, probably still invisible from the station, but there were a dozen or so Kansans on the platform waiting to see Old 97 pound through. Presently they caught the roar of our motor and their white faces were turned upward as we hurtled down. They began to shift here and there uneasily. Then they broke and ran like disturbed ants—apparently fearing our crate was out of control and going to crash right on the station platform.

I strained my eyes upon the end of the station. Against the general brown of the building I could make out a white streak that would be the name of the town. I could see a blur of letters and at last the blur resolved itself into a word: SYRACUSE.

I yelled the word to the pilot and he pulled back on the stick and pushed the throttle forward. Our old war-time Hispano-Suiza let go the Bronx cheer of a thousand giants and we rocketed up toward the turreted clouds. I craned my neck down and there was not a soul in sight. The train was a little closer to Syracuse across the dun and lavender plains. A small white plume of steam blossomed from the locomotive as Old 97 whistled and the Arkansas River glistened in the sunshine.

This western Kansas country was the scene of that curious phenomenon of town booming in the 1880's. It also was the scene of numerous county-seat wars. The one followed the other as a natural consequence.

Of course, town booming was not limited to southwestern Kansas. There has been town booming in practically all new countries. But in *eastern* Kansas, for instance, there was not such a disparity between anticipation and realization.

As a rule in town booming, the boomers have built far in advance of any needs that a calm and disinterested person could visualize. That was true in the case of Kansas City, Missouri. But in the case of Kansas City, Missouri, and other sections of the fertile Midwest, there were potentialities to be realized. The building was only slightly premature and time justified the wildest claims of the most optimistic optimists.

Sadly, those potentialities were lacking in the shortgrass country of Kansas.

In the 1880's, when that region was being settled, there was no reason in the speech of the boomers. If 160 acres was enough for a good farm in Illinois or eastern Kansas or Nebraska, they argued, why, a 160-acre farm in western Kansas was even better. There were no trees and brush to cut out. There was no wasteland. The soil was sandy and rich. All that was needed to make this region a garden spot was water and anyone with faith in God should know the Almighty would provide water when it was needed.

There were those in the 1880's who stoutly held there was sufficient rainfall in western Kansas even then to provide bumper crops. The current year, they were convinced, was just one of the dry seasons one has to expect anywhere. They held that the climate of the shortgrass country was changing. The basis for this argument was a theory that cultivation of the soil retained moisture, thus increasing evaporation, and that the evaporation of the moisture promoted more rain.

There was a saying in those days that "Rain follows the plow." And this epigram was believed as firmly as if it had come direct from the Holy Writ.

Of course, we now can look back and see how silly it was for anyone to believe that scratching the soil lightly here and there over a vast plain that had dried and baked under the wind and sun for centuries could possibly change the climate. We can see how silly that belief was—just as our children will be able to look back at many of our own practices and beliefs and marvel at our grotesque credulity.

There were some in western Kansas, however, who scoffed at the idea that plowing would bring the rains. They were the cattlemen. But the cattlemen were patently too prejudiced for their opinions to be considered by the wishful thinking homesteaders. It was plain for the homesteaders to see that cattlemen wanted only to discourage immigration. Let a few thousand farmers move in and where would the priceless unfenced range be?

Several more or less scientific gentlemen went out to western Kansas in those days and brought forth magnificent schemes for irrigating the sandy plains. They weren't popular, either. Plans for irrigation, in the first place, showed a reprehensible lack of faith in the Lord. In the second place, publicizing plans for irrigation might make timid investors and immigrants infer there was a lack of rainfall in this garden spot of the world.

To gain an adequate picture of the situation in western Kansas of 1880, it is necessary to tell something of Dodge City.

Dodge City was the metropolis of the short-grass country. The early history of Dodge City definitely is the early history of all that surrounding country.

Dodge City now is a modern-looking little city of about twelve thousand population. It is located a hundred and thirty miles downriver from the Colorado line and about forty-five miles north of the Oklahoma border. There are green lawns and geraniums and sunflowers and lots of big cottonwood trees and good schools and neon signs and red-fronted ten-cent stores and churches. You can buy two per cent beer in Dodge City and, if you know the proper place down by the Santa Fe tracks and have that sort of inclination, you can buy illegally something much stronger than two per cent beer, something which probably is made of ensilage juice. There is practically no crime in Dodge City—unless you count driving an automobile too fast a crime.

Dodge City was founded in September of 1872 when the railroad reached that point. It was named for Colonel Richard Dodge, commander of Fort Dodge and one of the founders of the city.

Almost at once the community achieved three distinctions: It became the northern terminus of the Texas cattle trail. It became the center of the buffalo hide industry. And for a period it was known as the toughest town in the West.

Some of the boom cattle years saw half a million head of longhorns brought into Dodge City to be loaded on cattle cars and shipped to Kansas City or Chicago.

The herders, released from the toil of driving bawling thousands up across the alkali flats and around quicksand sinks, dropped their cowboy inhibitions for cowboy entertainment. And to assist the cowboy in his quest for

joy unrestrained, there came to Dodge City gamblers and harpies and thieves and badmen and would-be bad-men.

At this time literally millions of bison were roam-ing the Kansas and Oklahoma plains. They moved in herds that sometimes extended for more than fifty miles. They were lumbering beasts and easily killed by a horse-man with the new repeating 45-90 rifle that could pump ounce slugs of lead into buffalo hearts at the rate of one a second.

At first the bison was sought for his meat. He was the Indian's staple. And buffalo flesh fed the Irishmen who graded the right of way and laid the tracks for the Union Pacific across Nebraska and the Santa Fe across Kansas.

Judged by any standard except an Indian's, it was not very good meat. It was too tough and stringy. Hunters killing for their own use customarily would slaughter half a dozen, cut out the tongues for food and leave approximately six tons of buffalo meat and bone for the coyotes.

When the thousands of Texas longhorns began walking their beefsteak up to the railroad in Kansas, the demand for buffalo meat dropped to almost nothing. Then the buffalo hunting business increased tremendously.

That is not a paradox. The railroad not only took western beefsteak east, but it took knowledge of the buffalo also. Easterners discovered what the western Indian had known for generations—that buffalo robes were astonishingly warm. More important, however, eastern manufacturers discovered that tanned buffalo hides had prodigious wearing qualities as power belting.

This was a period of great industrial expansion. More and more belts were required for more and more machinery. So there soon was a booming demand for buffalo hides. The belting manufacturers were paying $5 a hide, f.o.b. Dodge City. And the supply was, or seemed to be, unlimited.

Young farmers who could ride a horse and fire a rifle rushed out to western Kansas from Missouri and Iowa and Illinois and soon the buffalo hides were stacked ten feet high beside the Santa Fe tracks at Dodge City. They were stacked in odorous piles ten feet high and a hundred yards long waiting for shipment.

Pretty soon the inevitable happened. The supply caught up with the demand and by and by the price of raw buffalo hides dropped to $1. Most of America's "unlimited" buffalo herds were killed off at a dollar a head, which included the killer's trouble of skinning and transporting to the railroad. Three million buffalo hides were shipped east from Dodge City in the five years from 1872 to 1877.

It was in 1874 that Dodge City got so tough it frightened itself. On May 13th of that year the county commissioners adopted a resolution providing that,

"Any person who is not engaged in any legitimate business, and any person who has ever borne arms against the government of the United States, who shall be found within the limits of the town of Dodge City, bearing on his person a pistol, Bowie knife, dirk or other deadly weapon, shall be subject to arrest upon a charge of misdemeanor, and upon conviction shall be fined in a sum not exceeding one hundred dollars or by imprisonment in the county jail not exceeding three months, or both, at the discretion of the court, and the same to take effect from date."

One of the troubles in Dodge City was that the interests of the cowboys off the Texas trail and the interests of the buffalo hunters conflicted. So the cowboys took to eliminating the buffalo hunters, and vice versa. Also, the soldiers from Fort Dodge were inclined to pick fights not only with the cowboys and buffalo hunters, but with the lordly gamblers.

One of the first big fights occurred in a dance hall between troopers and gamblers when a soldier named Hennessey, who fancied he had been cheated, undertook to clean out the place. The soldier and his buddies managed to kill half a dozen gamblers and bystanders before Hennessey went down with half a pound of lead in his body.

By 1874 a gravedigger had practically steady work in Boot Hill providing final resting spots for hardy fellows whose draw was too slow or whose luck had run out.

To halt this wave of killing, the Ford County commissioners followed the example of Abilene, Kansas, and Austin, Texas, in the selection of a town marshal. These other towns had decided the way to handle tough men was to hire the toughest of the lot as peace officer.

Dodge City tried a whole platoon of badmen as mar-

shal. First was Jack Bridges, the scout, who killed several
before he gave way to Billy Brooks, whose reputation was
that of a wanton killer. It is reported that Brooks shot
fifteen men in his first month at Dodge City. Following
Billy Brooks were Ed Masterson and his more notorious
brother, Bat; the fearless Wyatt Earp, "Mysterious"
Dave Mathers, Charley Bassett and the great Billy Tilghman and his deputy Ben Daniels.

Until Tilghman's time, the gunmen marshals of
Dodge City killed a number of minor thugs, but the
town failed to quiet appreciably.

In 1879 President Hayes passed through Dodge City
and was to have been accorded a splendid welcome. The
president was scheduled to make a speech to this vigorous
frontier community from the bunting-draped rear platform of the train.

Unfortunately, however, the spirit of celebration
got moving too soon. The saloon business was too rushing
before the train arrived and when the presidential special

steamed up to the station the raucous yells of the wel-
coming committee and the alarming drumfire of revolvers caused President Hayes to stay discreetly in his car,
not even showing himself at the windows.

"Uncle Billy" Tilghman and Ben Daniels finally
tamed Dodge City. Tilghman was a just man and not
given to dealing favors to friends and bullets to op-
ponents. He was as fast on the draw and as accurate with
a pistol, apparently, as any gunman of the old West.
It has been declared often, however, that Tilghman never
fired at a man except to save his own life when making
an arrest.

Unlike some of the marshals (Hickok, for instance),
Tilghman was not one to play a friendly game of poker
with a hunted bandit and then shoot down a drunken
soldier who cursed him. Tilghman's word was law. For
fifty years as a peace officer in the wild West, Uncle
Billy captured scores of desperate outlaws without firing
a shot. His method was to approach the badman casually
and with no display of firearms. Then he would say with
deadly quietness, "Son, you'd better give me your gun."

Tilghman was a huge man and powerful. He captured Bill Doolin, the Indian Territory bandit, with his
bare hands even after Doolin tried to draw his gun.

After Dodge City had been turned into a law-abid-
ing community, comparatively speaking, Uncle Billy accepted a bid to clean up several Oklahoma towns. He
was still in Oklahoma after the World War and still a
peace officer during the hectic days of the Volstead Law.
A man well along in his seventies, Tilghman sought to
quiet a drunken prohibition agent who was creating a
disturbance in a Cromwell, Oklahoma, dance hall. The
prohibition agent did what hundreds of badmen of the
old West had failed to do—end Tilghman's career with a
bullet. The peace officer's body was taken to Oklahoma

City and lay in state at the capitol, where it was viewed by thousands.

This was Dodge City in the days preceding and during the period of town booming and county-seat wars in western Kansas.

There was no county-seat war in Ford County, which was dominated, of course, by Dodge City. It was more or less the same story with Finney County and Garden City. But there were a number of other counties which had no dominant community and trouble developed. Optimistic settlers developed an exaggerated estimate of the wealth that would result from designation of their particular hamlet as county seat and they were willing to go to almost any length to obtain that designation.

The crimes committed in the interest of county-seat designation ranged from subornation of perjury through bribery and ballot box stuffing to murder.

In Grant County, south of the Arkansas River, the battle was between the communities of Ulysses and Appomattox. The Appomattox folk believed it to be in accordance with the general fitness of things for an Appomattox Courthouse to stand in Grant County. Ulysses had been built hopefully in accordance with that same law. In addition, Ulysses had more money than Appomattox.

As the day of election neared, the civic leaders of Appomattox and Ulysses held a conference and both sides agreed to abide by the election results and to support the victorious town. It was agreed, moreover, that the victors would reimburse their defeated rivals for expenses in the attempt to build up an opposition county seat. It was agreed that the losing town should be abandoned after election.

The Appomattox boomers operated the time-honored but haphazard system of influencing voters, making extravagant promises, on the one hand, and warning of calamity, on the other. The Ulysses boomers were more direct and employed the simple expedient of paying $10 cash for every Ulysses vote. Consequently, it was a glorious victory for Ulysses.

Immediately after the election results were posted, the stunned Appomattox residents learned of the agreement entered upon by their civic leaders and the cry of treachery rang across the prairies. Homesteaders came tearing into Appomattox with lathered horses and guns loose in their holsters.

The perfidious civic leaders were taken into custody and locked up in the building that had been erected fondly as a courthouse while the hotter heads cried out to lynch their false leaders en bloc. After forty-eight hours' imprisonment the leaders promised to pay off all losses of the Appomattox boosters and they were released. They paid off the claims without argument—paid them with checks. The civic leaders were safely out of the county before the checks bounced back.

So in Grant County the victory and the spoils went to the city of Ulysses and the city of Appomattox, betrayed by its sponsors and routed by $10 ballots, died in its infancy. Ulysses, in the intervening half century and more, has grown to a population of 436.

In Wichita County, north of Garden City, the battle was between the towns of Leoti and Coronado. Some of the Leoti adherents deduced they could win the election if they could frighten the Coronadans sufficiently. So a party of Leoti bully boys galloped the three or four miles over to the rival community, shot up the place and made the leading Coronado boomers dance with bullets splintering the board sidewalks around their feet.

Finally some of the Coronadans managed to slip away and pick up their own hardware and a general battle was held along the town's main street. Three men were killed and several others seriously wounded.

All those killed were Leoti invaders, among them their leader, Jack Coulter, a cowboy who fancied himself as a badman. There is a legend around Leoti that bad, bad Jack Coulter's trigger finger twitched for half an hour after his death.

But Coulter and his pals didn't die in vain. Leoti won the election and now it has a population of 618. Coronado has survived with less than a hundred.

To my mind the most interesting of the county-seat wars was in Gray County. One of the principals in that affair was a friend of mine—a picturesque old gun fighter named Jim Marshall.

I knew Jim Marshall in his closing days, when he was a deputy sheriff in Denver—a dignified, handsome old fellow with white Vandyke and stiff-brimmed Stetson. He had been marshal in Cripple Creek during some of the wild days and peace officer in various parts of the West. His body was scarred by bullets and his legs were full of buckshot, put there, so he attested, by a dead man—a bandit killed by Jim's bullet who discharged his shotgun as he fell. Marshall's trigger finger had been shot away in one gun fight, so he had taken the trigger off his Bisley model Colt and "fanned" the hammer with his broad thumb.

Jim Marshall was in Dodge City during the tough period. I don't know what he was doing there, but probably it was gambling. Years later he was to operate a gambling house in Denver.

Anyhow, Jim and the more widely known Bat Masterson were hired for a special job in the Gray County war and that job nearly cost both their lives.

From Rochester, New York, there had come an adventurer named Asa T. Soule, who was impressed with the seeming opportunities of this new land. Mr. Soule was a man of means. As a matter of fact, he was a man of millions. He had made his fortune manufacturing and merchandising a panacea called Hop Bitters.

Mr. Soule's first move was to make the short-grass country bloom like the valley of the Nile and he started an enterprise called the Eureka Irrigating Canal down south of Dodge City. He gave that up when he was unable to get water into his ditch.

Then Mr. Soule built a railroad from Dodge City down southwest some fifty miles to a hamlet called Montezuma. But after the railroad was built it appeared that no one in Dodge City wanted to ride the steam cars to Montezuma and there wasn't any freight in Montezuma to haul to Dodge City. So Mr. Soule gave that up too and went to work booming the village of Ingalls to became county seat of Gray County.

At this time the town of Cimarron was county seat on a temporary basis. Mr. Soule had acquired considerable property in and about Ingalls, six miles up the Arkansas River from Cimarron. He believed that if Ingalls were to become the permanent seat of county government the value of his property would be increased millions of dollars.

An election was held, but the vote went against the hopes of Mr. Soule, except that an Ingalls man was elected county clerk. In that one victory the Hop Bitters magnate believed he saw his opportunity.

In Dodge City he hired Marshall, Masterson, and several others with similar reputations to attempt a coup d'état at Cimarron.

The new county clerk swore in the hired gunmen as deputy sheriffs of Gray County and issued them shiny new badges just obtained from Kansas City. Then in a dray the new peace officers drove the nineteen miles up the river from Dodge City and stopped at the Cimarron courthouse to take over the county records.

It was assumed by Mr. Soule that, if the county records and seal could be removed to his town, Ingalls automatically would become county seat of Gray County.

The dray was driven up to the courthouse door with a great deal of shouting and firing of revolvers. This was designed to frighten the Cimarron citizens into meek submission. But it didn't work. Perhaps the Cimarron folk failed to recognize the redoubtable Bat Masterson and Marshall. Anyhow, they weren't much frightened.

While the rest of the Ingalls gang stood guard over the dray, Masterson and Marshall rushed into the courthouse and began to pile the scant records of the new county together with the official seal and what not. By that time the Cimarron menfolk had answered the tocsin and came running from every direction, firing buffalo rifles, shotguns, and pistols at the invaders' outer guard.

This guard by the dray was composed of rough, tough Dodge City bullies. But they weren't quite rough enough and tough enough to stand up before the guns of the outraged Cimarron citizens. They scrambled into their dray, lashed the horses into a gallop and clattered out of town as fast as they could travel, leaving Jim Marshall and Bat Masterson in a very embarrassing position.

The two were alone in the courthouse and the courthouse was surrounded by a hundred or more irate townsmen who unmistakably were out for blood.

Glass from the courthouse windows was crashing and clinking and Masterson and Marshall took refuge on the second floor, firing out whenever they could get near a window.

All day long they were prisoners in the courthouse with bullets spattering into the window jambs each time they ventured to peek out. Neither Marshall nor Masterson was hit and the attackers likewise escaped injury. But one traditional innocent bystander, standing with his hands in his pockets a block away, was struck by a bullet from the courthouse and instantly killed.

The siege continued through the night and early the following morning the besieged were out of ammunition. Bat Masterson took off his white, stiff-bosomed shirt and waved it from a shattered window.

"If you're surrendering," a voice yelled from the dawn, "come on out with your hands up."

So the weary mercenaries marched out of the Cimarron courthouse with hands aloft and the Cimarron people organized a court immediately to place Masterson and Marshall on trial charged with killing the innocent bystander.

The defendants offered a unique defense. They weren't guilty of killing the man because they didn't even know him. They had no grudge against this stranger and hadn't shot at him. The death was an accident because the man just happened to get in the way of a bullet fired in defense of the prisoners' lives.

This seemed reasonable to the Cimarron jury and the jurymen brought in a verdict of acquittal with two qualifications. First, Masterson and Marshall must pay for the window glass the Cimarron boys had shot out of the courthouse. Second, neither of the defendants must ever set foot in Cimarron, Kansas, again under penalty of immediate hanging.

So Jim Marshall and Bat Masterson left not only Cimarron, but the state of Kansas.

"By God and by Jesus," drawled Jim Marshall, pawing his white Vandyke with the stub of his trigger finger, "there wasn't a doubt that Cimarron jury meant just what it said. Their verdict went right down in the county records—if Bat Masterson or Jim Marshall ever showed up in that town again there was to be a necktie party.

"I was willing to believe 'em. So was Bat Masterson. Even when Bat Masterson went back to New York he went out of his way to keep from going through Cimarron. Didn't even want to go through there on a train."

So Cimarron became permanent county seat of Gray County and it now has a population of a thousand. Ingalls is just a little town of 273.

Mr. Hop Bitters Soule gave up trying to do anything for Gray County and founded Soule College in Dodge City.

CHAPTER THIRTEEN

Great White Paternalism

THIRTEEN miles east of Dodge City, the Arkansas swoops abruptly northward for forty miles to Great Bend, as if it had decided to cut a beeline to the Missouri River. But at Great Bend, scene of a disastrous tornado in 1916, the river remembers its destiny and turns back down southeast to pass through the enterprising city of Hutchinson and, sixty miles farther on, the city of Wichita.

Wichita, as far as population is concerned, is the second city in Kansas, surpassed only by Kansas City, Kansas. Kansas City, Kansas, has a population of about 125,000. Wichita has about 120,000. But to look at the retail business districts alone, one would judge that Wichita was at least twice the size of Kansas City. The reason for that mistake would be, first, that Kansas City, Kansas, is overshadowed by the adjoining Kansas City, Missouri, and, second, because Wichita itself is an exceedingly live town.

Wichita started booming about twenty-five years ago when an oil field came in at her back yard. Wichita started booming with oil and when the white-hot enthusiasm for the Eldorado field wore off, Wichita had the booming habit and kept it up from sheer momentum.

At present Wichita is one of the leading airplane manufacturing points in the nation as well as being something of an aerial crossroads. The busy airplane industries attract other enterprises. Other enterprises attract people. So Wichita seems destined to be the largest city in Kansas.

From Wichita the river wriggles its course forty or fifty miles southward to Arkansas City, which is right on the Oklahoma border. Arkansas City has about fifteen thousand population and I personally can attest it's a hot spot. I have seen the thermometer register 114° there at midday and 100° at midnight.

Perhaps the Arkansas City Chamber of Commerce will be disposed to challenge that record—especially the midnight figure.

Lots of western towns will admit it gets warm there in July and August, but they always declare it cools off at night, influenced by the gulf winds or the high altitude or the low humidity or the ancient spell cast by an Indian medicine man in honor of his beautiful daughter.

But I still say I have seen it very hot at night in Arkansas City, too insufferably, sticky hot to sleep, and that the perfectly reliable-looking thermometer in front of a drugstore registered 100° at midnight.

Also, in the days when it was against the law to sell cigarettes or cigarette papers in Kansas, you could buy cigarettes with little trouble in Wichita and Topeka and Independence and Pittsburg and Salina and Junction City and Lawrence and Emporia but, as far as I could discover, there were no cigarettes for sale or barter in Arkansas City.

In 1889 Arkansas City was the scene of one of the most exciting and remarkable episodes in all of America's strange history. But this episode had to do with Oklahoma rather than Kansas.

It was the rush into the Cherokee Strip when at a cannon shot a hundred thousand men, women, and children dashed south from the environs of Arkansas City in a mad race to file on land which the government once ceded to Indians, but took back again when someone decided the land might be good for something after all.

The United States government in dealing with the American aborigines has a record of Indian giving that bewildered even the Indians.

The Oklahoma end of Uncle Sam's double-dealing with the red man reverts back to the beginning of the nineteenth century and the five tribes of Indians that lived in southeastern United States from Florida up to Tennessee. They were the Seminoles and Choctaws and Chickasaws and Creeks and Cherokees. Generally speaking, these were pleasant brands of Indians and highly intelligent. The whites, presumably as a compliment, called them the Five Civilized Tribes and set out to bilk them. Stories were spread among the Five Civilized Tribes about what lovely land there was out west for Indians and some of the trusting aborigines took the lordly white man at his word and moved out.

This seemed like a mighty fine idea to the administration of Andrew Jackson and a parcel of western land was set aside to be called Indian Country. The parcel consisted of the present states of Oklahoma, Kansas, and Nebraska. There was an agreement that the whites would not encroach on this domain.

Very soon, however, the whites discovered that Nebraska and Kansas were not utterly worthless. They immediately began to rectify the error by moving in on the Indians' posted property.

The fact that eastern Kansas and Nebraska held some of the best farming country on the continent led to another discovery—the territory of Oklahoma was plenty large enough for the original Oklahoma Indians and the Five Civilized Tribes too. So the government promised the Five Civilized Tribes that they and all their descendants unto the hundredth generation would not be molested if they all moved into Oklahoma and settled down.

The peaceful and trusting members of four of the Five Civilized Tribes sent thanks to the Great White Father and complied. But the Seminoles down in Florida were less credulous and large numbers of them refused to be driven from their ancestral hunting grounds. They felt that Florida might well be as good as the pictured Garden of Eden to the north and west and they refused to budge.

So the Great White Father sent troops and there were bloody battles. To an extent the Great White Father, John Tyler, was successful and he drove large numbers of the warlike Seminoles up to Oklahoma. Some hundreds escaped the enforced exodus by fleeing into the Everglades where their descendants live to this day.

They call the trail followed by the Seminoles and by the Choctaws to Oklahoma the Trail of Tears. Hundreds died on this march.

Finally most of the Five Civilized Tribes were moved into what now is Oklahoma with the promise of the Great White Father that nevermore would they be bothered. That did not imply, however, that the Great White Father would not be paternalistic toward his red children. The government split Oklahoma into three sections. The northern strip was ceded to the Cherokees to have and to hold throughout eternity. The middle strip went jointly to the scrappy Seminoles and the Creeks, and the southern slice was allocated to the Choctaws and Chickasaws.

The Five Civilized Tribes had relinquished all their land to the east and south. The Great White Father had given them all this fine land in return. Everything was binding and satisfactory—that is, for about twenty years.

When the course of empire was taking its westward way and the railroads were being pounded down to the Pacific coast and the buffalo were being killed by the millions for leather belting, the plains Indians went violently mean and tough over the ruination of their hunting grounds. Cavalry and Gatling guns were sent to teach the Christian life to the outraged red man and, tribe by tribe, the bad red warriors were subjugated.

Now the Great White Father—this time Andrew Johnson—decided that *all* the Indians of America should be herded into one pasture. There still was that great territory of Oklahoma very sparsely populated by the Five Civilized Tribes. Surely the Cherokees *et al* would like to have some more nice Indians come to live with them.

The government made a deal with the Five Civilized Tribes. The Five Civilized Tribes would sell some millions of acres of western Oklahoma for an average price of twenty-five cents an acre, and the subjugated western warriors would be moved into that district. The deal was consummated without undue trouble because the stipulation was that the Indians would sell the land or else.

All this time there were bitter interdepartmental rows over Indian affairs in Washington.

In Congress and all through officialdom there was a very noisy minority which held that the Indian Bureau should be transferred from the Interior Department to the War Department. It was well known that on various occasions troops had provoked peaceful tribes into warfare, but the military leaders held they could settle the Indian troubles in short order, if given the authority.

Many good Christians in high positions declared the only method of solving the Indian problems was by exterminating the Indians. Senator E. G. Ross of Kansas, on July 18, 1867, declared from the floor of the Upper House that war was the only method of bringing about peace with the Indian. "The conflict," he said, "is between barbarism and civilization, and civilization must win."

James A. Garfield, then chairman of the House Military Committee, fought valiantly for several years in the late 1860's to have Indian affairs transferred to the War Department so the "red devils" could be dealt with adequately.

Opposition pointed out that the Indians had *some* reason for indignation and that every treaty made between the United States government and the natives up to that time had been broken by the whites.

So at length it was decided (and bitterly assailed by the virile western press) not to exterminate the Indian, but to move him one and all into the territory previously assigned to the Five Civilized Tribes and their heirs for the duration of the human race.

Into Oklahoma then were driven seventeen tribes of western Indians, among them the Apaches and Cheyennes and Arapahoes, who, according to Choctaw lights, were definitely from across the tracks.

The Five Civilized Tribes liked to raise corn and potatoes and to hunt and fish. The seventeen new tribes liked to hold scalping parties. They liked to capture strangers, either red or white, and throw hatchets at them. They did not like Oklahoma and they didn't like the Five Civilized Tribes.

There followed such violent intramural discord that the Great White Father finally gave up his pretty dream of one big red union and quit sending savage tribes into Oklahoma.

Time went on with Missouri settling up and Kansas

settling up and Arkansas settling up with white farmers and cattlemen until the population of Missouri, for instance, averaged forty to the square mile.

Forty to the square mile was pretty crowded farming for those days and a lot of settlers began to look longingly across the line into the Indian Territory.

Despite the influx of western Indians into the land of the Five Civilized Tribes, there still was less than one Indian to the square mile and there was some mighty good farming land in eastern Oklahoma. And what, after all, did the Indians do with that rich land? They went hunting on it. Very little ground was plowed and planted and the Indians were heathens who ate with their fingers instead of their knives.

Cattlemen began to move over the border into western Oklahoma. They were quite legal about it. They didn't attempt to take the land away from the tough Apaches and Arapahoes and Cheyennes by force, because they would have needed several troops of cavalry with Gatling guns to do that. It was easier to lease a hundred thousand acres for fifty moons at a price of, say, a bottle of whisky per section.

The Great White Father kept troops in the Indian Territory. The purpose of the troops was to preserve order, to prevent enterprising businessmen from selling too large quantities of liquor to the Indians at one time, and to keep the "boomers" out. The boomers were men who were moving across the border, whether or not, and squatting on Indian land. And despite the quasi vigilance of the federal agents, they moved across in droves.

At last, by 1889, there were so many boomers squatting on Indian land that they became a federal problem and the Great White Father—Grover Cleveland now—took cognizance of the problem and settled it. He settled it on March 22, 1889, by announcing that all the "unassigned" land north of the Arkansas River in Oklahoma, commonly known as the Cherokee Strip, would be thrown open to white settlers one month from that date.

It was great news for Arkansas City, Kansas, dozing there in the spring sunshine on the banks of the Arkansas River.

The month gave seekers of free land time to move in from every state in the Union. They came by the thousands—on trains, on horseback, driving covered wagons, even riding high-wheeled bicycles. The roads were jammed with their prairie schooners and Arkansas City became a boom town.

The immigrants camped along the river and sang songs and got drunk and spent money—those that had money—in the Arkansas City emporiums of trade.

Then, on April 21st, the day before the great run into the Indian lands nearly a hundred miles to the south, the horde was permitted to cross the border into what now is Oklahoma. Twenty thousand homeseekers traveled down to the dead line and camped. Eighty thousand more waited at Arkansas City and other border towns for the fifteen trains which would race south the next morning. In all there were at least a hundred thousand waiting for the greatest race in America's history which would start when the sun crossed the meridian the next day.

But there were thousands already inside the lines. They had got there by various subterfuges. Some wore the badges of government officers, gained by greasing the proper palms, and these temporary officers would resign their posts shortly before noon that they might stake out preferred land and town lots at the stroke of twelve. These foresighted fellows were called "sooners," and there were enough of them to give Oklahoma its nickname of the "Sooner State."

They had their land staked out well in advance of the rush and were sitting under canvas shades with barrels of water which they had thoughtfully provided for the land rushers—to sell at a dollar a drink.

Everyone knows what the actual rush was like when the cannons boomed at high noon of April 22, 1889. Much romantic fiction has been written about that stirring scene. Several exciting motion pictures also have been made, showing the lurching prairie schooners and bouncing buggies and galloping horsemen and men and women running desperately on foot through the choking dust, showing the dastardly deeds committed, and the heroic actions of the better people.

I am not bold enough to question the authenticity of a single Hollywood incredibility in this case. *Anything* can happen when a hundred thousand people launch on a mad, hysterical dash into a new country as they did on that first land rush into Oklahoma. There were fist fights and gun fights and free-for-all fights when half a dozen or more men staked out the same preferred ground and, while they were fighting it out, some calmer head frequently slipped in, put in his own stake and recorded it.

The city of Guthrie was staked out by government men before the rush. It was to be the metropolis and the capital of Oklahoma after Oklahoma was separated from Indian Territory by a crooked line running north and south.

On the day before the rush Guthrie was all ready for the citizens, except that there wasn't anything in the town but a Santa Fe Railroad water tank and a shed which housed the government land office. That was Guthrie at 11 A.M. on April 22nd. But at 5 P.M. there were fifteen thousand persons camped on Guthrie's staked-out eighty acres, each one of whom expected to be a first citizen of this Chicago of the Southwest and a millionaire.

Not many went on down the line to Oklahoma City where opportunities for town lots were equal, but where opportunities for wealth were considered poor.

Today, however, Guthrie's population is less than 10,000. It was a couple of thousand larger in 1920. Oklahoma City, on the other hand, is one of the livest cities in the West with a rapidly growing population of well over 200,000.

That is today. But by midsummer of 1889 Guthrie had grown from a water tank and a shed to a city with 3 daily newspapers, 15 hotels, 97 restaurants, 50 groceries, 27 pharmacies, and 40 general stores.

Guthrie was the territorial capital of Oklahoma. It was the capital when Oklahoma and Indian Territory, once more joined under the name of Oklahoma, were admitted to the Union as a state. But Oklahoma City, after a long and bitter battle, won out in 1913.

The 1889 land rush was the greatest and most desperate of the ten which followed. Some of them were not runs but lotteries in which the land was drawn by chance.

In 1930 Oklahoma had a population of 2,396,000. Of that number about 2,301,000 were whites and Negroes. The rest—about 95,000—are descendants of the original Osages, who roamed around Arkansas and eastern Oklahoma, of the Five Civilized Tribes, to whom the Great White Father ceded the territory without qualification, and of the other Indians herded into the country against the wishes of all concerned.

Fate played one real joke on the intruding whites of Oklahoma, however. When, in 1906, the great Glen Pool oil field came in near the banks of the Arkansas River, it was on Indian land. All the Oklahoma oil fields have had a predilection for coming in on Indian lands and pouring millions into the laps of bewildered aborigines.

There are about 3,500 Osages living under their socialistic government in Oklahoma now. Their oil and gas royalties in 1935 had totaled $247,857,000, or about $70,000 for each Osage man, woman, and child.

I have seen a number of copper-faced fellows with silk hats on their braided black hair, riding luxuriously in $10,000 foreign-built limousines driven by uniformed white men.

CHAPTER FOURTEEN

From Whence to Where?

Across old Oklahoma Territory, the Arkansas River snakes its general southeastern course past Ponca City and crosses into old Indian Territory at Tulsa.

The city of Tulsa is one of the great oil centers of the world. It also is one of the fastest growing cities in the country. Washington Irving, touring the prairies in 1832, visited the site of Tulsa and predicted a great city would rise there, and grateful Tulsa has erected a monument to his prescience. Between 1920 and 1930 the population of Tulsa doubled, from 70,000 to 141,000. It is estimated that the city has from 170,000 to 200,000 now.

Sixty miles downstream is historic Fort Gibson, which was established in 1824 as military headquarters for settling and protecting the Southwest. Then on, with slightly less winding, until the river enters the southwestern fringe of the Ozark Mountains and crosses the border into Arkansas at Fort Smith.

I suspect the Ozarks are unique among American mountains.

First, the name is another of those strange Anglicizations of a French phrase. The hills were called Aux Arkansa by the early voyageurs, meaning they were in the territory of the Arkansas Indians. For the English-speaking settlers who followed, it was an easy step from Aux Arkansa to Oz-Ark—almost as easy as turning the Purgatoire River into the Picketwire.

Geologists say the Ozark range is one of the oldest in the world. Down in south Missouri and Arkansas they will tell you the Ozarks are the oldest in the United States. In New York State they'll tell you the Catskills are older. I personally don't believe it's anything to quarrel about. I think both ranges are pretty.

Sliding from geology to anthropology, archaeologists (or at least *some* archaeologists) suspect the Ozarks boasted a civilization of sorts before the Catskills did.

Apparently there were two brands of prehistoric people who lived in the Ozark region and both antedated the Indian, as we know the Indian, by many centuries.

There were the Cave Dwellers who lived in the northwestern corner of Arkansas near Oklahoma. They seem to have had no knowledge of metals, for the implements found in their caves are all of stone. Because they were careless at table, it is easy to check up on the Cave Dwellers' diet even now and to see that they lived largely on game supplemented by a little corn. It was not Golden Bantam or Country Gentleman green corn they ate, nor Boone County or Leaming field corn. The cobs were small and thin, more like popcorn cobs.

The Cave Dwellers manufactured robes from feathers and from rabbitskins. This is known because skeletons have been found with remnants of such robes wrapped around them.

This race was small physically, averaging less than five feet and a half in stature. Their skulls indicate a rather high degree of intelligence, taking the modern Caucasian skull as par. But none of the relics of handicrafts is equal to those of the Cro-Magnon man. The Cave Dwellers of Arkansas seem to have been closer to the Neanderthal. Their arrowheads and spearheads were not well made, compared to the later Indian variety.

Their crude jugs did not have even primitive decorations.

The Mound Builders, on the other hand, were different. As far as I know, there is nothing to prove that the Cave Dwellers and Mound Builders were not contemporaries, but it seems to be assumed that the Cave Dwellers came and departed before the advent of the strange race of Mound Builders.

Every once in a while the newspaper Sunday supplements have an article about the Mound Builders. There is a standard "lead" for articles on Mound Builders and it is in effect: "Who were the mysterious Mound Builders of North America? From whence did they come? What were they like? Where did they go?"

Scientists, of course, are contemptuous of Sunday supplement articles on scientific subjects. But when archaeologists write scientific articles about the Mound Builders they usually begin with the premise that the Mound Builders are "one of the major puzzles of American archaeology" and end up by asking the reader, "Who were the mysterious Mound Builders of North America? From whence did they come? Where did they go?"

They used to assume that the Mound Builders were a totally different breed of men from the Indians or any known aborigines. They used to estimate the Mound Builders were living in America fifty thousand years ago or a million years ago or any impressively large number of years gone by.

Now, however, they seem to have the date of the race's advent pretty well (although loosely) pegged. This would go also for the Arkansas Cave Dweller and the Colorado Cliff Dweller and the rest of the prehistoric families of this continent.

Men lived in Europe before the glacial ages. They know this because they find relics and skeletons of prehistoric men in and below glacial debris. In North America, although thousands of archaeological investigations have been conducted, no signs of men have been found except above the glacial deposits.

This would seem to prove that no one lived in the region of the United States earlier than ten to twelve thousand years ago.

There once was a theory that the Mound Builders were living up to a couple of centuries ago because skeletons have been found in mounds with comparatively modern metal implements beside them. That is explained away now by the fact that Indians liked to bury their dead on high spots and probably intruded their departed relatives in the tops of these prehistoric mounds.

Down farther in the mounds no such modern metal weapons and tools are found. As a matter of fact, when the investigators dig below the upper crust of a mound, they find no weapons or tools which were in European use later than the opening of the Neolithic period.

This tends to prove that the Mound Builders arrived in America soon after the retreat of the last ice pack—probably about eight thousand years ago. Otherwise, they would have brought with them domesticated animals and cultivated food plants known to their original home, as well as the mechanical inventions of their day.

The Sunday supplement writers still are speculating whether the Mound Builders were the Lost Tribes of Israel or whether they were refugees from lost Atlantis, but present-day anthropologists are pretty well agreed that prehistoric Americans and the ancestor of the American Indian were Mongoloid and came from Asia across Bering Strait at about the beginning of the Stone Age in Europe.

They have traced several migrations down the west

coast of North America, following the trails then east and south.

When the Mongolian nomads struck the rich lands of the Midwest and South, they paused and the native seed-bearing grass held their attention and turned them into an agricultural race. They cultivated this seed-bearing grass and it became Indian corn.

As the centuries passed and the so-called Mound Builders spread across eastern North America, they built a series of cities in the state of Arkansas. There were walls and moats for protection with springs of water inside the court. They made community threshing floors which were baked and hammered to such hardness that they remain like solid brick to this day. They constructed curious mounds, apparently for places of worship as well as for burial vaults.

Usually these mounds cover an area from one acre to a hundred acres. But in Arkansas there is one that measures more than a square mile in extent.

Daniel Boone was the first to report the remains of an ancient city in Arkansas and he declared he found an oak tree at least four feet in diameter growing from the ruined wall of what appeared to have been an ancient fort in Washington County. This was in 1804.

In 1898 an archaeologist named Edwin Walters was digging for relics near Fort Smith and he reported finding what he first believed to be a prehistoric burial ground along the south bank of the Arkansas River.

Mr. Walters wrote that as his research proceeded he found no diminution of skeletons. Then he observed two things, curious things for a large burial ground. One was that there seemed to be few women in this graveyard and no children at all. The other was the number of weapons in evidence.

Presently he noted that in a majority of cases there

either was a stone spearhead lying between the dished ribs of the skeleton or that the skull had been split as from the blow of an ax.

So Mr. Walters concluded he had stumbled upon a prehistoric battlefield in which approximately a hundred thousand men had been killed and left to molder in this little valley of about thirty acres. That would be a little better than three thousand dead men to the acre—which seems to be a mighty big yield of dead men.

But allowing 6 x 2 feet per man, that would be only 36,000 square feet covered by bodies, while there are 43,560 square feet to an acre. So I suppose it could be done.

However, they have found numerous skeletons of Mound Builders which measured about seven feet long. Now, if all the dead soldiers required 7 x 2 feet, that would total 48,000 square feet of soldiers to the acre and necessitate overlapping.

In so-called civilized times the bloodiest battle in North American history was at Gettysburg on July 1-3, 1863, when a total of only 7,058 Union and Confederate soldiers were killed.

It was Professor Walters's theory that some Mayas came up from the Southwest and engaged the Mound Builders in a pitched battle at this point. The Mound Builders must have had something the Mayas wanted pretty badly to have brought on such a fight.

I have no information about the winner of this war. Professor Walters, being an archaeologist, didn't bother to report the score.

Much has been loosely written about the great culture of the Mound Builders—about their culture and artistry. That, I believe, was written by congenital enthusiasts.

True, good pottery has been unearthed, some of

it really artistic in design. There were some ingenious Mound Builder artists who could turn a mug into an effigy of their medicine man or make a teapotlike urn roughly resemble some unidentified animal. They carved stone into strange images or faces. They were able to hammer copper into knives and other utensils.

But the Mound Builders had no written language, even in hieroglyphic form. By and large, their objects of art are not superior to those of the Cliff Dwellers of Mesa Verde, Colorado, and certainly cannot be compared with those of the Mayas.

One of the first mounds to be explored in Arkansas was in Greene County where the St. Francis River widens into a swampy lake. The great earthquake of 1811 split a group of mounds open here and led to the discovery of skeletons and pottery.

Again in Crowley's Ridge, in Poinsett County, a railroad excavated seventeen mounds to get gravel for its roadbed and revealed a number of interesting things about the Mound Builders.

Dwellings were exposed in cross sections, showing horizontal strips of burnt clay which were floors of prehistoric homes. In one mound, ninety feet in diameter, three connected rooms were uncovered. They lay roughly in the shape of a T and burned logs showed where the roof timbers had been set. There was even lathing of cane still visible on the walls. In this building pottery was found with elaborate decorations incised in the shape of crosses and swastikas.

This Crowley's Ridge excavation also produced a number of stone images which are among the most remarkable Mound Builder relics ever found. As a matter of fact, some of them are remarkable enough to have baffled the archaeologists. It even has been hinted that perhaps some modern tombstone cutter has perpetrated a hoax similar to Barnum's famous Cardiff Giant.

These specimens are on view at the Arkansas State Museum in Little Rock and the attendants attest their authenticity, saying an ancient oak had wound its roots around the cache of relics at the bottom of the excavation.

The oddest and most interesting of these relics is a head of stone called King Crowley.

King Crowley is in a fine state of preservation, except that the severe, flat-topped headdress is pitted, apparently by time. He is a determined-looking fellow with beetling stone brows, round comic-strip eyes, a straight short nose, unwavering mouth and square chin.

His eyes are inset round buttons of copper with silver pupils. There are gold plugs in the ears and inlaid in the bronchial region is a copper heart.

This heart bothers me. The Aztecs went in for human sacrifices and it is probable that the Mound Builders did too. Cutting out human hearts and offering them to the sun or moon as a bribe for good farming weather has been common custom with aboriginal races. At least, all aborigines knew what a human heart looks like. The Egyptians used it as a motif in some of their art work. So did the Aztecs. So did the Mayas.

But the heart inset at the thorax of King Crowley does not look like the human cardiac engine. It is a well-nigh perfect representation of the conventional St. Valentine's Day symbol. Where would the prehistoric Mound Builders of Arkansas get that?

On the other hand, one might ask where they got the swastika symbol, which is incised on many Mound Builder relics. If the swastika spread from ancient Persia and India widely enough for the Mound Builders' ancestors to have brought it across Bering Strait in the waning days of the Paleolithic period, why not the red, red heart?

My own theory of what happened to the Mound Builders is not worth a cent because I am not an archaeologist. But my theory is that nothing happened to the Mound Builders. My theory is that they merely got tired of building mounds and settled down to raise corn and children and to fight among themselves. Then they developed and scattered out and invented the birchbark canoe and feathered bonnets and lacrosse and after a few score centuries the white man came across the ocean, killed off some of the Mound Builder descendants and chased a lot more into Oklahoma.

CHAPTER FIFTEEN

The Ozarks

THE Ozark highlands form sort of an island rising from five hundred to twenty-five hundred feet above the surrounding plains—the plains which separate the Appalachians from the Rockies.

Of course, there is a geological theory about how the Ozark Mountains came to be. But I prefer the Indian story, which sounds suspiciously as if it had been lifted from Genesis.

It seems there was a tribe of beautiful Indians named the Massatonguas who inhabited a beautiful plain through which flowed a beautiful river. It seems that everyone was happy because the land was fruitful and the squaws were fruitful and the Great Spirit blessed them with fine weather and made the trout leap to any bait whatever.

The Great Spirit, however, imposed one restriction. The Massatonguas must never attempt to explore a cavern which opened mysteriously from a cliff on the riverbank.

Naturally, this restriction was the source of much conversation and speculation on the part of the Massatonguas. It was commonly agreed that the cave was the portal to a new world unbelievably beautiful, a world which doubtless was the home of the departed, where beautiful maidens fed you with amazingly tasty dog meat to the thump of gloriously tuned tom-toms.

The stories got better and better until some of the tribe couldn't stand it any longer. They built some strong canoes and one day paddled right through the portals of the cave in defiance of the Great Spirit's injunction.

Immediately there was a tremendous peal of thunder and the cavern mouth closed behind the canoes. The water boiled terrifically. The ground heaved upward toward the very clouds and for hours the sky was black as a burned stick. The Great Spirit was expressing his displeasure in no ambiguous terms.

Finally the earthly convulsions quieted enough for the remaining Massatonguas to look around and they saw that, figuratively speaking, the fit had taken the crease out of Nature's pants and the whole countryside looked as if it had been slept in. The beautiful plain was rumpled into the Ozark ridges and peaks, and down south the air was filled with sulphurous reekings while the water of the lakes steamed and boiled like the magic concoctions of a medicine man.

The too curious adventurers who caused this horrific upheaval never were seen again. They were walled up permanently in the cave, but their agonized moanings still can be heard inside the bowels of the earth on quiet nights.

That's how the Ozark Mountains were made and that, too, is how Hot Springs, Arkansas, came about.

Since then, however, the Ozarks have improved a lot in appearance with the addition of beautiful groves of pine and hardwoods—white oak, hickory, maple, walnut, and elm. It is a land of fireflies, redbirds, and strawberries. It is an isolated land largely, even in these days of automobiles—a land of strange people and strange superstitions.

De Soto undoubtedly was the first white man to visit the Ozark region. And the French adventurers, drawn by the fur trade rather than gold, were the first to explore and to exploit the country.

Marquette wrote of the Ozarks. But he never saw them. He obtained his doubtful data from the Indians at the mouth of the Arkansas River when he was smoking the calumet with them and being convinced by them that the Mississippi did not flow to China, after all.

Baron Armand-Louis de La Hontan, French-Canadian soldier, is credited with being the first white man to see the Ozark ridge, but that is the French story, which ignores Señor De Soto altogether. La Hontan wrote about his travels, publishing his book in France in 1703.

Probably the first English-speaking man to visit the region was Edmund Jennings, a North Carolinian. He called it the "Land of the Six Bulls," and the pioneers accepted that designation although they had no idea wherefore the six bulls.

The French had called the country "Terre de les Six Bouilles," because of the six great springs that feed the Indian, Shoal, Center, Spring, and North Fork Creeks, and Jennings Anglicized the phrase.

The country was settled in the late eighteenth and early nineteenth centuries largely by English-speaking people from Kentucky and Tennessee. The settlers found the Ozarks to be the sort of place sportsmen dream about but almost never see.

In 1806 Lieutenant Zebulon Pike, on his way west, passed through the Ozark region and recorded that he killed thirty-two deer in one week. Lots of people have beaten Pike's record since. And that's the reason deer are not so plentiful in the Ozark highlands now.

Over the line in the Missouri Ozarks, it is a matter of record that the hamlet of Warsaw shipped 144 bales of deerskins in the year 1854. The historian neglected to state how many deerskins go to make up a bale, but I suspect it is too many for the best interests of game conservation.

The hills were alive with wild turkeys, pigeons, quail, grouse, and even parakeets. The ponds and lakes were crowded with great wild geese, ducks, and swans. And the streams were so filled with trout that they choked the water wheels of the primitive gristmills.

So, living in this land of abundance and beauty, where the climate was not too hot in summer and almost balmy in winter, the early settlers developed an indifference to the rest of the world. They grew apart. They formed their own codes. And they espoused an astounding number of gorgeous superstitions that seem to fit in with the mystic haze which so often hangs over the Ozark country.

As to the codes, I can tell a story about my brother Glen and an Ozark farmer, which I believe illustrates one facet of the Ozark character.

It was watermelon season and Glen drove by a ten-acre melon patch that set his mouth watering. He stopped at the farmhouse where the farmer was sitting comfortably in the shade of a huge pecan tree while he whittled a stick.

"You've got some fine-looking melons there, mister," said Glen. "What's the chance of getting one?"

"Sure enough, stranger," said the farmer. "You never et a better melon than I've got there. I'll go right out and pick you a good one."

So the farmer dropped his whittled stick and ambled out into the watermelon patch followed by my brother Glen and half a dozen hound dogs. The farmer pushed one gigantic green ellipse with his foot. "How's that one look to you?" he asked, squinting at Glen.

"Wonderful," said Glen. "I'll take that one."

"Well, now, wait a minute. We'll just see is it any good first."

So the farmer slashed the seven-inch blade of his jackknife into the melon, looked at the red center shading into a pink near the green rind and shook his head sadly.

"No," he said, "sure couldn't ever let you take that one. Ain't ripe enough."

"Looks pretty good to me," said Glen. "If I never got a greener melon than that I'd have no kick."

"No, sir, stranger. Wouldn't never let you take a green melon like that away from *my* farm. Let's see how this one looks."

He slashed into another giant and again shook his head as he lifted a morsel from the flaky red center. "This here one," he mourned, "is way too ripe. Practically almost rotten. Couldn't never let you take that one away."

And while Glen protested, the farmer cut into melon after melon until he finally found one that seemed to his critical eye to have reached just the proper state of ripeness and texture.

"Now, mister," he drawled, "this here's a watermelon I'm proud to let you take."

"That's great," said Glen. "Never saw a better-looking melon in my life. How much is it?"

The pride and the joy in the Ozark farmer's eyes clouded over. "What you mean? Don't understand you, how much is it?"

"Well, how much you want for it?"

"You mean how much money? My God, stranger, you ain't thinking I'm *selling* watermelons, are you?"

Glen gulped and looked over the acres of watermelons. "Well," he said, "if you aren't selling watermelons, what are you raising all those for?"

The farmer spat. "I guess," he said, "you don't know about watermelons very well. There's kind of a sentiment-like with us folks around here. You say what I'm raising this patch of melons for? Well, I raises 'em for social fruit.

"You come by here and ask can you get a melon. Well, I never seen you before, but you seem likely to like watermelons and I got watermelons I'm proud of, so I want to pick you a good one. Well, suppose I take and sell you this fine watermelon for money. It's like you send to Montgomery Ward for a pair of gum boots. Just like that—you pay the money and you get the gum boots. That's all there is to it. It don't mean nothing at all.

"Now you come by here and you're a stranger and I never seen you before and you never seen me before.

You want a watermelon and I pick you a good one. I give you the watermelon and you say, 'Much obliged,' and you go on and eat the watermelon and you say, 'Holy God, I never eat such a bodacious watermelon,' and you feel good to-wards me and you feel friendly-like to-wards me from then on even don't you ever see me again.

"And I feel good because I know you're going to like that watermelon and feel friendly to-wards me and I feel friendly to-wards you because I know I done a good turn giving you that fine watermelon. See what I mean?"

"Yes," said Glen, "I see what you mean and I think it's mighty fine—just mighty fine. But you can't be raising all those watermelons to give away to folks that come traveling along this road here."

The farmer grinned and spat again. "Hell's afire, no," he drawled. "You might call giving 'em away to strangers that come along just kind of a by-product. I raises these melons mostly to eat ourselves and for our friends and kinfolks."

"But your friends and kinfolks raise watermelons too, don't they?"

"Oh, my, yes, they raises watermelons too, and when we goes to their houses we eat their watermelons and when they comes to our house they eat our watermelons. We gets rid of a power of watermelons just in our family. We'uns had a party here just 'tother night for our kinfolks and got rid of 115 watermelons. I picked 125 before the party and only had ten left."

"Heavens and earth," said Glen, "you must have a sizable family."

"Kind of sizable," the farmer admitted. "Take Pap. He got eighty-seven grandchilder right around here and there's no end of cousins and all. We all get together a lot in watermelon time, I tell you."

That is watermelon philosophy in the Ozarks.

There seems to be something about the Ozarks that either breeds or attracts strange characters with strange philosophies. I believe this is more or less true with all isolated hill countries where the evening mists seem surcharged with mysticism and the inhabitants talk of ghosts and spells and curses around the fireside of an evening. And I believe this is especially true of the Ozarks.

One of the most curious Ozark characters I ever knew was not a native of the Ozarks. His name was William Hope Harvey and he was born in West Virginia. He was nationally known when I was a boy, although most people had to think back to recall his greatest fame which had blossomed in 1894 with publication of his first book, *Coin's Financial School*. The book was a small, paper-bound volume advocating bimetallism. It sold upward of a million copies and did a great deal toward advancing the lost cause of young William Jennings Bryan two years later.

"Coin" Harvey followed his first success with *A Tale of Two Nations,* and *Coin's Financial School Up to Date,* the succeeding year and several other works on the same economic line within the next decade. He made a good deal of money from his publications and then set upon a career to save the world from moral ruin.

Coin Harvey was an elderly man when I first knew him—a straight, slim, gray-haired elderly man with a leaning toward checkered suits and red neckties. Despite his West Virginia antecedents—he was a graduate of Marshall College, West Virginia—Coin Harvey had a pronounced Harvard accent, until he grew eloquent with anger. Then he would revert to plain West Virginia cussing with a slag-heap accent.

This was about the time the first World War was breaking loose in Europe and Mr. Harvey had written a book which he believed would bring about a better understanding between nations and between individuals. The book was called *The Remedy* and it was expected to startle the world with the assertion that all human troubles were caused by greed, anger, selfishness, irreverence, sexual immorality, and divorce. I remember thinking it was very broad-minded of Mr. Harvey to include this last evil, because I knew he had been divorced from his first wife.

Anyhow, Mr. Harvey had rediscovered the Golden Rule, and he sent complimentary copies of *The Remedy* to the German Kaiser and the Czar of Russia and the President and Premier of France and King George V of Britain and the rest of the European rulers, and one to President Wilson. But apparently the rulers of Europe were too busy prosecuting their war to read *The Remedy*, for the war went right on. No considerable number of private citizens found time to read *The Remedy* either, so greed, anger, selfishness, irreverence, sexual immorality, and divorce continued to exact fearful toll from the human race.

This reluctance on the part of the world to read his book and heed his warning convinced Mr. Harvey there was no hope for the present civilization, so he voiced his opinions in fluent West Virginia speech with no trace of Harvard accent and he retired to his mountain lodge at Monte Ne, Benton County, Arkansas.

Mr. Harvey was the first citizen of Monte Ne. He built his hotel in the wilderness and he founded the settlement and named it. He originally sought a musical Indian name for the place, but all Indian names with suitable meaning seemed too harsh to his sensitive ear, so he made a combination.

"Ne," he told me, was Indian for water and "Monte" was French for mountain, so the name meant Mountain Water. He said he combined the French word with the Indian word because the French were the first white men to enter the Ozarks.

But, as a matter of fact, Mr. Harvey was in error. "Monte" is Spanish instead of French. But that is all right because the Spaniard, De Soto, was in the Ozarks before the French. Which may prove that two wrongs make a right, or something.

Mr. Harvey was a candidate for president on the Liberty party ticket in 1932. When Franklin Roosevelt beat Mr. Harvey out (to say nothing of Mr. Hoover), Mr. Harvey again lost all hope for the human race and builded a pyramid which would tell future civilizations about the fall of the present system.

Before he died in 1936, Mr. Harvey had spent something like $75,000 on his pyramid, which is 130 feet high and 60 feet square at the base. In the inner vault he placed relics of this dying civilization to enlighten future humans. These relics include copies of *Coin's Financial School* and *The Remedy*, etc. That future civilizations may be able to read his books after English has become a dead language, Mr. Harvey thoughtfully included a key. He firmly believed these coming civilizations would appreciate his greatness where he had been neglected by this.

Coin Harvy, ragtime economist of the Gay Nineties and would-be referee of world politics, now has become as much a tradition of the Ozarks as the curious Ozark superstitions.

Many of the superstitions prevalent in the Ozarks

have some universality. Others are, I believe, peculiar to that region.

Among the weather portents are some which I suspect have no circulation beyond those hills, but superstitions travel on mysterious wings and I may well be wrong.

There, for instance, is the belief that it's going to rain when you see a dog eating grass.

There is the belief that it is six weeks until frost after the first katydid song in August.

Lightning seen in the southern sky means a spell of dry weather is in prospect.

When the turkey buzzards arrive, spring is surely here.

There will be frost in May if it thunders in February.

The most accurate weather portent, however, is a saying of the Ozark Indians that, "The drought will be broken when it's black all around and pouring in the middle."

Here are some other Ozark superstitions which I like—

If you would grow good, strong pepper, you should lose your temper while planting it.

When you set eggs, if you would have the chicks all turn out to be pullets, have a woman carry the eggs in her bonnet. But never set eggs on Sunday or they'll all hatch into roosters.

Here are some suggestions on how a girl may add to her wardrobe:

If she will catch a butterfly and bite off its head, she'll get a new dress the same color as the butterfly.

If she will but shake her old dress at the new moon, she'll get a new dress before the next moon.

And here are some beauty hints the damsel probably

never will find in the women's pages of the daily newspapers:

If she will catch rain water on the first day of June, it will wash off freckles effectively.

She can cure chapped lips, not by applying lipstick or camphor ice, but by kissing the middle rail of a five-rail fence.

To cure the skin of blemishes, she should wash with dew blended with buttermilk and honey.

Cutting off the ends of her hair at new moontide will make her locks grow glossy and thick.

Some of the more valuable Ozark therapeutics are as follows:

Rheumatism—Wearing a buzzard's feather in your hatband is an excellent preventive. So is a heavy leather belt worn low on the hips. So is a buckeye carried in the pocket or a string of buckeyes worn around the neck. Rheumatism may be cured with water dipped from a stream on Ash Wednesday. The water should be rubbed on the afflicted spot as well as taken internally.

Sore eyes—Rub the eyelids with the tip of a black cat's tail.

Whooping cough—Drink mare's milk three times daily.

Toothache—Carry a hog's tooth in the right-hand pants pocket. Women have to let it ache.

Foot cramp—Turn your shoes upside down when going to bed and your feet won't cramp.

Colic—Drink catnip tea.

Bee stings—Poultice of well-chewed tobacco.

Asthma—Mullein tea.

Nosebleed preventive—Wear a string of red beads.

Croup preventive or cure—Wear a black silk cord around the neck.

Nightmare—Sleep with a sharp knife under pillow and the incubus will be frightened away.

General Hygienic Measures—Wear a piece of sheep gut sewed up in a seam of the clothing to escape contagious diseases. A woolen string tied around a child's neck is a good preventive for any malady contracted through respiratory or digestional channels. A bag of asafetida worn around the neck is highly regarded in the Ozarks for its pharmaceutical properties, but that preventive's value is widely recognized. Any germ will shrivel if it comes within six feet of a child wearing a bag of asafetida in a warm schoolroom.

It must be noted that the potency of all these medicines is increased greatly when the moon is waning.

Now for affairs of the heart, with philters, charms portents and auspices—

There is one philter which I refuse to record. It is too realistic for one born during the reign of Queen Victoria.

However, if a girl will drop a mixture of perfumed sugar, flour, and milk into a young man's moonshine, the blend will act as an aphrodisiac.

If she will hang the breastbone of a turkey over her front door, it will have an amatory influence on every eligible young man who enters.

Wearing a cherry pit around the neck has a romantic influence on a girl's suitor.

If a redbird flies in front of a girl it means she'll be kissed before night.

If a girl is thinking of her sweetheart as she works in the kitchen and the fire blazes up brightly, it means the suitor can be depended upon.

If a girl stubs her toe she should kiss her thumb immediately if she would be lucky in love.

If a damsel's skirt flies up it means her boy friend is thinking of her.

On the other hand, if the cornbread burns it means a girl's suitor is angry with her. And if she sees a cobweb over the door after he has gone home it means he'll never call again. And if she watches the caller out of sight he'll never return. And if she sits on the table she can't be married for another year.

For the young man, he can find if a girl loves him by bending a mullein stalk in the direction of her house. If she loves him the mullein stalk will grow up again. If she loves another, the mullein stalk will die.

For general useful Ozark information—

If you should happen to have money in your pocket when you see the new moon, you should turn the money over immediately. Then you'll have money all the rest of the year.

Shingles cut in the dark of the moon will lie flat on the roof.   Shingles cut in the light of the moon will warp.

Make a wish when you see a redbird: if he flies upward the wish will come true; if he flies downward you won't get your wish.

Hang a colored cloth in front of a mare's manger and the mare's colt will be the color of the cloth.

If you drop a dishrag, you're going to have a dirty caller. Should the rag fall spread out, the dirty caller will be a woman; should the rag fall in a wad, the dirty caller will be a man.

Always cover the mirrors in a house of death. Cover them with white cloths immediately after death comes, because if anyone sees his own reflection in that house before the corpse is removed, that person will die within the year.

In moving to a new house always carry the salt and pepper over the threshold first.

It is unlucky to—

Carry ashes from the house on New Year's Day, look at the moon through bushes, walk across the room with only one shoe on, sing before breakfast, move cats from one house to another, or stand under a walnut tree during a thunderstorm.

Outside of the Ozarks it is unlucky to stand under any kind of tree during a thunderstorm.

CHAPTER SIXTEEN

Grand Duchy of Arkansas

To Henri de Tonty, or Tonti, goes the title of "Father of Arkansas."

This title might have been bestowed upon John Law, a renegade Scot, who started the first real colonization of Arkansas—but John Law died in dishonor.

On the other hand, de Tonty was a romantic figure and an honest and loyal man.

He was born in Italy about 1650, the son of Lorenzo Tonti. In his youth he joined the French Navy, changed his name from Tonti to de Tonty, and became a subject of the French king. Later he transferred to the army, was a brave soldier and suffered the loss of one hand in a grenade explosion. Following this injury, de Tonty obtained a cleverly fashioned hand of iron and thenceforth wore gloves summer and winter to hide his misfortune.

In 1678 La Salle was back in France planning an expedition which would form an empire for France in the New World. He wanted a few brave, resourceful, and strong young men for his party and his attention was called to the twenty-eight-year-old Italian-born officer, whose record already was brilliant.

This was the beginning of an association which resolved into a close friendship that endured until 1687 with La Salle's murder in Texas.

La Salle's plan was to build a line of forts from the Great Lakes to the mouth of the Mississippi, thus holding this tremendous territory for Christ and the glory of King (l'état, c'est moi) Louis XIV—to say nothing of lining up a monopoly in the fur business.

De Tonty was engineer for the party and it was he who built the 45-ton *Griffin*, the first sailing vessel on the Great Lakes. The *Griffin* was lost, somewhat mysteriously, on Lake Erie while bound for the Niagara River laden with pelts.

Near the present site of Peoria, Illinois, de Tonty built a fort, naming it Fort St. Louis, and La Salle left his young friend in charge while he went on to plant more crosses and to make arrangements for more furs.

Almost immediately on La Salle's departure, trouble fell upon Lieutenant de Tonty. His men didn't like Illinois. They'd rather be back home in France where the wine flowed freely and the mademoiselles had more spirit than the copper-colored wenches of America. So the soldiers walked away from Fort St. Louis, leaving the commander only four men.

De Tonty sent two of his loyal musketeers on La Salle's trail to tell the commander into what a state Illinois affairs had fallen. And about that time in came an army of Iroquois Indians.

As a matter of habit, the Iroquois opened war upon the Illinois Indians. That was bad, because de Tonty had been negotiating with the Illinois Indians for a treaty to exchange friendship for friendship and Christianity for furs.

At once the negotiations broke up. The Illinois chieftains charged de Tonty with perfidy because it was known that the French already had a treaty with the Iroquois. It was assumed that de Tonty had induced the Iroquois to come and wage war upon the Illinois tribe or, at the very least, that the French were sympathetic to the invaders' cause.

The Illinois chiefs seized de Tonty and, handicapped by a very sketchy knowledge of the Illinois language, the brilliant Italian had difficulty in talking himself away from the torture stake. He promised the Illinois he would go before the Iroquois council and induce them to call off the war and on this promise he was given what amounted to a suspension of sentence.

De Tonty went to Iroquois headquarters and fervently urged that the Iroquois go fight someone else, if they had to fight. That brought forth a storm. Cries of traitor were hurled at the lieutenant once more. If he was a treaty brother of the Iroquois and in good faith, why ask them to call off a potentially profitable war with such a push-over as the Illinois tribe?

In a burst of patriotic enthusiasm, one young brave leaped upon de Tonty and stabbed him. De Tonty, seriously wounded, still had the stamina and courage to lash out with his Iron Mike hand and fractured the skull of the patriotic warrior. That move saved his life. A slim young fellow, de Tonty appeared to be anything but a Samson. Yet one blow from his gloved open hand nearly killed this muscular warrior.

The Iroquois chieftains looked at one another in amazement. Then they looked at de Tonty with new respect and called the squaws to stanch his wound. They told him gravely that he was a great man and that, since he wished peace between the Iroquois and the Illinois, the Iroquois would move back east.

Unfortunately, however, the Illinois did not know de Tonty's negotiations had succeeded. Because of his wound, the lieutenant was forced to stay with the Iroquois several days and the Illinois assumed he had fled their wrath. When de Tonty returned to Fort St. Louis he found nothing but ashes. His two men were gone— either slain or chased into the woods.

The Iroquois had departed now and winter was at hand. So de Tonty, still weak and shaky from his wound, constructed himself a rude shelter as best he could with his one hand. He lived on roots and acorns and what small animals he could trap. But he lived and he stayed by the ruins of Fort St. Louis until La Salle returned the following year.

De Tonty joined La Salle in the journey down the Mississippi in canoes. Originally they had planned to make the trip in comfort with the *Griffin,* but that craft was at the bottom of Lake Erie.

At the mouth of the Arkansas, La Salle's canoes were met by a party of Indians who paddled out into the stream, making signs of welcome and of friendliness.

The tradition of the kindly Marquette and Joliet had spread among the Arkansas Indians during the nine years since their visit. La Salle profited from the wise and humane deportment of his French predecessors.

The Arkansas Indians entertained La Salle's party elaborately with feasts and dances and also warned the white men against the dangers of warlike tribes and supernatural terrors downriver.

La Salle, however, was not one to be frightened, and it was only a minor annoyance to him to hear that the Mississippi failed to flow to China. Wherever it flowed, it was his business to claim the territory for Louis XIV, arrange fur treaties, and erect the cross of Christianity as well as military outposts.

They left the mouth of the Arkansas River and floated down the Mississippi to its mouth, where La Salle established another Fort St. Louis. Then La Salle went back to France to get four shiploads of soldiers and settlers for his trading posts in Louisiana—which he had named the Mississippi River country just so he wouldn't forget who was king of France. De Tonty returned to his old Fort St. Louis in Illinois.

Coming back to Louisiana from France, La Salle's ships missed the mouth of the Mississippi and the admiral, Beaujeu, sailed the fleet into Matagorda Bay in Texas, ridiculously insisting that the little Texas Colorado River was the Mississippi.

La Salle knew better, but there seemed to be room on Matagorda Bay for another Fort St. Louis, so he built it, erected crosses and made fur treaties with the Texas Indians. Sickness and dissension swept over the little colony, however, and presently through death and desertions, La Salle's force of 280 soldiers and settlers had dwindled to 35.

In March, 1687, La Salle decided it was time to find the Mississippi and move up to where Lieutenant de Tonty was rebuilding Fort St. Louis in Illinois. But before the journey was well started the great La Salle was assassinated by his own men.

Meanwhile de Tonty had become worried about his chief. With a small party he started downriver in search of La Salle and he stopped again at the mouth of the Arkansas to visit with his old friends, the Arkansas Indians.

De Tonty had been so enchanted with the beautiful, lush country of Arkansas and with the quaint hospitality of the Indians four years before that La Salle had made a concession of several thousand acres to his lieutenant in the vicinity of the Indian village. Now in 1686, de Tonty felt it would be an honor to his Indian friends to establish a post or fort in their midst.

This he did now, and with considerable restraint refrained from calling it Fort St. Louis. Instead, he named his fort, "Poste Aux Arcansas."

When he departed down the river to hunt for his commander, de Tonty left half a dozen men at Poste Aux Arcansas to hold the fort and to see what fur business they might pick up. This was the first settlement in Louisiana Territory, and, of course, the first white settlement in what now is the state of Arkansas.

De Tonty started for the mouth of the Mississippi in search of La Salle and while he was gone seven survivors of La Salle's north-bound party reached Arkansas Post with news of the ill-fated Texas colony and of their chief's murder.

Among these seven was Henri Joutel, who recorded these events in his journal. He described their joy at sighting from the river the village of Arkansas Post. They felt certain it had been built by French hands even at first sight, both because of the type of architecture and because of the great cross on the riverbank.

De Tonty journeyed to the mouth of the Mississippi and, finding no trace of his superior, sadly retraced his steps to Arkansas Post where Joutel and the others told him of La Salle's death. De Tonty was desolated by the news. He immediately organized another party and set off again downstream with some of the Texas survivors to recover La Salle's body.

They proceeded to the mouth of the Red River and then struck off inland, cutting their way through dense underbrush and vines, wading in swamp water up to their waists, their faces pulpy from insect bites, in constant danger from hostile Indians and water moccasins.

The men grumbled and finally rebelled openly. They would go no further in such a country to recover any dead body—even La Salle's. They were going back. And back they went, the ailing and disconsolate de Tonty with them.

Grieving for La Salle, de Tonty turned his grant of land over to the church and maintained a missionary at Arkansas Post for several years at his own expense.

Despite the inroads malarial fever made on his not too rugged constitution, de Tonty continued making explorations and kept the Mississippi forts of Louis XIV in repair until the fever finally killed him in Alabama at the age of fifty-four.

The tiny village of Arkansas Post held to life after the death of its founder—a group of log buildings on the edge of the swampy forest crowding down to the north bank of the Arkansas River. In the village were a priest, a handful of French soldiers, and a fur-trading merchant or so. And on the edge of the log village were the wigwams and huts of the original Indian inhabitants.

Nothing at all happened to this strange village in the wilderness for thirteen years following the death of de Tonty in 1704. Then came a remarkable succession of events which might well have settled this Arkansas country more than a century before it actually was settled and which might have made Arkansas a grand duchy of France.

Early in the eighteenth century rumors still persisted that there were rich gold and silver deposits in the territory of Louisiana. Antoine Crozat, an enterprising merchant, sensing magnificent opportunities, wormed a concession from Louis XIV, in which Crozat should exploit the resources of Louisiana for fifteen years, of course, turning a liberal percentage over to the crown.

This was in 1712 and de la Mothe Cadillac was governor of Louisiana, which included the whole Mississippi-Arkansas countries. Under the king's concession Governor Cadillac was virtually working for Crozat.

In 1715 some samples of silver were brought to Cadillac. They were samples, so said the bearer, from the rich mines up in the Arkansas mountains.

Excited, Cadillac headed an expedition northward, journeying with great discomfort along the St. Francis River from above Helena, Arkansas, to the headwaters in southeastern Missouri. He did find some lead. But he found no trace of gold or silver.

Cadillac was disgusted. He wrote to Crozat:

"This colony is a monster. Has it not been asserted there are mines in Arkansas? It is a deliberate error. Has not a set of novel writers published that this is a paradise? I never saw anything so worthless."

This report was very discouraging to Merchant Crozat back in Paris. He would have dropped the concession, but Louis XIV wouldn't let him. And Louis XIV kept hounding the concessionaire to produce some Louisiana gold at once. Louis needed more money for the prosecution of wars and for pogroms against the Huguenots and to maintain eight or ten mistresses and to keep up the court of Versailles.

Then Louis XIV died after reigning seventy-two

years and establishing a royal endurance record. (Queen Victoria of Britain reigned sixty-three years.)

On his deathbed, Louis le Grand passed the scepter of France down to his great-grandson along with some sound advice. The great-grandson, however, was only five years old and didn't know what great-grandpère was talking about when he counseled the boy to be warned by his lot and keep away from wars and wild women.

The boy, who was to be Louis XV, engaged in a war before he was six, married a Polish princess at thirteen, and became the angel boy of Mesdames Pompadour and Du Barry, to whom he turned over management of the French government, which was an awful bore to him— but not to them.

This first war was with one of his Uncle Phils, who was King Philip V of Spain. Another of the child king's Uncle Phils was Philippe, Duke of Orleans, who was appointed regent of France for the period of the little boy's minority. The conflict could have been called the War of the Uncle Phils, but it wasn't.

The Spanish Uncle Phil was a grandson of Louis le Grand and consequently should have been a step closer to the French throne than the little boy, Louis XV, except for one thing. That one thing was the Treaty of Utrecht in which King Philip V solemnly swore to renounce all claims to the French throne forever and ever if he could be recognized as the king of Spain.

In these days when treaties between rulers and states are held sacred, it will be difficult to understand the action of King Philip. But on the accession of his little nephew to the throne of France, this Uncle Phil forgot his vows at Utrecht and set about to claim his birthright by force of arms. For his pains he was soundly thrashed by Uncle Phil, nephew of Louis le Grand, Duke of Orleans and regent over the kingdom of little Louis XV.

After the war Uncle Phil of Spain made another treaty never to covet the throne of France again and no harm done, except that a few thousand good Spaniards had laid down their lives for the holy cause of Philip V and a few thousand good Frenchmen had laid down their lives that France might be governed by a great-grandson of I-am-the-state Louis instead of by a grandson of that self-sufficient monarch.

Victorious though he was, the Duke of Orleans found his war had cost a lot of money. And Louis le Grand hadn't left the treasury in very good shape.

One night Philippe went to one of the fancier gambling houses, perhaps to see if he couldn't balance the national budget with cards or the dice. He won no money, but he made the acquaintance of a tall, handsome, yellow-haired Scot named John Law who seemed to have all of the world's luck sitting in his lap.

It is barely possible that Law's good fortune could not be attributed entirely to luck, for he was a professional gambler with more than a million francs hoarded away from his winnings. He was a fugitive from a British gallows. He had been deported from Venice and Genoa as a swindler. He had a way with women that evoked admiration from the popeyed and lascivious Philippe.

So John Law and the regent of France became friends and the Scot outlined a bold financial plan to Philippe which had been rejected earlier by the canny Parliament at Edinburgh.

The trouble with France's financial structure, Law told Philippe, was deficiency of a circulating medium. He wanted to start a private bank and issue currency against specie held in the bank's vaults. This plan, he assured the regent, would bolster France's lagging domestic trade and make collection of taxes infinitely easier.

The request was granted and pretty soon the private bank of John Law & Company became the Banque Royale of France with the renegade Scot as director-general.

Shrewd and suave John Law soon had the bewildered Philippe at a point where the regent would have agreed to almost any financial arrangement Law suggested.

Periodically Antoine Crozat, Louisiana concessionaire, would come to Philippe and tearfully plead to be freed of his responsibility. And Philippe, following the course of Louis XIV, would refuse bluntly and demand that Crozat produce some Louisiana gold in the next month or two if he knew what was good for him.

One day Crozat made his plea in the presence of John Law and John Law's blue eyes flashed as he smelled opportunity.

"Let the man out of it," he urged Philippe. "I'll take over that concession myself."

Law took the charter for twenty-five years, agreeing to settle six thousand colonists and three thousand slaves in Louisiana. He agreed as well to see that the native Indians were instructed in godliness, which was a nice touch from John Law.

There is some doubt whether Law ever had been in America. Some say he had explored the Mississippi Valley and knew of its potentialities at first hand, that he had crossed the Atlantic after escaping from Newgate Prison in London. Others say his information came only from his agents. In any event, Law did have a pretty fair knowledge of America and its possibilities. And he was convinced that France needed new natural resources and that he personally could use a few billion more francs.

He formed the Compagnie d'Occident, or Western Company, broadcasting stories of the unheard-of riches and resources of Louisiana Territory. He exhibited gold in Paris, which was said to have come from the wealthy mines of Arkansas. He characterized the collection of shacks at the mouth of the Mississippi as the "beautiful and flourishing city of New Orleans." And yes, M. Law issued stock in the Western Company and put it up for sale.

The stock sold. It increased in value. It doubled in value. It tripled in value.

John Law then extended his concession. He, with the agreement of Regent Philippe, extended his concession to include China, the West Indies, and the South Seas. He extended his concession to take in Senegal and the East Indies and he renamed the firm, Compagnie des Indes.

Money-hungry peasants were rushing to Paris from far provinces to buy this marvelous stock. Astute Britishers were crowding into fishing boats even to cross the Channel and buy Law's shares.

The Scot had promised Philippe to wipe out the public debt of France if he could have his way, so purchasers were required to pay for their share in the bonanza with one-fourth hard money and three-fourths paper issued by the Banque Royale.

The shares issued originally at $100 mounted to $1,000 and to $1,500 and to $2,000 and the printing presses were running night and day to meet the demand for paper money—money now backed by practically nothing at all. Well, there was approximately $700,000,-000 worth of coined money in France as compared to more than three billions in circulated currency.

By this time Law was councilor of state and comptroller general of finances and getting worried over the economic state. But he was serious about settling Louisiana Territory. In all, forty-three shiploads of people were sent. Some of the "settlers" were kidnaped, it is true, and some were delivered from jail. But Law bought Negro slaves with his own money and paid the expenses of seven hundred German families in emigrating to settle Louisiana.

John Law took a personal grant of twelve miles square just above Arkansas Post, which included the old de Tonty concession and several Indian villages. He planned to establish a personal grand duchy on this land.

Hundred-dollar shares in the company climbed to $3,000 and tents were erected in all vacant spots around Paris to take care of the thousands rushing in from all parts of Europe to gain riches from this remarkable stock. Brokers were doing business in kiosks and, because they had no means of rapid communication, one broker might be selling shares several hundred dollars cheaper than the fellow a dozen blocks away. Chambermaids and coachmen became millionaires in a week trading in India Company paper. The city was mad. Celebrations continued from dusk until dusk and then started over again.

John Law, more astute than other members of the government, became truly alarmed. He tried to shut off the flow of fiat currency from the presses, but the Duke of Orleans was drunk with joy and wouldn't listen now even to the man who ostensibly had made France the richest land in all history.

Meanwhile things were not going so well in America. Some of John Law's ships were wrecked and the emigrants drowned. An epidemic struck the German colonists, wiping out most of them.

But on paper at least, John Law, professional gambler and fugitive from a British murder warrant, was the richest man on earth. He purchased fourteen of the finest estates in France, and the titles of nobility went with the estates. He poured at least a million and a half of his own francs into the Louisiana venture—especially into his own grand duchy on the Arkansas River. He intended to build a model city there and to live like a king in his Arkansas palace while his German and French serfs brought him the bounty of the rich soil.

Well, his colonists made a start all right, plowing the fields and planting crops—mostly wheat. And the French troops, sent over to protect the colonists from the red Indians, had nothing to do but make love to the colonists' wives and daughters because the Indians were friendly and needed no scaring by soldiers.

In Paris the towering structure of the Compagnie des Indes was trembling at its insecure foundation.

"What France needs is more credit," John Law had told curly-locked Philippe before he started his private bank. He planned moves to give France more credit and he succeeded only too well. France found itself in the position of a $20-a-week clerk whose misplaced credit has allowed him to buy a fine automobile, radio, and diamonds.

The $100 shares mounted to $4,000 and more. And when the crash finally came it was like nothing the world had seen before—or since.

When the wave of selling started and panicky throngs began to mill about the brokers' kiosks, John Law, comptroller general of France's finances, took time only to stuff a few hundred livres in his pockets and fled the country. He had planned to take refuge in his grand duchy at Arkansas Post. But the apparent necessity for flight came so suddenly that Law had no time to take any large quantity of money with him. When he escaped France he didn't have enough cash with him to buy passage across the Atlantic.

Five months after John Law had become the most powerful man in all Europe he was living practically in poverty in Venice. That's how fast these extraordinary events took place. And because Law once had been deported from that city, Venice police kept him under surveillance and Law was unable to promote any extensive gambling schemes. He died in Venice nine years later, still poor.

The fiat currency was pounded down to no value and was repudiated. But the government of Louis XV acknowledged its partnership in Law's enterprise and assumed $340,000,000 of the Compagnie des Indes's obligations.

Jean Baptiste Bienville, new governor of Louisiana, took back Law's personal grant in the name of Louis XV and sent a friend named Dufresne to Arkansas Post as director of the colony.

Already, with the flow of money from John Law's personal pocket, the colonists had a hospital in their settlement, adequate cabins and large storehouses in which to hold their patron's crops.

But Governor Bienville had no money with which to continue this subsidy. A drought ruined the crops. The soldiers' pay was not forthcoming and their grumbling annoyed the officers who took out their grouches on the settlers and the Indians—both of whom replied in kind.

The several hundred German colonists erected spite fences against the French colonists and civil war was in prospect in the Arkansas grand duchy until some articulate colonist made a speech suggesting that they all throw up this life in the wilderness and return to Europe where, if they had no venison and turkey on their tables, they at least had no red Indians for neighbors.

The speech was met with cheers from the homesick Germans and French and they immediately began construction of boats and rafts to transport themselves and goods to tidewater.

When they reached New Orleans, however, Governor Bienville persuaded most of the colonists that they were making a grave mistake, that Louisiana was a beautiful new land and that Europe, after all, was afflicted by wars and politics. So they settled on what now is known as the "German Coast" in St. Charles Parish, west of New Orleans.

A few of the sturdy French stayed on at Arkansas Post after Bienville removed the troops.

Father Poisson, their priest, wrote in 1726 of the situation there:

"The French settlement on the Arkansas would have been an important one had M. Law continued his subsidy four or five years. . . . His intention was to found a city here, to establish manufactories and to found a duchy.

"The property he sent here amounted to more than 1,500,000 livres. . . . This was not a bad beginning for the first year, but M. Law was disgraced. Of the 3,000 or 4,000 Germans who already had left their country, a large number died in the East. The others were recalled. The Company of the Indies took back the grant and shortly abandoned it. The entire enterprise has therefore fallen to pieces. About 30 Frenchmen have remained here. Only the excellence of the soil and the climate have kept them, for in other respects they have received no assistance."

Governor Bienville in 1721 directed that Sieur Bernard La Harpe take sixteen soldiers and ascend to the headwaters of the Arkansas River, keeping a journal, noting the navigability of the stream, and ascertaining particularly if any Spaniards had settlements in this region. Bienville was conscious that De Soto had explored this new land of France nearly two hundred years before and he suspected there might be some Spanish communities that necessarily must be wiped out.

La Harpe found only forty-odd colonists left at Arkansas Post. He helped them improve their stockade according to military ideas and he started up the Arkansas River on March 10, 1721.

One of the special things La Harpe was instructed to look for was a rock of gigantic proportions on the river, a rock rumored to be composed of purest emerald.

He found the rock a month later and satisfied himself it was not emerald. In the general vicinity of the big rock he also found a smaller rock on the north bank of the river and on April 9th he and his party camped at "Petit Roche" because practically the whole detachment was ill with the fever.

They stayed there several days and, when the men's health grew worse instead of better, La Harpe was forced to abandon the expedition to the river's headwaters and return to New Orleans. The swampy country in eastern Arkansas even then was filled with malaria which laid the sturdy explorers low. For a hundred years those unwholesome marshes steered the course of westward immigration to the north and to the south of Arkansas.

Under the governorship of the pouch-eyed and purse-lipped Bienville, the French colonies in what now is the state of Louisiana were growing. But it was a long time before Arkansas Post and environs again attained the population held during John Law's ascendancy.

In 1744 there were only twelve male inhabitants and ten slaves. One hundred years after de Tonty founded the settlement, there were only 196 inhabitants.

King Louis XV hated the very name of Louisiana, hated it despite the development around New Orleans.

Perhaps it reminded him of John Law and of Uncle Phil, the Duke of Orleans, and the Mississippi Bubble which well-nigh brought a revolution about his boyish ears. At any rate, he regarded the whole territory as a white elephant and when, as result of being badly whipped in a war with England, he had opportunity to cede the whole sorry region to Spain, he did so gladly and the country returned to the land of De Soto, its discoverer. That was by the Treaty of Paris in 1763, by which England gained all French territory east of the Mississippi and south of the Great Lakes.

CHAPTER SEVENTEEN

Forty Years, Three Flags

SPAIN held the Louisiana territory for thirty-seven years and did exactly nothing toward developing it. Then came Napoleon in 1800 with plans to establish a French empire in the New World that made John Law's grand duchy seem like the modest ambitions of an unimaginative peasant.

Bonaparte made a secret treaty with Spain, by which France again became possessor of all territory ceded to Spain in the Treaty of Paris. Napoleon's treaty was secret and his plans for mighty developments were secret because the United States of America had come into being seventeen years before. The consul divined correctly that this new republic would be hostile to a French empire along the Mississippi River.

It was impossible, however, for Napoleon to keep his scheme secret for long. The news reached Thomas Jefferson, then president, and Jefferson was alarmed. New Orleans must not be a French port if the United States was to grow westward.

Jefferson concluded that New Orleans must be purchased from the French and he sent James Monroe to Paris to work together with American Minister Robert Livingston toward buying the city at the mouth of the Mississippi.

Napoleon scorned the offer. So Monroe and Liv-

ingston went away and tried to think up new arguments
and inducements.

Unknown to the Americans, however, more potent
arguments were being prepared north of the English
Channel. Another war between France and Britain was
brewing and Bonaparte knew he would need money to
prosecute it.

On April 30th Monroe and Livingston received a
message from Napoleon's secretary, Marbois. The consul would reopen the subject of purchase himself.

To the amazement of the Americans, Bonaparte
declared forthrightly that he would sell the whole territory of Louisiana, comprising 875,000 square miles, and
not just the town of New Orleans.

Monroe and Livingston had no authority to purchase anything except the town, but Napoleon imperi-
ously made his offer on a "take it or leave it" basis and
would not wait for an exchange of letters between the
envoys and Jefferson.

Monroe and Livingston were in an uncomfortable spot. But they were men of initiative and moral courage. They went beyond their authority and sealed the negotiations, agreeing that the United States would pay $15,-000,000 for the territory.

As they fixed their signatures to the bill of sale they felt they had done a good day's work. Livingston laid down his pen and said to Monroe: "We have lived long, but this is the noblest work of our whole lives. It will change vast solitudes into flourishing districts. From this day the United States take their place among the powers of the first rank."

However, there were many, many people in America who did not feel so jubilant. They blamed Jefferson bitterly for the purchase, for spending such a gigantic sum of the taxpayers' money to buy a howling wilderness that never in the world could be of value.

The howling wilderness comprised all or a part of thirteen states—Louisiana, Arkansas, Missouri, Iowa, Minnesota, South Dakota, North Dakota, Nebraska, Kansas, Colorado, Wyoming, Montana, and Oklahoma. The purchase made almost inevitable the annexation of Texas, Oregon, California, Arizona, and New Mexico. The purchase *made* the United States. And its immediate effect was to open the way to settlement of this vast territory.

In 1789 the population of Arkansas was estimated at 368. In 1810 it was 1,062. In 1819 it was 14,000.

The present state of Arkansas was made a part of Missouri Territory in 1812 and was organized as Arkansas Territory in 1819, with its boundaries including the Indian Territory.

Thus, Arkansas has been in both Louisiana and Missouri, as well as having been a French colony and a Spanish colony.

The English-born naturalist and explorer, Thomas Nuttall, traveled up the Arkansas River in 1819, about the time the rush of immigration was starting. He reported that practically no one was living in the low, swampy lands along the lower reaches of the Arkansas and White rivers, characterizing it as a vast and solitary wilderness.

He described the town of Arkansas Post as situated on the first prominent elevation on the Arkansas River, a scattered town of thirty or forty houses. It was a trading center for furs, hides, bear oil, and wild honey brought down the Arkansas and White rivers and traded for guns, powder, cloth, etc., which had been brought up the Mississippi from New Orleans.

At that time Francis Notrebe, a Frenchman, was the principal merchant in Arkansas Post, which meant eastern Arkansas.

Nuttall found a few shiftless, malaria-ridden squatters living in the bayou country even then. But a short way up the river he also found a goodly number of refined and educated folk living in clean, frame houses built after the old French style with high gable roofs and wide verandas.

This was the great period not only of exploration, but of settlement. The Arkansas River was the broad highway for immigration. The immigrants traveled in keelboats and by canoe, often cordelling the heavily-laden keelboats for many miles where the current was swift.

They established communities at Mooney, about thirty-five miles up from Arkansas Post. They formed a settlement at La Harpe's little rock and another at Fort Smith, then called Belle Point, at the confluence of the Poteau and Arkansas rivers.

Before the Louisiana Purchase the enterprising

Frenchmen of Arkansas Post had made numerous trips up the river to Belle Point, trading beads and other ten-cent-store trinkets to the Indians for furs. But the first real white settlement there was a fort built by Major Stephen H. Long in 1817. Major Long named his fort for his commanding officer, General Thomas A. Smith, and he reported: "The situation is secure and healthy with a complete command of both rivers, elevation 30 feet above the water. The fort is supported on a base of stratified sandstone."

When the second Fort Smith was built this sandstone bluff was blasted away.

Major Long's fort was a mere wooden stockade surrounding a blockhouse and barracks. But it was a symbol to the natives that the white man had come to stay.

At sunrise and at sunset a ceremonial cannon shot would boom across the river, echoing from Sugar Loaf on the south to the Boston Mountains on the north, and it impressed the Indians mightily. They never essayed an attack on Fort Smith nor on the settlers in its vicinity.

The first permanent settler in western Arkansas was Captain John Rogers, fresh from the Battle of New Orleans, and he built a great log house with stone chimneys where the eastern pier of the Fort Smith bridge now stands. Others soon followed Captain Rogers, building houses and planting crops along the river. On the west side of the stream, which now is Oklahoma, there was a community of Canadian voyageurs with their Cherokee wives. They live in legend as French Jack, Louis Layee, and Frank and Louis Rafield.

A Major Ben Moore of Virginia was the first to grow cotton and tobacco in western Arkansas. And Major Moore not only built a gristmill downstream from Little Rock, but he cut a channel through the bedrock of the river for vessels.

A settler named John Billingsly was one of a party of eighteen families that worked their way up the river in 1814. In 1876 Billingsly wrote of the pioneer life as follows:

"We had all the luxuries of life that a new country could afford, such as buffalo, bear, deer and elk meat and fish and honey. We had pound cake every day, since we beat all the meal that we ate in a mortar.

"The first year our corn gave out about six weeks before the roasting ears came. The substitute for bread was venison, dried by the fire in a mortar and made into small cakes which we fried in bear oil. That hoap [sic] us out until forward Irish potatoes came in. We had all things in common. We had no doctors or lawyers in those happy days. The first legislature was held at the Post of Arkansas. My father was a member. We had no tax to pay but county tax.

"When Major Bradford came to Fort Smith we furnished him with buffalo meat for the soldiers and then we got some flour from him, which was a great treat for us.

"We soon got strict enough to hold camp meetings and everybody went and left their houses for a week at a time.

"When we came back everything was all right. We generally built our chimneys up to the mantle-piece and hung our meat outside on the ribs of the house. If any man would have a lock on his doors in those days he would have been looked upon with suspicion.

"Men clothed themselves by dressing deer skins and making full suits of the same. When the French traders came up the river we bought some goods. We paid 50 cents for calico; 37½ cents for domestics and 40 cents for checks.

"I gave $4 for the first teacups I ever owned, and

very common they were at that. I had to pay $4 for a set of common knives and forks. We paid all things in beaver, otter, bear and deer skins, bear's oil and beeswax."

Before the gristmills came, the settlers were obliged to resort to even more primitive means to grind their corn into meal.

A large tree was cut down and the stump smoothed off. Then a fire would be kindled on the center of the smooth surface and kept burning there for days, burning deeper and deeper into the body of the stump.

Finally the charcoal was scraped out of the hole. A pestle or maul would be hung from the end of a long pole and the pole balanced in a forked stick set up in such a manner that the maul would hang over and fit into the burned hole.

The settler and his wife would put their corn into the stump hole, take hold of the loose end of the sweep-like pole and work it up and down. This would cause the pestle to pound the corn into a rough meal and incidentally mix up a lot of charcoal with the flour. Maybe the charcoal kept the pioneer digestions in good shape.

Mr. Billingsly recounted that all travel was by either boat or horseback and that a party was something to be planned for weeks. Young women would pack their finery in saddlebags and joyfully ride horseback fifty miles or more to attend a dance.

The dancing would last all night until the dawn dimmed the lights of tallow dips and pine knots, and the fiddlers and tambourine players were exhausted. Then the celebrants would do what chores were necessary, sleep a few hours, and resume the party at nightfall. Sometimes a special party would last as long as five days.

The great social events, then as now, were weddings. The bride's trousseau usually would consist of a new calico gown and some new homemade shoes of home-tanned deerskin. The groom's outfit would include a new coonskin cap, linsey or cotton shirt, and jeans or coarse linen breeches.

At a wedding there had to be entertainment in the daytime as well as at night, and that would consist largely of shooting matches, foot races, wrestling and feats of strength, lubricated by mountain dew and fortified by barbecued game.

David Crockett wrote of one of these pioneer shooting matches at Little Rock.

It was in 1835 after the mighty hunter had been defeated for re-election to Congress from Tennessee and was making a tour of the western territories with his famous gold- and silver-inlaid rifle which had been presented him by Philadelphia admirers.

Crockett had accepted an invitation to attend a banquet in Little Rock and that afternoon it was suggested, after "liquoring up a bit," that some of the Little Rock crack shots and the scout hold a shooting match on the outskirts of the village. It was commonly declared that Crockett not only could hit a deer fly in the left eye at seven rods, but that he could climb a thorn tree with a wildcat under each arm.

The Arkansans had heard many such extravagant tales about the great Davy. They wanted to see him in action.

Crockett described the event as follows:

"I shouldered my Betsy, and she is just about as beautiful a piece as ever came out of Philadelphia, and I went out to the shooting grounds, followed by all the leading men of Little Rock, and that is a clear majority of the town, for it is remarkable that there are always more leading men in small villages than there are followers.

"I was in prime order. My eyes were as keen as a

lizard's and my nerves were as steady and unshaken as the political course of Henry Clay. So at it we went, the distance 100 yards.

"The principal marksmen led the way, and there was some pretty fair shooting, I tell you. At length it came my turn. I squared myself, raised my beautiful Betsy to my shoulder, took deliberate aim, and smack! I sent the bullet right into the center of the bull's eye. 'There's no mistake in Betsy,' said I, in a careless sort of way as they were all looking at the target, sort of amazed, and not at all overpleased.

" 'That's a chance shot, Colonel,' said one of the gentlemen who had the reputation of being the best shot in these parts.

" 'Not as much chance,' said I, 'as there was when Dick Jackson took his darky for better, for worse. I can do it five times out of six any day in the week.' This I said as confident as the government [meaning Andrew Jackson] did when he protested that he forgave Colonel Benton for shooting him, and he was now the best friend he had in the world. I knew it was not altogether as correct as it might be, but when a man sets about doing the big figure, half-way measures won't answer, nohow, and the 'greatest and best' had set me the example that swaggering will answer a good purpose at times."

Crockett then wrote how the Little Rock men insisted on a second round and how he demurred:

"Knowing that I had nothing to gain and everything to lose, I was for backing out and fighting shy, but there was no let-off, for the cock of the village, though whipped, determined not to stay whipped, so to it again we went.

"They were now put on their mettle, and they fired much better than the first time. It was what might be called pretty sharp shooting.

"When it came my turn I squared myself and turning to the prime shot I gave him a knowing nod by way of showing my confidence, and says I, 'Look out for the bull's eye, stranger.'

"I blazed away, and I wish I may be shot if I didn't miss the target.

"They examined it all over, but could find neither hide nor hair of the bullet and pronounced it a miss. I says, 'Stand aside and let me look and I warrant you I get on the trail of the critter.' They stood aside and I examined the bull's eye pretty thoroughly, and at length cried out, 'Here it is. There is no snakes if it ain't followed the very track of the other.'

"They said it was utterly impossible, but I insisted on their searching the hole and agreed to be stuck up for a mark myself if they didn't find two bullets there. They searched for my satisfaction and, sure enough it all come out just as I told them, for I had picked up a bullet that had been fired and stuck it deep into the hole without anyone perceiving it.

"They were all perfectly satisfied that fame had not made too great a flourish of trumpets when speaking of me as a marksman. They said they had enough of shooting for the day, and they moved that we adjourn to the tavern and liquor."

Davy Crockett was not the only famous frontier figure who visited Arkansas. There was, of course, Daniel Boone, who has been mentioned as the discoverer of the first prehistoric ruins in the state. There was Zebulon Pike, the gallant army lieutenant, who explored the Ozarks and plotted the course of the Arkansas River from its mouth to Colorado. There was Zachary Taylor, who commanded the troops at Fort Smith.for three years, and Jefferson Davis, and the great Sam Houston.

One of the best Arkansas legends of Zachary Taylor has to do with two young lieutenants, fresh from West Point, who had been assigned to duty at the frontier post of Fort Smith.

General Taylor was a most unpretentious man and rarely even appeared in uniform except for formal occasions.

The general went aboard a newly arrived boat shortly after sunrise one morning, looking for some important mail that was overdue. He was accosted by the spick-and-span young subalterns who took the general to be a backwoods farmer.

"How's crops, old fellow?" they inquired.

"Oh, purty good," replied General Taylor. "Could stand a mite more rain, but purty good, considering."

The lieutenants invited the "old fellow" to have a drink, joked with and at him for some time, and then went ashore singing out, "Well, old fellow, give our love to the old woman and the gals."

A few hours later the adjutant very formally ushered the new subalterns into the commanding general's quarters for introduction and the boys nearly fainted. With supreme dignity and apparently no recognition, General Taylor received their credentials. Then he called his wife and daughter, Bessie.

"Boys," said Old Rough-and-Ready, "I want you to meet the old woman and the gal."

Samuel Houston was a resident of Arkansas for one period of his remarkable life. As a boy he had run away from home and lived with the Cherokees for several years. He returned to his Tennessee home when eighteen and took up civilized life, studying law and teaching school He enlisted as a private in the United States Army at twenty, fought in an Indian campaign, won promotion, became a district attorney, major general of militia,

congressman, and governor of Tennessee by the time he
was thirty-four.

He served one term as governor with distinction
and was re-elected. Shortly after re-election, Houston,
who then was thirty-six, married Miss Eliza Allen, a girl
of culture and family. But his bride left him in less than
a week.

There is some mystery connected with this separa-
tion and numerous explanations have been offered gratu-
itously by persons who don't know any more about it
than I do.

Houston wrote a note to his wife's father, vaguely
taking all blame on his own head—which may have been
justified and may have been mere chivalry.

Immediately, Houston resigned his governorship,
donned buckskin, and left in search of his old Cherokee
friends. He discovered they had moved across the Mississippi into Arkansas and he followed, bestowing brief
prosperity upon each barroom on his trail.

There is a story about General Houston traveling
with a jug of whisky and a lush lawyer named John
Linton.

Houston was drowning his sorrows and Linton also
had something or other to be sad about, according to
tradition.

So the Arkansas barrister spoke some classical Latin
extolling the virtues of Bacchus, and Houston bellowed:
"That's the spirit. Got to make a sacrifice to Bacchus
before you can have another snort. There ye go, Bacchus!" He tossed his wide-brimmed hat into the campfire and took another drink.

That seemed a noble gesture from the former governor of Tennessee, so Lawyer Linton heaved his som-
brero into the flames and took a drink.

Houston stripped off his jacket and tossed it into

the fire and tipped up the jug. Linton stripped off his coat and tossed it into the fire and tipped up the jug.

The blazing beaver and buckskin and wool made a horrible stench and about that time they probably sang a song—it might have been "Green Grow the Rushes, Oh!"

Then Houston tossed his shirt to the flames and Linton did likewise and both had a drink.

Then in went the ex-gubernatorial undershirt and the Arkansas lawyer's undershirt—if he had one.

Then to Bacchus went their trousers and drawers and socks and shoes and Sam Houston, the only man ever to become governor of two of the United States, stood up stark naked, six feet four or five inches tall and roaring drunk.

"Time to get on the trail," he shouted. "Got to find my Cherokee family."

So into the next village rode General Sam Houston and Lawyer Linton while the good housewives covered their blushing faces with sunbonnets and chased their innocent offspring indoors behind drawn blinds.

Houston finally found his old Cherokee friends and his old sweetheart, Tiana, and he was adopted into the tribe officially as a Cherokee. The Cherokees gave him the name "Big Drunk," apparently with some reason.

For three years he lived happily with the Indians and his Indian wife, who, according to historians, was exceptionally comely—for a squaw. As a matter of fact, Houston later declared these three years were the happiest of his life.

Then Tiana died and Houston went to Little Rock where he lived somewhat mysteriously, organizing forces for a Texas revolt.

He left Little Rock for the campaign which was to make him president of the Texas republic and later governor of the state of Texas, riding a pony which was so small Houston had to use short stirrups to keep his feet from dragging. To make the picture complete, it is recorded that the pony had no tail.

One of the most famous and picturesque appurtenances of Arkansas pioneer life was the bowie knife. The bowie knife is supposed to be distinctly Arkansas. They call Arkansas the "Bowie State," as a matter of fact, and they called the bowie knife an "Arkansas toothpick."

However, Webster's International Dictionary states the knife was named for its inventor, Colonel James Bowie. And Colonel James Bowie had little or no connection with the state of Arkansas. Colonel James Bowie was a Georgian by birth and migrated to Texas, where he died in the Alamo massacre.

In Arkansas there is a feeling that Webster's International errs on this score. Evidence is offered that Colonel Bowie was not the inventor of the bowie knife at all, but that it was invented and manufactured by a blacksmith in Hempstead County, Arkansas, a man named James Black, and that the knife was named for Colonel James Bowie's brother, Reason Bowie, who popularized the blade.

The first bowie knife, according to former Governor Daniel W. Jones, was made by Black for Reason Bowie and its temper and sharpness proved so remarkable that other frontiersmen came from afar to get "a knife like Bowie's."

Governor Jones believed the Washington, Arkansas, blacksmith had rediscovered the secret of Damascus steel. As a boy he had known and admired James Black, so when the blacksmith was an old man and blind the governor called on him.

Jones asked his old friend if he would bequeath the secret of his marvelous steel to him.

"I'll do that," said the old man, "if you'll go out someplace and get a pen and paper. There's a dozen or more stages to this process and you'll have to write them down."

So the governor went out and got pen, ink, and paper. When he returned, the old blind man shook his head. "No use," he said. "Just been trying to remember the recipe while you were gone. But it's no use. I've forgotten the whole thing." So his secret died with him.

Black sold his bowie knives for $10 to $50, according to size, and it took a good many beaverskins to make $50 in the 1830's. But a bowie knife was a man's most prized possession, for with this legendary blade as his ally, one honest man was supposed to be the equal of half a dozen bandits.

There's a story that they found Colonel Bowie's body in the Alamo with his bowie knife still in his hand and that he was surrounded by the bodies of seven partially dissected Mexicans.

So maybe the Washington, Arkansas, blacksmith made a knife for the colonel, also, and sent it to Texas by parcel post. Or maybe the colonel just borrowed his brother's knife for the duration of the war.

I do like to think of that backwoods artisan, James Black, rediscovering the secret of Damascus steel and then forgetting the formula when senility clouded his mind. But I suppose there is more than a possibility that Colonel James Bowie invented the bowie knife after all.

More characteristic of backwoods Arkansas than the stories of these frontier heroes, of course, is the famous old tale of the Arkansaw Traveler.

Native Arkansas historians don't like this story very

well. Most of them feel obliged to tell some version of the legend, together with apologies, asserting the story never was typical of Arkansas, not even of the backwoods squatter.

"The Arkansaw Traveler" has been printed many times and told many more. One of the first phonograph recordings I ever heard—and that must have been around 1905—was of the Arkansaw Traveler.

A well-dressed traveler riding a splendid white horse had lost his way on one of the ambiguous backwoods trails. In some versions of the story this traveling gentleman is a wealthy planter named Sanford C. Faulkner. Anyhow, weary and drenched from a summer shower, the traveler approached a log cabin.

On a bench outside the door sat an Arkansas squatter with coonskin cap, buckskin breeches, and moccasins. He was scraping away at a miserable fiddle, playing over and over a few bars of a simple tune. Over his head on the wall of the cabin was a sign bearing the single word, "Whisky."

"How do you do, my friend," greeted the pompous gentleman on the white horse.

"Ain't your friend. Never seen you before," said the squatter, scraping away on the fiddle.

"I have lost my way," said the traveler plaintively. "It's growing dusk. May I stay with you for the night?"

"You can git to hell if you want. But you can't stay here."

"But, my friend, I am weary and drenched. Have you any spirits here?"

"Loads of spirits. My woman Sal saw one down by the holler gum tree last night and it near skeered her to death." Again the fiddle squeaked away.

"Oh, I don't mean that kind of spirits. Have you some whisky?"

"Had some, but drank the last this morning."

The traveler pointed to the sign on the cabin. "What's that sign mean, then?"

"Oh, that. That there sign means I run a tavern here. I keep the tavern here and sell whisky to make a living."

"Well, that's what I'm getting at. I want some whisky. I asked you if you'd sell me a drink."

"Stranger, I tell you how it is. My woman Sal and me went partners on a bar'l of whisky last week. I sticks a spigot in my end of the bar'l and Sal sticks a spigot in her end of the bar'l. When I wants a drink I takes it from her end of the bar'l and pays her the shilling. When she wants a drink she takes it from my end of the bar'l and pays me the shilling back. It works splendid until that damn skunk Buck bores a hole in the bottom for to suck on and this morning when I goes to buy a drink the bar'l's plumb empty."

"Well, I'm sorry your whisky is gone. But I'm hungry. If you run a tavern can't you sell me a bite to eat?"

"Nope. Not a dern thing in the house. No meat. No bread. No meal." Again the fiddle rasped away.

The weary traveler shook his head. "Well, at least," he said, "you won't mind me tying my horse to this tree and resting my tired bones a minute."

The squatter shook his head. "Don't dare you tie your hoss to that tree," he warned. "That's a persimmon tree and Sal allows she's going to make some persimmon beer and we don't aim to have the persimmons shook down."

"All right, I'll move on. How far is it to the next house?"

"Don't know. I never visit."

"Well, where does this road go?"

"Don't go nowhere's far as I know. It's always right there when I get up in the morning."

"All right. I suppose my horse and I can get along tonight without anything to eat. But at least you can't refuse me shelter for the night."

"Got no shelter for you. That there roof leaks. Only one dry spot in the house and me and Sal sleeps there."

"Why don't you put some new shakes on the roof and stop the leaks?"

"Been raining all afternoon. Can't fix the roof when it's raining."

"Why don't you fix the roof when it isn't raining, then?"

"Don't leak when it ain't raining." And on went the fiddling on the same monotonous bars.

"Well, I'm sorry. Tired and wet and hungry as I am, I suppose I must be on my way and try to find a more hospitable house. But why don't you play the rest of that tune?"

"Don't know no rest. Think maybe you could play it all yourself?"

"I believe I could if you'd lend me your fiddle."

"Well, you don't look like no fiddler. But here. Try it if you think you can."

The traveler took the fiddle and played "The Arkansaw Traveler" through with some spirit. And before he had gone far with the tune the squatter had lost his lassitude. He was on his feet dancing wildly. Sal was at the door pounding in time on the doorjamb and half a dozen tow-haired children were grouped around the traveler.

As the fiddle scraped to the tune's conclusion the squatter loosed a war whoop. "Buck, you lazy good-for-nothing, whyn't you take the gentleman's hoss? What you gawping there for? Take that hoss to the shed and give him all the corn he can eat.

"Here, there, stranger, take a chair. Take half a

dozen chairs if you can find 'em. Sal, get busy there.
Get busy like six hosses in a mudhole. Run you down to
the holler where I killed that buck this morning, run you
down there and cut off a venison steak. Get the best steak
on that buck and fry it up for me and the gentleman.
Jen, shake a leg there. You hear me, Jen? Lift up that
floor board by the bed and get the black jug I hid from
that skunk boy Buck. Pour me and the gentleman some
whisky and don't be stingy about it either. Lil, you chase
the dog out of the bread box and set the table. Be quick
now."

"Pappy," whined Lil, "they ain't enough knives to
set the table."

"What you mean, they ain't enough knives? There's

big butch and little butch, cob-handle and granny's knife, and where at's that knife I found yesterday? Them's enough knives for any gentleman.

"Yes, sir, stranger, we'll feed you and drink you and sleep you if you just play that fiddle some more. Play right on, stranger, and you can sleep in the dry spot."

So the traveler played for a couple of hours and then, thinking he best get directions while his host still was in good humor, inquired again about the road. "I'll want to get an early start in the morning," he explained.

"In the morning! What you mean, stranger? You-all won't be getting away from these parts for six weeks. You're going to stay right here and play that old fiddle."

"Well," said the traveler, pleased that at last he had won over his host, "I'm more than a little obliged for

your hospitality, but I really have to move on. Where will I find my road?"

"All right," said the host, "when you cross that slough over there and pass a weed field that has a little measly corn growing in it, you go on a couple of miles along the bank of a swamp where the mud'll come up to your hoss's withers, then in a mile or so further you'll come to a place where there's two roads.

"If you want to, you can take the right-hand road and follow it another couple mile and then the road'll run out.

"Then you'll see that ain't the road and you'll have to come back and take the left-hand road. You ride along over that road through a couple swamps for about three mile. Then that road will run out too, and you'll feel mighty lucky if you can find your way back to my house and live with us and fiddle as long as you want."

The Arkansas squatters of whom "The Arkansaw Traveler" settler may or may not have been typical were fierce, ignorant and suspicious characters who held "title" to their land with rifle and knife. But by and large, the pioneer settlers of Arkansas seem to have been people of enterprise and of some culture and honor.

In the Fort Smith district, for instance, a community of settlers raised the money for their pre-emptions and sent one man on horseback back to the land office to pay for their claims. This man had two lead horses laden with silver and he was gone for several weeks. Yet he was not under bond and there seems to have been no special worry that the bailee might give way to temptation and keep on riding past the land office with his cargo of money.

The first outside business done by these pioneers of Crawford and Sebastian counties was with Mexico. Ponderous two-wheel carts drawn by oxen or donkeys were driven up from the south laden with laces, silver, and bricabrac to trade for furs and corn several years before the steamboats began bringing large quantities of supplies from New Orleans.

The steamboats not only brought an end to the picturesque Mexican trade, but they seem to have brought on the beginnings of that strange era of near feudalism and rather ridiculous chivalry which lived in Arkansas up to the Civil War.

CHAPTER EIGHTEEN

Pistols at Dawn

THE curious chivalry of pre-Appomattox Arkansas, of course, was not limited to Arkansas. It was a condition or aberration which saturated the entire South. It was sired, probably, by Sir Walter Scott and nurtured by a whole legion of very romantic and very bad writers of the early nineteenth century.

With this wave of romantic fiction oozing across America, it was easy for the southern planters and their women—particularly their women—to cast themselves in the roles of plumed knights and highborn ladies. This was easy because of the institution of slave labor. If a planter owns body and soul a company of laborers, black or white, he may readily come to regard himself as a liege lord—especially if his mind is filled with the sort of fiction which filled the minds of southern ladies and gentlemen in the three or four decades preceding what they like to call the War Between the States.

They built themselves castles. They decked themselves out in gorgeous imported clothing. They acquired courtly manners—very courtly manners. And they were most serious about their personal dignity, which they euphemized as their honor.

This whole world of moonshine and magnolias revolved on the axis of slavery. And when the liege lord's serfs were emancipated, American feudalism died a violent death.

To this day one may find many intelligent Arkansas
men and women who will sigh for the old days Before the
War, as they recount legends passed down by their
parents and grandparents. There are many intelligent
Arkansas men and women who also will defend the institution of Negro slavery which made the old Arkansas
chivalry possible.

They will say:

"Oh, there probably were some cruel masters, but
they were in the great minority and they usually were
punished for their sins. Mostly, the slaveowners were
kind to the darkies. They treated the darkies as children
or as mentally incompetent adults and the slaves loved
their masters."

They will tell stories of slaves who refused to leave
their masters when freedom came. They will tell of
Negro servants who virtually are slaves now, who have
remained with their white families for many generations.
They will tell of Negro mammies who rule their white
families with rods of iron and are loved by the white
children as a second mother.

Well, that all is the usual nostalgic defense of the
Good Old Days in the South, which disregards the fact
that slavery was uneconomic and impossible of survival
even if the moral side of the question were disregarded.
And it's overlooking the fact that, after all, the chivalric
actions of those early Arkansans were pretty silly.

A by-product of chivalry in Arkansas inevitably
was dueling. If Mrs. Hopkins snubbed Mrs. Smithers at
the foreign missions barbecue, it well might mean coffee
and pistols at dawn for Mr. Hopkins and Mr. Smithers.
There is no record of the number of duels fought by
Arkansans during the period of chivalry, but there were
a lot of them. Some of the best people and people highest

in official standing fought duels, as well as some of the people in lowest standing.

Robert Crittenden, first secretary of the Territory of Arkansas, and counted as the first great statesman of the new state, fought a duel with Henry Conway and killed him. Crittenden was undisputed head of the Whig party in the state. Conway was boss of the Democratic party and Arkansas representative in Congress. The duel came at the end of a bitter political campaign and followed a duel between Ambrose H. Sevier, a cousin of Conway and also a state builder, and Colonel T. W. Newton, partisan of Crittenden. Both duels came from bitter words passed in the campaign.

Superior Court Justices Andrew Scott and Joseph Selden, both of Little Rock, fought a duel one May morning and Judge Selden was killed.

On the night before the duel the two jurists were playing whist with two young women.

Judge Scott's partner, who no doubt was a highborn lady, but probably poor at arithmetic, spoke gleefully to Judge Selden, "Aha, Judge, we have both the tricks and the honors on you."

And Judge Selden, being a stickler for accuracy, said, "Madam, that is not so." He is supposed to have said it bluntly, just like that, "Madam, that is not so," in a tone of voice no well-plumed knight ever employs when addressing a lady.

The startled young woman raised her tiny lace handkerchief to hide her tears, and she sobbed, "Why, Judge Selden, I did not expect to be insulted."

The plumes of Judge Scott, however, were unsullied. He pushed back his chair. He stood erect with the lace ruffles of his shirt gleaming white in the candlelight. And he spoke to Judge Selden with hauteur: "Sir, you have insulted a lady. You have insulted my partner and I de-

mand that you apologize immediately for your rude-
ness."

It is difficult to understand Judge Selden's actions.
He was of a period of chivalry and had he not been a
plumed knight himself it is inconceivable that he would
have been appointed to the Superior Court bench. Yet
here he was crassly exposing this tender flower of Arkansas to harsh realities. He had brought tears to her beautiful eyes by a forthright statement that she was wrong
in claiming both tricks and honors.

Moreover, when challenged by Judge Scott, Judge
Selden was crude enough to insist he had not insulted
the lady.

"I have merely told her a fact," said Judge Selden
firmly.

Perhaps it was several generations back, but there
must have been a drop of low blood in Judge Selden.
Surely no thoroughbred Arkansas gentleman could have
failed to see the insult in presenting any cold fact to a
lily of the Southland, let alone the more culpable crime
of contradicting her.

"She said," insisted Judge Selden, "that you had
taken both tricks and honors. By gad, sir, you yourself
can see that isn't so."

"That's neither here nor there," asserted Judge
Scott, with proper dignity. "The thing is, are you going
to offer apology?"

"Well," said Judge Selden, "I didn't insult anybody.
I just said you all didn't win tricks and honors and that
isn't any insult because you all *didn't* win tricks and
honors, so damn me I ain't going to apologize."

"Very well," said Judge Scott, "my seconds will call
upon you within the hour."

So at dawn the two Superior Court justices and
their seconds met on the dewy greensward and the whiter

plumes of Judge Scott were victorious and the honor of the unmathematical flower of Arkansas was vindicated in the lifeblood of young Judge Selden.

These are just a few of the many, many duels in Arkansas history.

John Hugh Reynolds, in his *Makers of Arkansas History*, says: "We should not be too severe in criticizing these duelists, for they were honorable men who insisted on the highest standards of gentlemanly conduct according to the customs of their own time."

There was an extraordinary duel in 1848 between General Albert Pike and John Selden Roane. Mr. Roane, a relative of Judge Selden, was the fourth governor of Arkansas. General Pike was a prodigious character who has become such a legend that he almost might be called the patron saint of Arkansas. He was a Paul Bunyan of the Southland. Even today, nearly fifty years after his death, when an Arkansas writer essays to put down words about General Pike, extravagances and hyperbole fly like goose feathers from a burst pillow.

General Pike, with his retainers, appeared on the field of battle smoking a fine Havana cigar. He took the cigar from his mouth and slowly expelled a cloud of aromatic smoke while he casually and dreamily pinked Governor Roane with a bullet. Then he deliberately and with apparent enjoyment took another draw on the cigar.

General Pike was an epicure. He was a gourmet and a gourmand. He was a soldier. He was a lawyer. He was a poetaster, and they will tell you General Pike could have been one of the great poets of all time had he wished to work at it. They will tell you General Pike was one of the most distinguished men, if not *the* most distinguished man America ever produced. No attempt is made to explain this statement. It's just a cut from the same pragmatic weave that proves the girls of Little Rock and

Helena are more beautiful than the girls of Herkimer, New York, or Fargo, North Dakota.

General Pike was a sullen-eyed, bewhiskered giant who was born in Boston and educated at Harvard. He went to Arkansas in his youth and began his career by teaching school, editing a country newspaper, reading law, and writing what passed for poetry.

He slept only five or six hours a night, consumed enough food and brandy, it is said, for a dozen men, and worked prodigiously. He became a most successful lawyer, traveling over the state to try cases before the Circuit Court.

As General Pike's fame as a barrister grew, he employed a brass band to travel with him and he would ride into a town to the blare of martial music. They say General Pike's appearance was so imposing that people would turn to look at him and I suppose this was particularly true when he had his brass band along.

Court day always was made something of a festival in these frontier communities and settlers rode in for many miles to attend trials. They would jounce in over the rough, muddy roads, bringing their families of swamp-depigmented children and baskets of picnic lunch which would be eaten on the courthouse lawn. During recesses the women would "visit" and swap recipes. The men would congregate at the saloons and swap lies. The barroom arguments on court days often developed raw material for more court days.

Arkansas court days were great occasions in pre-Civil War times comparable only to Christmas and the Fourth of July. After the Civil War, court days were comparable only to Christmas because the Fourth of July was no day of rejoicing south of Mason and Dixon's line. Grant had captured Vicksburg in 1863 on the Fourth of July. The Battle of Helena, Arkansas, was lost on the same day. News of Gettysburg also came on the Fourth of July. So, after the Civil War the children of Arkansas shot their fireworks on Christmas.

But both before and after the war, court days were fete days, especially when Albert Pike was coming to town as counsel for the defense, bringing his brass band to give concerts. It is possible that members of the jury enjoyed band concerts just as much as the spectators. At least it is a matter of record that juries seldom were prejudiced against clients of General Albert Pike.

Being a mighty man, the general also was a mighty hunter. When he was practicing law at Fort Smith he used to go goose hunting, but naturally a mere shotgun was no weapon for a character like General Pike.

He would borrow a cannon from the fort and load it with a bucketful of shot. Then he would have the cannon hauled out to the Mazzaed prairie where the wild geese fed in huge droves during migrations.

General Pike would have his men build a blind in front of the cannon and at dawn he would stroll out personally and touch off the howitzer. In that way this giant among sportsmen could kill a hundred or so feeding geese with a single shot. It was a system that brought added fame to General Pike, but it wouldn't be practical today. For some reason, there aren't so many wild geese in Arkansas now.

General Pike went to the Mexican War and served as a captain. He was a brigadier general in the Confederate Army in the Civil War and head of the Confederacy's Indian department. In this latter capacity, he succeeded in enlisting a brigade of Indians who proved better at scalping the dead Union soldiers than they were at fighting against artillery.

Before the Battle of Pea Ridge, General Pike showed his military acumen by anticipating defeat and having a servant go far to the rear and hide with $63,000 of Confederate treasury gold. In that way the money was saved and General Pike's stature was increased another cubit.

As a lawyer, General Pike made a great deal of money, but it is said his charities kept him poor. He built the finest mansion in Little Rock. And there is a story of his receiving $200,000 on winning a lawsuit and repairing to New Orleans where he put on a protracted party of such longitude and latitude that the whole legal fee was expended.

One of General Pike's services to the Confederacy during the war was revamping "Dixie." Certain verses of the original song were lacking in dignity, such as:

> While missus lived, she lived in clover,
> And when she died, she died all over,
> Look away, Dixie Land.

General Pike rewrote "Dixie" into a cotton belt "Marseillaise" with such verses as:

> Strong as lions, swift as eagles,
> Back to their kennels hunt these beagles!
> To arms! To arms! To arms in Dixie!

It is said that when Albert Pike was working on a lawsuit or perhaps composing a poem he would work night and day, sleeping only an hour or so a night and eating practically nothing. But when the case or the poem was finished, Albert Pike would relax in such a magnificent manner that his name even now is seldom mentioned in Arkansas without the qualifying adjective, "great."

He liked to go camping and to be camp cook himself, even when he had grown so portly that it was difficult for him to move around under his own power.

Other members of the party would scurry out into the woods to kill game while General Pike presided majestically over a huge iron kettle into which he dumped squirrels and rabbits and birds and chunks of bacon and potatoes and turnips and tomatoes and carrots and cabbage and possum and pork and onions and red pepper and garlic, stirring it all with one hand while he held a great bowl of brandy in the other, and discoursed over his big meerschaum pipe, as Colonel Marcellus L. Davis said, "Like the sage, the philosopher, the poet, the statesman that he was."

When the conglomerate was sufficiently stewed, General Pike would begin eating. He would eat day and night and drink raw brandy day and night for the period of the holiday, consuming as much food as a dozen lusty men and drinking enough brandy to jingle a score.

At the time of his death in 1891, General Pike was said to be the highest ranking Mason in the world. Most of his prose writings were on Freemasonry, although he translated some fifteen volumes of Aryan literature into English and wrote several treatises on ornithology. General Pike was a great bird lover and was an expert on migratory fowl, especially on wild geese.

One of the most beautiful buildings in Little Rock is the Masonic Albert Pike Memorial Temple, which was dedicated in May, 1924.

John Hugh Reynolds describes General Pike as follows:

"Albert Pike was a king among men by the divine right of merit—a giant in body and brain, in heart and soul. So majestic was he in appearance that wherever he moved, on highway or byway the wide world over, every passerby turned to gaze upon him—and admire him. His whole countenance told of power combined with tenderness, refinement and benevolence."

CHAPTER NINETEEN

Gunpowder and Hyperbole

WHILE few actual battles were fought within the state, the Civil War levied a terrible toll on Arkansas. The reconstruction days were scarcely better than the war.

Arkansas was one of the last southern states to secede in 1861. A potent minority of citizens favored the Union cause, strong enough to make itself felt politically, even though composed mostly of the nonslaveowners.

Bitter wrangling followed the election of Abraham Lincoln and continued even after the first gun of the war was fired on April 12, 1861, until May 6th when a secession ordinance passed.

Before secession, however, state troops had anticipated war. Under orders from Governor Elias Rector, two steamers loaded with troops and artillery splashed up the Arkansas River on the night of April 23rd. The troops were under command of Colonel Solon Borland, who carried a demand from Governor Rector that Captain S. D. Sturgis, U.S.A., commander of the Fort Smith garrison, surrender to the state of Arkansas.

The troops landed just below Fort Smith and were joined by local militia of Sebastian County and from Crawford County across the river.

In this joining of commands there may have been some jollity and even conviviality. At any rate, Captain Sturgis was warned of hostile approach in ample time to move his troops and munitions and other supplies across the west loop of the river into Indian Territory.

Nearly a year passed before a real battle was fought in Arkansas. That took place up in the timbered hills of Benton County in the extreme northwest corner of the state on March 7 and 8, 1862. It was the greatest fight of the war within the boundaries of Arkansas and it is known variously as the Battle of Pea Ridge and the Battle of Elkhorn. Southerners prefer the latter term because in the first day's action Confederate troops drove the Northerners half a mile back from Elkhorn tavern and captured several cannon.

Even now Arkansas historians say 15,000 Confederate troops under goateed General Earl Van Dorn won a "partial victory" over about 24,000 Federals commanded by General S. R. Curtis.

Contemporary northern writers declared that General Curtis with 11,000 men won a "glorious victory" over General Van Dorn, who had a "motley army of approximately 30,000." In these contemporary northern reports, Confederate losses were placed at 3,000 and northern killed, wounded, and missing at "a few hundred."

In view of records, it doesn't take a military expert now to see that the battle actually was a Union success. The Confederate General Benjamin McCulloch and his successor in command, Colonel James McIntosh, were killed and their brigade was demoralized. The Confederates were forced to retire and General Van Dorn moved his army across the Mississippi, leaving the state of Arkansas practically at the mercy of the Federal forces.

Official records show the Union command at the Battle of Pea Ridge (or Elkhorn) consisted of 10,500 infantry and cavalry and 40 cannon. The Confederates had 16,202 infantry and cavalry and about 50 cannon.

However, about 2,000 of the Confederate force were practically untrained and ineffective, being Albert Pike's Indians and farmers armed with shotguns and squirrel rifles.

The great General Pike's Indians reverted to type wholeheartedly in the first hours of the battle, charging over the battlefield and scalping scores of wounded Union soldiers. When the Federal artillery opened up, however, the red men were terrorized by the uproar and retreated into the brush to take no further part in the battle.

Reports of this Indian barbarity shocked the North —just as the South was shocked at the use of Negroes in the Union Army.

Some of the Southerners also were shocked at the Indian scalpings at Pea Ridge. Outside of Arkansas these Southerners comforted themselves with the thought that Albert Pike was born in Boston. In Arkansas Albert Pike's greatness in a way sanctified even the deeds of his Indians.

At Pea Ridge the Union troops actually lost 1,351 instead of the "few hundred." General Van Dorn's report of his own casualties was between 800 and 1,000 killed and wounded and 300 missing.

Van Dorn's retreat from Arkansas and the subsequent advance of the Union soldiers must have been most disconcerting to the Arkansans. There had been a great deal of patriotic whoop-la about the war and a great deal of loose oratory about the general worthlessness of northern men as fighters and about the magnificence of the southern soldier. Especially after the first Battle of Bull Run one heard on every hand that one Southerner could lick four or five or half a dozen Yankees. The Arkansans accepted that legend as gospel.

To show the Arkansas contempt for northern factory workers and shoe clerks who "didn't even know which was the business end of a gun," a public-spirited orator in White County started recruiting a company of schoolgirls, who, he declared, could keep all the Yankees out of the state.

At the outbreak of the war the population of Arkansas was 435,450. A considerable number of Union sympathizers found their way north to enlist with the Federal forces. And more than 50,000 Arkansans saw service with the Confederate Army—more than 10 per cent of the total population. Comparatively few of Arkansas' soldiers shed their blood in their native state, but they laid down their lives by the thousand in battles east of the Mississippi.

Shortly after General Van Dorn's retreat from Arkansas (or strategic removal, if you will) a Helena lawyer named Thomas C. Hindman started recruiting an army to drive the hated Yankees from the state. He raised and trained a fairly well-equipped army of 11,000 men and in the fall of 1862 started north on his crusade.

Across the line in Missouri was Brigadier General James G. Blunt with about 7,000 men, mostly from Kansas. He got word of General Hindman's advance and sent a call for General Francis J. Herron to come on and help fight the Arkansans. In response, General Herron moved east to meet Blunt, who was marching down into the oak- and pecan-clad hills of Washington County.

General Herron and his Iowans sighted a body of troops near the town of Prairie Grove on December 7, 1862, and assuming they had made the expected juncture with Blunt's men, marched on singing.

To their sorrow, however, the troops were not Blunt's Kansans, but General Hindman's Confederates.

There was a desperate battle for several hours, with Hindman's cavalry having the advantage. Herron was driven back a mile or so. Then Blunt's army, hearing the firing, double-timed into position and the Confederates were forced to retreat, retiring across the Arkansas River to the southern part of the state.

Confederate casualties were 1,317. Union losses were 1,251.

To this day children in Arkansas schools are taught that Prairie Grove was a Confederate victory, that General Hindman retired south of the river only because his supplies had given out after he had driven the Yankees from the field of battle.

Over in the eastern end of the state, the Mississippi River town of Helena had been occupied without a struggle by General Curtis when Van Dorn strategically had retired into Tennessee.

Virginia-born General Benjamin Mayberry Prentiss was holding the town with 4,129 Union men and he had fortified the surrounding hills until Helena was a Federal stronghold controlling that section of the river.

Along in June of 1863, when the siege of Vicksburg was under way, the Confederate command resolved to take Helena. They hoped a strong attack there might turn General Grant's attention away from Vicksburg. They hoped, moreover, that even if Vicksburg fell, they still might control the Mississippi with Helena.

Theophilus Hunter Holmes, West Point graduate Confederate general, moved up from Little Rock with 7,600 men and attacked Helena at dawn on the Fourth of July. Holmes used fine military strategy, but the Federal positions were too strong.

At ten-thirty in the morning Holmes was obliged to retire with 1,636 men killed, wounded, or missing. The Federal losses officially were 57 killed, 146 wounded, and 36 missing.

That was the Battle of Helena, a distressing defeat

for the western Confederates. Vicksburg fell on that very day.

With the occupation of Vicksburg, Grant ordered General Frederick Steele to move his forces to Helena and there to organize an assault upon Little Rock.

With an army of 14,000 (3,500 of them sick with malaria) General Steele marched down to the Arkansas River on September 7th.

General Sterling Price with about 7,700 effectives, apparently was prepared to make a desperate defense of the state capital. He had 6,500 troops entrenched on the north side of the river and 1,200 on the south side.

Steele marched up the river. For the last ten miles there was almost constant skirmishing between cavalry units, but the Confederates retired. When the Federal forces reached Little Rock General Price's army was gone, leaving seven steamers and one gunboat blazing furiously in the river. The city was formally surrendered to the Union general at 7 P.M. of September 10, 1863.

Price reported a loss of 64 men. Steele's casualties were 137.

One week before Little Rock surrendered, General Blunt had taken Fort Smith almost without a struggle and that practically ended the fighting in Arkansas. It did not, however, end the war for the Arkansans.

Arkansas continued to send its able-bodied men into the Confederate armies. Arkansas continued to give what money it had left to the cause. Arkansas continued to eat its meat without salt—when it could get meat.

The Arkansans drank coffee made of okra seeds or parched rye. The Arkansans starved and patched their ragged clothing and prayed fiercely.

They prayed fiercely for a cause they believed in their hearts to be a just cause. They believed in their cause just as strongly when the economic structure of the

Confederacy finally was worn to shreds and the tide of battle turned against General Lee's starving heroes. They wouldn't believe it was a lost cause until Appomattox— and some of them refused to believe even then.

And while the real battles in Arkansas were over by the autumn of 1863, skirmishes continued and the bitterness continued and the loyalists of Arkansas never lost an opportunity to put in a lick or two for the Confederacy.

I have personal knowledge of one obscure sortie after northern Arkansas officially was in Union hands. It occurred at the village of Clarendon in Monroe County, which was not important enough from the Union viewpoint to waste a garrison on.

Clarendon is on the White River, perhaps seventy-five miles up from its juncture with the Arkansas. It has a population of about two thousand now and I suspect it was considerably less than a thousand in 1864.

Word was circulated in Clarendon one day that a

Union gunboat was on its way up the river with a safe full of gold to pay the troops stationed upstream. So the patriotic Clarendon citizens wheeled out an old cannon that had been abandoned in some retreat, loaded it up to the muzzle, and pushed the cannon up on the levee, commanding the river at the downstream bend. They piled brush in front of the gun to hide their operations. Then they waited.

Presently the gunboat hove in sight, splashing slowly against the considerable current. She swung in toward the right bank to take advantage of an eddy, swung in toward Clarendon and the hidden gun. The Clarendon men waited until they knew they could not miss their target and then let drive at the gunboat's water line.

It was a direct hit. A gaping hole was torn in the boat's side and she immediately listed to starboard and began to settle. But as she sank, the gunboat made Clarendon pay for her death. She raked the town with volley after volley from her cannon.

When I was a boy my father had a sawmill on the banks of the White River at Clarendon. At low-water stage the rusted smokestack of the sunken Federal gunboat still was visible. No one ever had made an attempt to raise her and salvage the cargo.

It was taken as a matter of fact in Clarendon that the safe still was aboard at the bottom of the river and that the safe held several thousand dollars in gold.

My brother Glen once tried to initiate a project to recover that safe when he found he could rent a diver's suit in Memphis. He took the matter up with several young fellows around town, fellows who ordinarily were ready for a fight or a frolic or anything else that offered entertainment, night or day. But Glen found everyone singularly apathetic to this proposal.

Yes, they reckoned there was a lot of gold down

there in the gunboat. They reckoned there was more gold than they could make in several years' hard work. It wasn't that the gold still was technically the property of the United States even after passage of half a century. No, it wasn't that. They just didn't want to mess with that old gunboat.

You see, quite a passel of Yankees had gone down with that old boat. The Yankee skeletons would be down there still, guarding that safe of Yankee gold. The Clarendon young men hadn't lost anything down there with those Yankee skeletons. And they wanted no truck with *any* skeletons at the bottom of the White River.

So, as far as I know, the Yankee gold is still there —if, indeed, there ever *was* a safe of gold aboard the Yankee gunboat.

CHAPTER TWENTY

Carpet Bags and Crime

ARKANSAS suffered with the rest of the South from the stupid, vicious reconstruction legislation.

In 1868 practically every able-bodied white man in the state was robbed of his citizenship—because he had borne arms against the Union. The Negro, utterly untrained for citizenship at that time, was given the franchise.

For three years following the close of the war, under the governorship of Isaac Murphy, Arkansas made progress toward reconstruction, even with the military occupancy. Deserted plantations were being occupied again. The hundreds of farmhouses burned by marauders were rebuilt. The fields once again were growing cotton and grain. The returned Confederate soldiers renewed their oath of allegiance to the United States. There was a surplus in the state treasury.

Then Congress enacted its punitive legislation. Then came the rule of the carpetbagger with embezzlement of public funds and crass mismanagement of public affairs. In less than six years the Arkansas treasury surplus had been supplanted by a state debt of more than $7,000,000.

It may be unnecessary to explain that "carpetbagger" was the term applied in the South to those northern adventurers who came down after the close of the war and made expedient personal use of the chaotic political and economic conditions. More often than not, it appears, the carpetbaggers were corrupt politicians and heartless opportunists. The term "carpetbagger" was applied because these men were reputed to carry all their worldly goods with them in their traveling bags.

The climax of the carpetbagger days came politically to Arkansas in 1872 with the campaign for governor.

The carpetbag Republicans had as their candidate Elisha Baxter, North Carolinian by birth, but a citizen of Arkansas since 1852. Baxter had commanded a regiment in the Union Army.

Strangely enough, the Democrats had for their candidate a native of Ohio who had come to Arkansas as a carpetbagger. Joseph Brooks was a severe, chin-whiskered man who looked like a New England preacher. Outraged by the iniquities of the carpetbaggers, Brooks had turned against his own group and had thrown his not inconsiderable power as an orator to the defense of the Arkansans.

It was a bitter campaign. And the election was so close that it was necessary to call upon the legislature to decide it.

Of course, the carpetbag legislature was favorable to the Republican and Baxter was inaugurated.

The square-jawed Baxter was a great disappointment to the carpetbaggers, however. He fundamentally was an honest man and a just man. He opposed legislation which would impose added oppressions upon an already distraught people. He refused to appoint unfit carpet-

baggers to office and he stood stanchly by his principles although his Republican partisans threatened to impeach him.

Then came a strange switch. Brooks still was protesting Baxter's election, still was querulously claiming that he and not Baxter was governor of Arkansas. Now Baxter's own partisans suddenly moved over into Brooks's camp and the Democrats who had voted for Brooks swung to the support of Republican Governor Baxter, who so diligently had been protecting their interests.

In April of 1874 the Republicans went to a carpet-bag court and got an order ousting Baxter from office. With a mob of armed men they marched upon the state-house and forcibly ejected Governor Baxter and installed Joseph Brooks.

Immediately armed men began rallying to the cause

of the evicted Baxter. More armed men rallied to the cause of Brooks. There was some skirmishing and several men were killed. A major battle was in prospect until United States troops came in and dispersed both irregular armies.

President Grant then declared it was the duty of the Arkansas legislature to determine who should be governor, which the Republicans believed was tantamount to vindication of former Democrat Joseph Brooks's claims. True, the legislature once had elected Baxter. But that was before he had vetoed all their pet schemes. That was before the Republicans had switched to Brooks and the Democrats had switched to Baxter.

But again a strange thing happened. The legislature stood by the theory that once a Republican always a Republican, and voted as they voted before—installing Elisha Baxter as governor.

All this time the Ku-Klux Klan had been busy in Arkansas. It grew in strength until it was almost a super-government, and the Negroes, being frightened out of their postwar imperiousness, were becoming subjugated almost to the state of their ante bellum slavery.

The white-robed Klansmen, mostly former Confederate soldiers, committed many crimes themselves, even to murder. But they also moved effectively against the wave of outlawry that afflicted Arkansas following the war.

From the days of the fabulous Murrell gang up through the early decades of the twentieth century, Arkansas was plagued with outlaws. The geography of the Ozarks and the Boston Mountains had more than a little to do with that. There were so many good hideouts. And it was possible for the bandits to make forays upon settlements and escape to their lairs before organized search could be made.

It is most difficult at this time to separate legend from fact about the Murrell gang. This curious organization of cutthroats and thieves seems to have assumed the proportions of a secret society. It existed for twenty-five to thirty years, ending sometime before 1860. According to the common stories, this organization preyed upon the wealthy from New York to Texas, but particularly in Arkansas.

Headed by John A. Murrell, the gang was said to have been numbered in the hundreds, most of the membership being passive, however, rather than active. One of the legends is that the gang was organized after the manner of a corporation with stockholders and regular dividends paid to members who may have done nothing but turn in an occasional report concerning prospects in their neighborhoods.

It does seem to be verified that residents of St. Francis and Lee counties, Arkansas, did live mighty close-mouthed lives for years, afraid that any friend or neighbor might be a member of Murrell's dreaded secret police. Murrell's vengeance was swift and terrible upon those who opposed him.

It appears that the Murrell gang started modestly by stealing horses and mules and later branched out into the slave business and plain and fancy banditry.

Murrell is known to have boasted that he had stolen and resold more than a thousand slaves, sometimes being bold enough to sell the Negro back to the original owner.

If a slave turned up missing and a few days later the plantation owner was approached by a stranger who blandly offered to sell a fine field hand for $500 or so, the planter felt he was face to face with a Murrell gangster. If he was a prudent man he would pay the money and buy the slave sight unseen and not be surprised when his missing slave stumbled in that night shaking with terror.

Murrell's victims often paid tribute, receiving nothing in return except an implied immunity for an indefinite period. In that respect, Murrell's operations were similar to those of a modern racketeer.

They point out Murrell's trail across eastern Arkansas by lone pine trees. In a country where pines are rare, it is related that passive members of the gang planted pine saplings in front of their houses indicating that therein shelter and food could be found by active members of the gang.

Legend attributes hundreds of murders to Murrell and his unholy crew. The characteristic Murrell system was this: A traveler would be waylaid, his throat slit, and his horse and all identifying clothing taken. Then the body would be eviscerated, filled with stones, and sunk in the river.

Murrell had a house near Forrest City in St. Francis County, and the story now is that there was a regular dime novel trap door and dungeon beneath the house where traitorous members and others displeasing the gang czar were hurled to die of starvation.

Murrell and his gang disappeared shortly before the Civil War. The chieftain's fate is something of a mystery, but some say he was killed by his own gang. Others declare he was hanged in Mississippi. Still others believe he died a natural death in his house and that his henchmen, afraid to be caught with the body, fled, leaving it to molder in the cabin.

Murrell was only the first of a legion of spectacular bandits and murderers who operated in Arkansas.

William Quantrell, the guerrilla, came to Arkansas with his band of cutthroats after murdering a hundred and forty men, women, and children in Lawrence, Kansas, and sacking the town. In Arkansas the gang wore either the blue or the gray uniform, as best suited their current purpose, fought against both sides, and pillaged the homes of Union and Confederate sympathizers alike.

Wild Bill Hickok operated briefly in Arkansas, but killed only one man, a youth named David Tutt, who was rash enough to object to Hickok's cheating at cards.

There were Jesse and Frank James and Cole Younger, who shuttled across the Missouri border. There were Wade Thompson and Jesse Roper and a score of others.

But the fame of Arkansas regarding outlaws rests largely on the Federal Court of Isaac C. Parker, who for nearly a quarter century was known as the "hanging judge."

From 1875 to 1896 Judge Parker presided over the United States District Court at Fort Smith, which also had jurisdiction over all felonies committed across the river in Indian Territory. It was the Arkansas federal officers who waged war on banditry in that region, shot dozens of outlaws to death, and brought the rest before the stern bar of Judge Parker.

Petty offenses were handled by the United States commissioner instead of the federal court. But in the twenty-one years that Judge Parker presided at Fort Smith, 28,000 defendants stood before him charged with 13,490 felonies.

One hundred and seventy-four of these were convicted of capital crimes and 163 were sentenced to death.

Eighty-eight of these were hanged. Five died in jail. One was killed attempting to escape jail and 43 death sentences were commuted by the President of the United States.

The story around Fort Smith is that George Maledon, deputy United States marshal who officiated at the scaffold trap, once hanged twenty-one men in twenty-four hours.

The records, however, do not show this activity. In the twenty-two years Maledon was on duty at Fort Smith, he hanged sixty men. Twice he executed six men at once on the same scaffold. He hanged five men simultaneously on three occasions.

The Fort Smith scaffold was built for wholesale executions; it could hold twelve victims at once, but Maledon apparently was content to operate at cruising speed and not strain his apparatus.

There were many stories about the ghosts of hanged men frequenting the spot of their death and these stories were widely believed by Negroes and superstitious whites. Once a woman asked Marshal Maledon if he wasn't afraid the spirits of executed criminals would come back and haunt him.

"No, lady," Maledon said. "I do a good job on my hangings. I ain't yet had a man come back and ask to have it done over."

Judge Parker was an ardent baseball fan and was known to have adjourned court rather than miss a good game.

One time a delegation of Fort Smith players called upon the hanging judge with a sorrowful story. They were to play a crucial game with Van Buren that afternoon and their star pitcher—an Indian named Flatfoot—was in jail charged with a liquor law violation.

"I'll let him out for the afternoon," Judge Parker said. "I'll let him out to pitch and I'll be right there on the third-base line with a forty-five on my hip. If that redskin tries to run out on us I'll shoot him down right on the diamond. And if he doesn't pitch the best game that's in him, I'll throw the book in his face when they bring him to court."

So Chief Flatfoot took the mound for Fort Smith with Judge Parker's words in his ears. He saw Judge Parker's stern face there on the third-base line and he fanned the first twenty-one Van Buren players to face him. Van Buren got only one dinky scratch hit and no Van Buren player reached second base. Fort Smith won the game, 2 to 0.

Judge Parker was delighted. When Chief Flatfoot was brought to the bar, the hard-boiled jurist almost beamed at the frightened defendant. After the evidence was in, which convicted the Indian beyond a doubt, Judge Parker read him a kindly lecture. Keep away from liquor, he advised, and Chief Flatfoot would make the big leagues. Then he gave a suspended sentence.

Among the notorious criminals of Arkansas and Indian Territory to face Judge Parker were Cherokee Bill, who was hanged in 1896; the Dalton boys, Henry and Frank Starr, Ned Christie, and Bill Doolin.

CHAPTER TWENTY-ONE

Rambunctious River

THE river has been both the first friend and the worst enemy of Arkansas.

It comprised a highway for the first explorers and settlers who made their way up from the Mississippi. But at the same time its swamps and attendant chills and fevers in the lower reaches delayed the march of immigration to the state of Arkansas, made the settlers move northward through Missouri.

It was the river that gave birth to the cities of Pine Bluff and Little Rock and Fort Smith and all the smaller towns between.

It was the Arkansas River and its keelboats that brought the settlers in and carried the settlers' produce out in exchange for supplies.

There were ten steamboats operating on the Arkansas as early as 1820, and in 1834 there were eighteen. At that time, however, the hand-operated keelboats and flatboats were carrying at least 90 per cent of the business. There wasn't so much hurry in those days.

A keelboat usually could make the trip from Little Rock to the mouth of the White River and return in two or three weeks. The record keelboat run was that of the *Robert Morris,* which made this round trip in nine days in April of 1822.

The most important steamboat period was from 1840 to 1870. In 1850, 115 trips to Little Rock were

made by eighteen steamers while lighter boats were making regular schedules to Fort Smith and even Fort Gibson.

Perhaps the most famous of the glittering side-wheelers that plied the Arkansas was that *Pat Cleburne*, named for the Irish-born Arkansas general. There was a good deal of pageantry about a steamboat coming into an Arkansas town with whistle booming and the black pitch pine smoke billowing from her stacks. And there were singing black stevedores and the steamboat mates cursing enormously because that was part of their role and there were the flashy river gamblers lounging on the hurricane deck in broadcloth and fine linen and the whole Mississippi River show, but in a slightly condensed version without the original cast.

Then, in about 1870, the railroads began to make much better schedules and the day of steamboating began to wane.

Travel today from Fort Smith to Pine Bluff and you won't see more than three or four rusty little steamers. But the rivermen are as optimistic as are the mining men at the other end of the Arkansas. They believe the government eventually will get around to keeping a deep channel open and then the Arkansas will be alive with gleaming packets. They believe that once the federal government gets a comprehensive flood-control plan in operation, the river's yellow current will be kept constant and perhaps the channel will be kept open automatically.

Theodore Brent's "Report on the Arkansas River Waterway of 1931," made to the Mississippi Valley Association, recommended improving the Arkansas for navigation over the 530 miles from Tulsa to the mouth, providing a dependable channel of not less than nine feet. He had table after table of statistics to show the great advantages and profits to be gained from an Arkansas River barge line, not only to the Arkansas valley, but to the nation at large, in carrying out Oklahoma's oil and Arkansas's coal and agricultural wealth.

General Arsene Perrilliot wrote that the proper system for controlling floods and for keeping a navigable channel is to maintain a constant current velocity.

He wrote that when a stream's velocity is doubled, as in time of flood, it is given power to carry sixty-four times as much silt as it can carry at normal current. He argued that a stream will not deposit its silt if the velocity of current is maintained, but the stream will enlarge its own bed, scouring out the bottom and becoming narrower and deeper where the river now is shallow and wide.

There are two theories of how to accomplish this end. One is the construction of reservoirs to hold surplus water during floodtime. This water would be released gradually during the dry seasons, keeping a regulated current in the stream. The other theory is that new channels should be constructed to take care of seasonal high water.

The government leans toward the former method.

Floods have been the bane of the lower Arkansas. From Little Rock up, damage never has been high because the hills keep the stream pretty well in its channel. But below Little Rock it is a different story.

The first real flood of record apparently was one of the worst. Incessant rains in the spring of 1833 caused the river to rise more than thirty feet in June. Water stood fifteen feet deep in the bottom lands from Little Rock to Arkansas Post. Thousands of acres of cotton and corn were swept away and plantations were ruined.

In 1862-1865-1867 floods wiped out the settlement of Cypress Bend, in Arkansas County, a few miles upstream from Arkansas Post. At this date there would be scant interest in the former location of this backwoods hamlet except that it once was the home of Sir Henry (Dr. Livingstone, I presume) Stanley. Stanley kept store at Cypress Bend for his foster father until the Civil War began. Then he enlisted in the Dixie Grays, was captured and held prisoner of war for two months. And, after sixty days in a military prison he decided that the Union cause was the just cause after all, and enlisted in the Federal artillery.

The most famous town to be wiped out of existence by floods in Arkansas was Napoleon—made famous by Mark Twain in *Life on the Mississippi.*

Napoleon was the county seat of Desha County (pronounced De-shay) and it was a town of some distinction with a good-sized Marine Hospital, churches, banks, a theater, courthouse, and stores. It stood at the confluence of the Arkansas with the Mississippi and it was an important river point when Mark Twain was a steamboat pilot.

In *Life on the Mississippi*, Mark Twain told of a fantastic errand he planned to perform at Napoleon. He described the utter amazement of the captain when his ex-pilot asked to be put ashore at Napoleon and how the captain finally recovered sufficiently to inform Mark Twain that the town didn't exist any more. He said: "The Arkansas River burst through it, tore it all to rags and emptied it into the Mississippi. . . . Just a fifteen minute job, or such a matter. Didn't leave hide nor hair, shred nor shingle of it, except the fag-end of a shanty and one brick chimney."

Actually the demolition of Napoleon took rather more than fifteen minutes. The destruction was accomplished, not by one catastrophic flood, but by a gradual caving of the land.

In the fall of 1865 the federal government deemed the location of Napoleon unhappy and moved the Marine Hospital, whereupon Desha County leased the big brick building for a county hall. Some of the hospital rooms were occupied by the city government for municipal purposes.

Occupancy of the building became dangerous by 1869 and two years later the county and city records were moved to a new building and the old hospital was abandoned to the river, which by that time had eaten under one end of the structure.

That same year the old jail was declared dangerously near the river and it was replaced by another.

During these six years both the Arkansas and the Mississippi had been crumbling away the banks, foot by foot. Every few weeks the residents would arise to note that a neighbor's house or store had disappeared in the night.

This all was discouraging to the chamber of commerce and county commissioners, who finally decided there was no way to cope with the two rivers and it would be the better part of valor to move the county seat elsewhere.

A public-spirited citizen named L. W. Watson offered to donate to the county five acres of land on the railroad to the south on condition that the new county seat be named Watson. The offer was accepted and Watson became county seat of Desha County, Arkansas, while the once proud city of Napoleon was abandoned.

However, in 1878, Jay Gould got tired of having the Arkansas River running over his railroad more often than his trains and moved his tracks westward to higher ground. That left the damp but thriving town of Watson several miles off the railroad and practically isolated back in the swamplands. The following year the Desha electorate voted to move its county seat once more and this time to Arkansas City.

The pretty city of Pine Bluff, which lies on the last ridge of hills before you run into the flat, alluvial "Delta Country," has had more than its share of floods. In 1890 Pine Bluff had the distinction of owning the longest pontoon bridge in the world, connecting the main section of the city with North Pine Bluff. It held that distinction until the next spring. Then high water boiled over the longest pontoon bridge in the world and took it to New Orleans in segments.

Eleven years earlier, in 1879, Governor William R. Miller had taken steps to save Pine Bluff from the hungry Arkansas. He memorialized Congress for a $20,000 appropriation to stop the river's encroachment on Pine Bluff and the request was granted.

The river makes a wide horseshoe from the north at Pine Bluff and, in swinging the loop, turns very sharply east right at the city. The United States Army engineers effected a baffle bar at this loop designed to throw the current farther from the Pine Bluff bank and save the sandy soil on that side.

Apparently this baffle bar was successful, for no more city lots and houses dropped into the river. At least the baffle bar was successful until the big flood of 1908 when the yellow torrent went to work cutting a new channel right through the heart of the city.

In the middle of the night Pine Bluff citizens, hastily organized, braved the flood to plant huge quantities of dynamite at strategic points and they blasted a new channel for the rampaging Arkansas. They saved Pine Bluff, but they left the courthouse and a hotel hanging over the brink of the old channel, where they still hang, although bolstered and cemented to apparent safety. There is a moot question in Pine Bluff as to who owns this strip of rich land which once was the river bed.

Pine Bluff is a city of wide, tree-shaded, clean streets, broad lawns and neat, middle-class homes. Its population is about twenty thousand and the business streets show more activity than is usual in a city that size. Also it is known locally for its plethora of electric signs.

Traveling down through the bayou country, I had a young driver named Melvin. Pine Bluff was Melvin's idea of a perfect place to live.

"I ain't ever seen," said Melvin, "such a pretty sight as Pine Bluff at night. I declare I ain't. Everywhere it's electric signs, red, blue and white and all the signs is doing something. Everywhere you look, sure enough, there's a red dog chasing a blue cat or the like. There's one sign that's got a lady changing a baby's diaper. That one's just as lifelike as could be. I sure enough never did see anything prettier."

Next to the historic flood of June, 1833, when the Arkansas hit an all-time high stage at Little Rock of 34.6 feet, a record of 33 feet was reached on April 19, 1927.

In this flood only the roofs of houses were visible at
Arkansas City and the residents camped along the levee
for days.

The normal river stage for July in Little Rock is 6.6
feet and flood stage is reached at 23 feet.

Human suffering greater even than that exacted by
the 1927 flood was brought by the breaking of the levees
in 1937, which inundated more than a hundred thousand

acres in eastern Arkansas. This flood came in January and
was followed by a prolonged and bitter sleet storm which
brought added misery to the thousands of refugees shel-
tered by National Guard tents.

Work is under way to put an end to these periodic
disasters under the Flood Control Act passed by Congress in June, 1938.

Reservoirs are being built on the north fork of the
White River, on the Buffalo River, on Wildcat Shoals
of the White, on Eleven Point River, Strawberry River,
Little Red River, and on Petit Jean Creek and the

Fourche la Fave River. The last two come into the Arkansas from the south.

There seems to be good reason to believe these reservoirs will eliminate or at least reduce the number and violence of floods. Whether maintenance of a comparatively constant current velocity will automatically deepen the river's channel, as General Perrilliot suggested, and bring profitable navigation back to the Arkansas, remains to be seen.

CHAPTER TWENTY-TWO

"Now laugh, God damn you"

THERE is a story about a man from Little Rock who went to New York looking for a job. He was interviewed by an elderly, dignified prospective employer who asked where the applicant was from. The Little Rock man squared his shoulders and jutted his jaw. "I," he blurted, "am from Arkansas. Now laugh, God damn you."

With the joke-makers, Arkansas is in the same class as mothers-in-law and brides. Judged by the standards of wit and humor on the radio, I'll admit there may be something wrong with my glands of risibility, but I can see nothing very funny about mothers-in-law or brides. And I certainly don't see anything about Arkansas that is funnier than New York or Iowa or Indiana, and nothing even approaching Southern California for eccentricity.

I suppose the custom of laughing automatically at mention of Arkansas started with the "Arkansaw Traveler" tale—that and the extravagantly obscene oration, "Why Change the Name of Arkansaw?" which West Point plebes from Arkansas are required to recite.

The notion that anything concerning Arkansas is funny per se was advanced in 1903 by publication of a paper-bound book called *On a Slow Train Through Arkansaw* by Thomas W. Jackson. It was sold mostly on railroad trains and newsstands, but it sold literally by the hundreds of thousands at twenty-five cents a copy. It was a collection of "funny railroad stories," anecdotes, and conundrums.

Here are a few samples:

"There was a lady on the train with a baby. When the conductor asked her for her ticket, she said she didn't have any, the baby had swallowed it. The conductor punched the baby."

"There was a young fellow on the train. He couldn't get a seat. He was walking up and down the aisle swearing. There was a preacher on the car. He said, 'Young man, do you know where you are going, sir? You are going straight to hell.' He said, 'I don't give a darn; I've got a round trip ticket."

"Little Rock is noted for pretty girls. I met one of the first girls in town. . . . Her name was Auto. I think she was from Mobile. . . . She was the most bashful girl I ever saw. She wouldn't go by a lumber yard where there was undressed lumber."

"I said when I got married I wanted a wife that was like an almanac. 'Why do you want a wife like an almanac?' 'Because I could get a new one every year.'"

Many Arkansans didn't see anything very funny about *On a Slow Train Through Arkansaw*, but maybe they were prejudiced.

The late Opie Read used to say he once shot a man to death when the man complimented him as author of *On a Slow Train Through Arkansaw*. Read said, moreover, that an Arkansas jury acquitted him on grounds of justifiable homicide.

I don't suppose there is any question that Opie Read was the outstanding literary figure ever to live on the Arkansas River. William Allen White's Emporia, Kansas, is approximately a hundred miles from the river.

There were some elements of greatness in this huge,

shambling humorist. His astounding spontaneity was at once his greatest asset and his chief liability.

He turned out fifty-two books in his lifetime, poured them out at white heat and mailed them in sections to his publishers without even bothering to read over his manuscripts, let alone revise them. His audience largely was that stratum of humanity which bought paper-bound books to read on the train. It was not a critical audience—it asked only to be entertained.

Well, Opie Read's novels entertained them. Read's novels also gave them some mighty shrewd character portrayals and an exhibition of the storytelling art rarely excelled—although the English sometimes grew turgid.

There wasn't a great deal of money to be made from writing paper-bound books for the railroad train trade. Read's greatest seller was *The Jucklins*, which sold nearly two million copies. But the author had surrendered his rights to the novel for $700.

Opie Read was not a native of Arkansas and the closing years of his life were spent in Chicago. But his first successes were identified with Arkansas and his best work had to do with quaint characters and dramatic incident connected with Arkansas. As a matter of fact he preferred to identify himself with the swamplands and the Ozarks.

Read was born in Nashville, Tennessee, on December 22, 1852. He took up newspaper writing at twenty-one when he was working as a printer in Franklin, Kentucky. From Kentucky he drifted across the Mississippi River to Arkansas and worked on the Little Rock *Gazette*.

The tramp printer, Opie Read, was remembered as a huge fellow with a drawling speech, an amazing talent for storytelling, and hollow legs as far as drinking corn whisky was concerned. He also was a poker player of no mean ability, being able to hold his own pretty well with the professional gamblers who plied the Arkansas and Mississippi rivers.

In 1883 Opie Read established a humorous publication in Little Rock, which he named the *Arkansaw Traveler*. Before Read gave up this editorship in 1891, the paper had a national reputation for humor and bucolic philosophy. To the end Opie Read loved the role of rustic philosopher, frequently going so far as to drop final "g's" and use double negatives in writing as well as speech.

When his books began to attract attention, Read took to the lecture platform, emulating Mark Twain, whom he knew and greatly admired.

Gigantic as he was in figure, Read's appearance still was that of a country youth wearing his father's clothing. His long black coat draped from his burly shoulders in folds. His shapeless trousers bagged not only at the knees, but hung in accordion pleats from thigh to ankle. He wore his hair as a bushy mane and affected a flowing tie.

But on the platform he was the most fascinating speaker I ever saw. He was a consummate actor and his booming, drawling voice charmed his audience equally with the humorous and dramatic incidents that made up his lectures.

After his retirement, Read was fond of telling the boys around the Chicago Press Club that he had lectured in every county in the United States and in virtually every city, town, and hamlet.

Critics say Opie Read was "almost" a great novelist. They say his profound knowledge of human nature, sense of drama, and disillusioned optimism gave him the potentials of a great writer, but that he was always in too great a hurry to meet the demands of the train "butchers" to turn out a truly great book.

In Arkansas Opie Read is remembered mostly for his aphorisms, such as:

"Genius sometimes works with the energy of despair."

"The happiest man I ever saw was the laziest. He was also the smartest."

"More men have been saved by their children than by all the moral lessons ever printed. There ain't nothin' more to be deplored than a childless old age. I'd ruther be a hungry dog shut up in a church."

"Compliments are almost worthless when they reach none but the flattered ear."

Opie Read's last book was published in 1927. Its title was *The Gold Gauze* and it wasn't a very good book. He died on November 2, 1939, near the close of his eighty-seventh year.

The state of Arkansas has an area of 53,335 square miles, of which 810 are water—when the rivers aren't flooding.

In 1930 the population was 1,854,482, but the 1940 census will show well over 2,000,000.

There are 35.3 persons to the square mile, under the 1930 census. By that count the urban poulation was only 382,878 and the farm population was 1,119,464.

The total accountable income for the state in 1937 was $440,000,000.

Mineral products in 1936 amounted to $21,517,000, including petroleum, coal, bauxite, gas, mercury, rutile, oilstones, and manganese.

There were 1,072 manufacturing plants in the state in 1935, turning out products to the value of $122,447,-739 and paying $18,941,721 in wages to 30,511 employes.

Farm lands in the state amounted to $33,616,000 acres valued at $376,087,716.

Arkansas farms produced 1,808,440 bales of cotton in 1937—more than any nation in the world exclusive of the United States—and surpassed in America only by Texas and Mississippi.

That same year Arkansas farms produced 40,640,-000 bushels of corn, 1,050,000 bushels of wheat, and 3,080,000 bushels of oats.

The livestock population of the farms in 1935 was, hogs 887,000, sheep 65,000, and cattle 1,187,000.

The above dry facts are just an attempt to prove by statistics that Arkansas isn't funny.

Following the Arkansas River as best you can, it is approximately 275 miles from Fort Smith diagonally across the state to the site of old Arkansas Post—which now is a state park.

Start with Fort Smith. The 1930 population was 31,000. It is the home of the black felt hat and rugged individualism among automobile drivers.

In the springtime the residential sections of Fort Smith are beautiful with redbud trees. In the summer, latticed half doors are in use in the hotel rooms and so are huge ceiling fans, for obvious reasons. The leading hotel features an eight-course chicken dinner for seventy-five cents—"all the chicken you can eat, don't hesitate to ask for more." The initial consignment is a large platter of golden-brown spring chicken. If you are glutton enough to polish off that big platter, the waitress will urge, "Oh, suh, couldn't you eat some more chicking? Just a teeny piece more?"

Part of the original fort has been preserved as a memorial, with stone walls twelve feet high and two feet thick.

The old garrison road is now Fort Smith's main

street, as Garrison Avenue. The streets are wide and clean. There are the conventional number of flaming neon signs and red-fronted ten-cent stores and movie palaces that standardize American cities today.

There is this slight difference: Prominent on Garrison Avenue there is a large harness store displaying fine yellow horse collars in the window, and the hardware stores exhibit fishing tackle with gaily-painted cork bobbers, and the meat markets advertise, "Salt meat for boiling, 10 cents; salt meat, best quality, 15 cents."

These things show you Fort Smith is not in Massachusetts or Oregon or Colorado.

Down the river, 170 miles or so to Little Rock, there are many villages, most of them sleepy in the sunshine, and not quite so clean looking as are the villages 500 miles to the north. There is scarcely a hamlet small enough not to have its monument to the Arkansas dead in the Civil War.

There is nothing sleepy about Little Rock, however. It is clean and modern and there is a sense of youth and electric activity which is difficult to explain. Little Rock is not a young city. It was founded in 1814, which is a long time ago when speaking of cities west of the Mississippi. Little Rock is seventy-five years older than Oklahoma City. It is forty-four years older than Denver.

The capital of Arkansas is a city with a bright, metropolitan retail district, big lawns, fine old trees, large, comfortable middle-class districts, and beautiful mansions. Maybe it was only good fortune, but Little Rock gives an appearance of intelligent planning from the beginning. I say maybe it was only good fortune, for it seems incredible that any city could have intelligent planning consistently over a period of a century and a quarter.

The only city I can think of that is comparable

to Little Rock in this respect is Lincoln, Nebraska, which was founded in 1867 and deliberately laid out as a model city. Lincoln is more of a "spotless town" than Little Rock, it is true, but Little Rock has a mellow flavor which no city in Nebraska ever could acquire.

Little Rock faced one major peril early in its career. On February 3, 1821, the year after the capital was moved from Arkansas Post, a "large and respectable gathering" of citizens was called for the purpose of changing the village name.

It was argued that there was no dignity to such a name as "Little Rock," which, of course, came from the stone on the north bank of the river and which distinguished the spot from the near-by larger rock.

Some of the patriotic civic leaders contended the adjective "little" was mighty poor psychology, that it tended to minimize the importance of their metropolis. This farsighted clique had a new name for the capital city all worked out. They would christen it "Arkopolis," an etymological miscegenation of Gallicized Indian and classical Greek. However, a majority of the assembly, being endowed with more common sense than erudition, voted down the hybrid name and held to the picturesque and meaningful Little Rock.

The city—and also a lot of the country along the Arkansas—now is faced by another peril. That is the "rock veneer" house. They build a frame house and cover it with neatly fitted stone about two inches thick.

There is no reason, as far as I know, why a rock veneer house couldn't be built just as attractively as any stone residence. But the tendency in Arkansas is toward a two-tone effect, alternating pink and gray stones in a drunken checkerboard design which is bewildering to the eye and somewhat nauseating to the aesthetic sense.

CHAPTER TWENTY-THREE

Lynching and Sharecroppers

THERE is nothing any Southerner resents more than the suggestion that his state is handling the Negro problem badly. Usually the Southerner will deny there is any such thing as a Negro "problem." He will insist that the situation is well under control in a manner equitable to both white and black races and that everyone is happy as long as the Yankees keep their hands off. He is particularly vehement in his denunciation of "Damn Yankee Communists who come down here agitating discontent among the darkies."

Of course, there *is* a Negro problem in Arkansas as well as in the rest of the South. In Arkansas, 25.8 per cent of the population was Negro in 1930—and if that doesn't present a racial problem there isn't any such thing anywhere.

The Arkansas method of conducting interracial affairs is about as consistent as most human systems. Old Negro servants are practically members of white households and Negro servants presume to criticize their employers to their faces in a manner amazing to a Northerner. White babies nurse at the black breasts of "mammies." Negroes are cooks, barbers, hairdressers, waiters. They perform every sort of intimate service for the whites. Yet the Jim Crow law is strictly in effect—an act which assumes that the Negro is unclean and must not come even close to the white lords in public.

Although a Negro has cooked the food and another Negro serves it, no Negro could think of eating in a white restaurant or hotel. In the theater a small place high in the gallery is reserved for Negroes. A negro cannot ride in the same railroad car with whites—unless he is the porter who makes the white man's bed and hands him his face towel. Not only this, the Negro cannot sit in the same railway station waiting room. Each public building has doors plainly labeled "White" and "Colored," and woe to the Negro who is bold enough and foolish enough to step across the line.

Official records show that 226 Negroes were lynched in Arkansas between 1882 and 1937.

According to these official records, lynching in the United States has been declining steadily in the last few years. But I have been told by reputable Arkansans that the decline is only ostensible and is caused by agitation for an antilynching law.

I have been told solemnly that there are just as many lynchings in Arkansas as ever, but that news of them is being suppressed. I was told of a case, supposedly in 1938, where a Negro rapist was dragged behind an automobile through Little Rock streets and his body finally burned publicly, and it was declared, "Not a word appeared in any newspaper."

From my knowledge of newspapers and newspapermen, I am inclined to doubt this—with all respect to my informers. I can't believe that good newspapermen and good wire service men would suppress news of this sort, even if a chamber of commerce did request it.

However, Monroe N. Work, director of the department of records and research at Tuskegee Institute, Alabama, tells me he has proof of southern newspapers suppressing news of lynchings, that he gets information from private sources of lynchings which have not been reported officially and publicly.

There was a lynching in Clarendon once which was more or less typical of that strange and ghastly human phenomenon, mob hysteria.

At that time in Clarendon there lived a young woman (a beautiful and highborn lady, of course) and her middle-aged and well-to-do husband. For romantic reasons, the highborn young lady wished to dispense with her husband in such a way that she could acquire his money and property.

Such a job of work would be dangerous, difficult, and perhaps even messy, so the highborn lady naturally commissioned one or more of her four house servants to do the deed and make it look as if there had been a burglar.

The servants were unskilled in murder and bungled the job so thoroughly that the burglar angle was untenable and the police finally frightened the Negroes into a partial confession involving madame.

That night the enraged townsfolk met and whipped themselves into a vengeful frenzy. They went to the young widow's mansion and took the four Negroes— two men and two women.

Spokesmen for the mob visited upon the lady in her parlor and they said to her:

"Ma'am, we're mighty sorry to bust in on you this-away, but it's a thing what's got to be done and you know it yourself. We're taking your niggers down to the Big Nora mill and hanging 'em for the murder of your husband.

"Now, we're leaving this here little box with you and it's full of morphine pills—strong morphine pills, sure enough.

"Come dawning we'll be back here and ain't you

dead by then, why, we're naturally obliged to take you down to the Big Nora mill and hang you alongside your niggers. We wouldn't want to do that at all and we reckon you wouldn't want us to go and do a disgraceful thing like that either.

"Sure enough mighty sorry, ma'm, there ain't any easier way, but them morphine pills ain't going to hurt you a bit—just put you to sleep and you won't wake up. You just take 'em all right down with some water. Good-bye, ma'm, and may God have mercy on your soul."

So the spokesmen bowed low and left the highborn lady and they took the two Negro women and two Negro men down to my father's sawmill and hanged all four of them to the log trestle.

At dawn the mob went back to the mansion and found their night's work was over.

The Negroes of Clarendon were terribly shocked. They freely asserted the Big Nora mill would be cursed from then on.

My father was scornful of such talk. He was scornful of it even after the Big Nora mill went broke and he lost it.

There was another curse levied on Clarendon and Monroe County once. An Indian was hanged for murder in Clarendon and before they sprang the trap he cried out his innocence and called upon the White River to come up and flood the b'Jesus out of the whole county. Well, every time there is high water and the rivers go out of their banks, Monroe County seems to catch the brunt of the flood. That happens year after year.

It is about forty-five miles from Little Rock to Pine Bluff and about sixty winding miles from Pine Bluff through the swamps and bayous to the mouths of the Arkansas.

It is a flat, dreary country most of the way, full of miasmic sloughs and swollen-trunked cypress. But here and there is a fine plantation with its grand pillared mansion and aura of romance.

Then there are the sharecropper districts where one seldom sees a white face, where hundreds of Negroes live in identical unpainted farm shacks with identical squalid outbuildings and identical hound dogs.

A great deal has been written about the southern sharecroppers, both black and white. It is barely possible that too much has been written by socially-conscious zealots who set out from New York with a fixed premise and make their research data fit their preconceived notions.

Sharecropping in the South started soon after the Civil War. Owners of huge plantations discovered this form of serfdom had advantages over even the slavery system, because the planters were relieved of direct responsibility for the well-being of the Negro workers.

In theory, a sharecropper is more independent than a farm laborer working for wages. His time is his own. If he wants to work, he can work. If he wants to go possum hunting, he can go possum hunting. But, of course, if he grows too utterly lazy to raise a semblance of a crop, the landlord will see that he doesn't remain on the land another season. Doubtless there are cases where sickness or other misfortune also have caused eviction of families from sharecropper shanties. Also, doubtless, there are kindhearted landlords who have maintained unfortunate tenants for years at a financial loss.

Most sharecroppers are in debt practically all the time. The landowner gives them credit at the store—up to a certain point. He advances them seed for the crop.

He takes the cotton and the corn when it has been picked and gives the sharecropper his portion of the proceeds after the debt has been deducted. Sometimes the sharecropper's portion of the proceeds isn't enough to liquidate the debt. Then, as a rule, he gets no money at all for his year's work. But he gets an extension of credit.

I suppose—landowners being human beings—that sometimes sharecroppers are shamelessly cheated. And, as sharecroppers also are human beings, I suppose there is cheating being perpetrated on that side of the fence. From my own limited observations of this form of crookedness, however, I should say that one must be a mighty keen wing shot to cheat a landlord—that is, the average landlord.

Conditions in some of the sharecrop districts are pretty bad. In some cases they are almost as bad as a city slum. There are places in the lower Arkansas valley

where some health hazards actually are worse than they are in New York City. New York's water supply at least is comparatively pure. But in the swamp country lack of proper sanitation, combined with water from shallow wells, makes for typhoid and other enteric disorders. Negro sharecroppers like to go barefoot in newly plowed ground. They like the feel of fresh earth on their bare feet and they probably would go barefoot a good deal in spring and summer even if they didn't have to economize on shoe leather. That practice opens the door to hookworm.

Pellagra is endemic in the swamps. There is a theory in Arkansas that pellagra is caused by eating moldy corn meal, but I don't believe that theory has any real scientific basis. Pellagra seems to be definitely a deficiency disease, the same as rickets. Naturally, pellagra victims probably have been eating moldy corn meal, for things

mold very quickly down the bayous. But their trouble is caused by lack of a balanced diet rather than by mold.

Of course, there is evidence of rickets among the children of impoverished sharecroppers, but this condition is not nearly so prevalent there as in the tenement districts of northern cities.

Generally speaking, I suppose the children of a city's welfare relief clients have a better diet than the children of a sharecropper because of some semblance of intelligent supervision. But in southeastern Arkansas there probably are two or three times as many hours of sunshine annually as in Buffalo, Detroit or Chicago, for instance. Also, the swamp people have a passion for greens—dandelions, mustard, turnip greens—and the growing season extends from about the first of March to well into December. That leaves less than three months to subsist on corn meal and cured pork augmented by a little game.

One soft morning in early spring I dropped in on Remmie Dunlap to inquire if he knew how I could get over to Arkansas Post. Remmie Dunlap didn't know. As a matter of fact, he had never heard of Arkansas Post —the first white settlement in the Louisiana Purchase— although Arkansas Post was not more than twenty miles away.

Remmie lived just off a winding dirt road where the razorback hogs wandered as wild and as aimless as rabbits. His house was one of about twenty-five on an alluvial flat at the edge of a cypress swamp where a mockingbird glee club was wrapping up the morning in gossamer song. These sharecropper houses were spaced at regular intervals in a sort of echelon formation. I should judge there were about forty acres for each house.

Remmie Dunlap's house, like the rest of the houses

on the flat, was shed-roofed and roughly square in shape. It was approximately twenty feet along a side.

The outstanding characteristic of this whole settlement was the universal weather-beatenness of everything. And this impressed me as odd, for the weather is notably kind in southeastern Arkansas.

Remmie Dunlap's shed-roofed house was gray and weather-beaten and the ancient gray boards of its walls had that peculiar slick look that old wood bears when its fibers are beginning to separate one from another in the initial stages of disintegration.

Remmie Dunlap's shed-roofed barn and shed-roofed privy were of the same identical shade of decaying gray as his house and of the houses and barns and privies of his neighbors. The wood parts of the superannuated plow and of the dish-wheeled wagon that lolled under the sycamore in the front yard were of a slightly lighter shade of gray. I suspect one day these implements had known paint. But I am satisfied no building within miles of Remmie Dunlap's house ever had been caressed by a painter's brush.

Remmie was sitting on the tongue of his wagon when I came up. He was giving directions to his fifteen-year-old boy, Warren, and Warren was working sadly with a wobble-jawed monkey wrench trying to tighten the share of the superannuated plow.

Warren was a thin youth, but his black face held that warm sheen characteristic of particularly healthy Negroes. He wore a faded pink shirt and faded and patched blue jeans and his big splay feet were bare. Remmie was lean but not thin. The muscles of his bulky shoulders were blocked out under his blue cotton shirt. He gestured languidly with a big, cordy hand now and then as he gave suggestions to his son. Remmie wore a shapeless and greasy black hat and heavy, rough leather plow shoes. He was somewhere between thirty-five and forty, apparently.

Because Remmie seemed friendly, I sat down beside him on the slick gray wagon tongue and offered him a cigarette. He accepted it and the proffered light and he drew the smoke in deeply.

"That dad-burn plow," said Remmie, "is wore out, sure enough."

"Looks kind of old," I admitted.

A tawny shepherd dog and a brown hound were lying together under the sycamore. The shepherd had come out to meet me, barking once or twice as a matter of record, then went back to his dust bed and slumped down with his chin on his paws. Now that I sat down on the wagon tongue, the hound got up with dowager dignity and ambled over to sniff at my feet. He sniffed one foot carefully and then the other. Then he looked at my face with gloomily contemptuous brown eyes, twitched a sneer from his pendulous lip, then turned and walked stiff-legged back to the sycamore and lay down with the shepherd.

Remmie scratched the wool up under his black hat. "That there plow, don't know how old it is," he said. "Them handles is wore down slick from my daddy's hands and from my granddaddy's hands, too."

"Your father and grandfather worked this place?"

"That's right. Yes, suh."

"And you've been here all your life?"

"Well, no, suh, I haven't. I was my pappy's least boy. They was four gals and three boys. When I growed up there weren't no place for me round here so I goes to Memphis and I works in the carshops toting lumber for a piece. When I hears about loads of money niggers can make working in automobile factories up in Dee-troit I saves up my money in Memphis and goes to Dee-troit and I gets a job in Mista Ford's automobile factory, sure enough."

"Did you like it there?" I asked.

Remmie took off his hat and rubbed his pate. Then he looked over at me and grinned broadly.

"No, suh," he said, "I didn't like it in Dee-troit a-tall."

"Why not?"

"Well, suh, I done got married in Dee-troit."

I laughed.

Remmie laughed too, and then shook his head. "No, suh, I don't mean it like that, the way it sounds. My wife, she's a good woman. She's a Mississippi nigger what was working in a kitchen up there and I meets her in the Baptist church. She ain't having very good time and I ain't having very good time, so's we gets married.

"Them Dee-troit niggers, they's mighty high-toned and biggety, I want to tell you. Get mad if you calls 'em nigger. It's colored folks this and colored folks that all over the place and they looks down on southern niggers like they was poor white trash. Won't have much to do with me and my wife a-tall.

"I ain't ashamed because the Lord made me a nigger. One the finest rivers in Africa is the Nigger and if the Lord's willing one the best rivers he got is named the Nigger, I ain't ashamed to be called nigger either. That's the way I looks at it.

"And I works in this Mista Ford's automobile factory all day just holding a nut with a wrench while a white man name Mista Robinson screws in a bolt and then I holds another nut while Mista Robinson screws in another bolt and I does that a million times ever' day and dad burn if I don't get just sick picking up nuts and holdin' em' in a wrench for Mista Robinson to screw in bolts ever' day for years."

"How long were you there?"

"Well, suh, I done lose track. Five, ten year. And when I gets through workin' all day I goes home and we lives with a million other niggers in a great big brick house and I climbs up four or five stairs and there is my wife, Magnolia, with the washing all over the place on account it's raining, and there ain't no fresh air and the other niggers all calls me Lynch Bait account I'm from Arkansas and they does nothin' but drink gin and shoot craps and I don't do neither because I'm a teetotal and a Christian. And we cain't get no real fresh vegetables and no decent greens and they ain't no place for Magnolia to go after dandelions even and no fresh catfish.

"And one time a nigger that lives across the hall name of Williams, he comes over all dressed up and he says, 'Mista Dunlap, I'd admire to talk with you a minute.' Yes, suh, niggers in Dee-troit all calls each other 'Mista' unless they got nicknames like Lynch Bait, and I's glad to be called Mista instead of Lynch Bait and I says, 'Come in, Mista Williams.'

"He comes in and he says, 'Mista Dunlap, you should ought come along with me to the Communist meeting where all the colored folkses going to get equality with the white folks, even Mista Ford.'

"So I goes this Communist meeting, which is mostly niggers, only some white folks, which is pooty low white folkses, because ever'body calls ever'body else comrade and mista, white or black, and they talks a lot of big words how splendid it's goin' to be for the colored folkses and other comrades when the Communists get to be president and they gives me a red card to sign and I says I'll think it over and tells Magnolia and Magnolia says she wouldn't join no lodge that was low enough to take in white folkses that was low enough to join a lodge with niggers, especially northern niggers, and so I never did sign that red card a-tall."

The boy Warren still was struggling with the rusty bolt on the plow. "Pappy," he drawled plaintively, "I cain't get this yere nut-bolt tighten up nohow onlest you goin' to hold t' other end."

"Look yere," said Remmie severely, "I done hold all the nut-bolts I is ever going to hold. Ain't never goin' touch another nut-bolt."

I started to rise from the wagon tongue to go to Warren's assistance. Then I considered my social status. If I, a white man, stooped to assist this colored youth, I very likely would so demean myself in the eyes of the father that he'd leave me in contempt.

But still—there was the Mr. Robinson in Mr. Ford's factory. Apparently Mr. Robinson was above reproach. There seemed to be a fine distinction between nut-holding and bolt-twisting.

"Here," I said to Warren, "you get on this side and hold the nut. I'll tighten the bolt."

Warren obeyed quickly and I tightened the rusty bolt while he held the nut. Warren grinned amiably. "Thank you, suh," he said. "Thank you, suh," said Remmie. "Mighty kind of you, indeed."

I resumed my seat on the wagon tongue. The wood was very smooth under my hand, but I could feel the outlines of the gray grain, standing in relief above the surface. A motley flock of scrawny chickens—some black, some dirty white, some brick red—scratched and talked under the wagon and beyond in the sunshine.

"How," I asked Remmie, "did you get back to Arkansas?"

"Well, suh," said Remmie proudly, "you see I can read and write. So can my big sister Florabelle what's the wife of Ermine Kinney over there third house. So sometimes when I'm in Dee-troit I writes a letter or picture card to Florabelle and she reads it to our daddy and mammy and the other folkses what can't read and sometimes when the cotton is picked and paid for, if they's any money left, why, Florabelle's got a lead pencil and she buys a piece of paper and envelope and postage sticker stamp at the store and she writes me a letter and tells me who-all's died and had babies and got sick and had fights and everything.

"So one time the cotton's picked and there's some money left and Florabelle gets the sticker stamp and paper and writes me about a muskroom sociable Ringling Weber and his wife Oh Susannah had with a lot of fried muskrooms what turned out to be toadstools and Florabelle and Ermine was lucky because their girl Rhododendron was mighty sick with stomach fever and they didn't go and Ringling Weber and Oh Susannah was dead and so was our pappy and mammy and big brother Walter and three, four other folks.

"Well, when I get that letter of Florabelle I say to Magnolia, 'Listen, honey, now they's got room for us back home in Arkansas and maybe, do we hurry up, Mista Blaisdell'd let us work that there farm I was borned on and there'd be fresh air for the children and plenty of fresh greens and catfish and we'd be away from dad-burn nuts and bolts and these yere biggety northern niggers.'

"So I writes Mista Blaisdell a letter and he writes me a letter and he says all right. So I got an old Ford automobile there in Dee-troit and I got about forty dollars in the saving bank and we sells off our household stuff except the bedding and a few things and we loads up the Ford automobile and I quits my job holding nuts for Mista Robinson and Mista Ford and we puts Warren here in the back seat on top the bedding with Mildred and the least boy Stanley and we drives all the way from Dee-troit back here and I trades that old Ford automobile for them old grizzle mare mules in the barn there name of Mary and Martha and we been here five, ten years now."

"Then you're happier here than in Detroit?" I asked.

Remmie grinned. "Sure am," he said. "Don't like Dee-troit nohow."

"But you certainly were better off working in the Ford factory."

"No, suh—not nohow."

Remmie's wife Magnolia—two hundred pounds of dark brown maternity—came out the door followed by a boy of seven or eight. Magnolia wore a clean pink house dress and probably nothing else except for heavy shoes and a bandanna on her head. The boy wore faded but clean bib overalls and a ragged straw hat. Magnolia was carrying a slender pole with a fishline wound around it. The boy Stanley was carrying a tin can.

Magnolia grinned. "I allows we-all going down the slough and get us catfish for dinner," she said.

"Oh, boy," drawled the youth, Warren. "Mammy, use Stanley for bait and get a big un."

"Hush your big mouth," said Magnolia. "We got good worms for bait, ain't we, honey?"

"Sure enough have." Stanley held up the can, but eyed me with distrust.

"But look," I said to Remmie, "in Detroit you had a regular pay check. You had money. You had a car. Your children had good schools—went to the same schools as the white children, didn't they?"

"Don't want my children go to school with white children. Just get a lot of foolishness in they heads. Just make 'em unhappy because they's niggers. Don't need no automobile down here nohow. Don't need no money much. Me, I don't have to punch no time clock down here all the time. Don't have to hold bolt-nuts all day long. Get money in Dee-troit and have to spend it all for chine bones and *in*surance. Down here don't need no *in*surance nohow. Nobody's got *in*surance down here excepts it's a lodge for town niggers' fancy buryings. See them hogs down across the road? Them's my chine bones now. Them's my ham and pork chops and tender-loins too."

A tall, yellowish Negro wandered around the house. "Hi, there, Remmie," he said.

"Hi, Raleigh," said Remmie.

"You-all got your cotton done bedded?" asked Raleigh.

"Not all," said Remmie. "I allow it's time to put in garden sass soon's Warren gets that old plow fixed up."

"Plow's all fixed—much as I can fix it," said Warren.

"Cotton sure enough can wait bedding until garden sass gets planted," observed Remmie, ignoring his son.

"I thinks so," said Raleigh, nodding his head. "That's what I thinks too." He squatted on the ground and rubbed the yellow shepherd's ears.

"Loads of time yet for bedding cotton," said Remmie.

"Sure enough," agreed Raleigh. "Mista Blaisdell say cotton should ought be bedded. But they's lots of time yet. Remmie, you know Sam Westfall's old mule?"

"Yeah, I knows him."

"Well, he done got thrush."

Remmie shook his head. "Sam Westfall keep his barn cleaner and old mule won't get no thrush."

Raleigh took out a long-bladed jackknife and went to whittling on a stick. "Remmie," he said, "you-all got ary tar? I told Sam Westfall I'd ask did you have ary tar for his old mule's thrush."

"Ain't got no tar," said Remmie. "I sees it Warren keeps our barn pretty clean so's Mary and Martha don't get no thrush."

A short, heavy-set black Negro came in languidly from the road.

"Hi, Remmie," he said.

"Hi, Rome," said Remmie.

Rome sat down on the plow beam and grinned. "Remmie," he said, "Sam Westfall's old mule, he done got thrush in his hoofses."

"I hear tell," said Remmie.

"If you got some tar," said Rome, "I'd take a mite over to Sam Westfall."

"Give it if I had it," said Remmie. "Ain't got a smidgen."

Rome dug into his overall pocket and brought out a cheap harmonica. He thumped it on his palm and began to tootle it softly. He played the old church hymn, "When the Roll is Called Up Yonder." He played it with prodigal interpolations.

Pretty soon two more Negroes came shambling across lots and joined us. One was middle-aged and the other was in early maturity.

Remmie pushed his shapeless hat to the back of his head and squinted up at the middle-aged Negro.

"Hear tell," he said, "your old mule, he got thrush."

"Yeah, Remmie, you hear tell right. I just wonderin' if—"

"No, I ain't got ary bit of tar," interrupted Remmie. "Had I got it, you's welcome, sure enough. But you keep your old barn clean out and your old mule don't get no thrush."

Sam nodded his head sorrowfully. "I knows it," he

admitted. "I knows it, but I gets a powerful misery in my back ever' time I picks up old manure fork."

Rome's harmonica whooped into a galloping refrain unfamiliar to me, but crowded with provocative rhythm.

Remmie turned his head and slowly winked at me and then nodded in the direction of Sam Westfall. Sam's foot was tapping with the beat of Rome's tune. His shoulders began to sway. His foot began to pound. And all at once he leaped into the air and went into a buck and wing with prodigious energy. For a man of his age, Sam was wonderfully agile. I also have seen worse dancers on the stage.

"Rome, he done that a-purpose," Remmie whispered to me. Then he shouted, "Hi, there, Sam Westfall, you-all better look out of that there back misery."

Sam leaped into the air and spun. "Ain't nothin' cure old back misery like this," he yelled.

"Maybe," said Remmie, "you better go home and bring you old mule too. Sure enough. Maybe you and old mule hoedown together and it cure you both."

Rome's harmonica screeched on a high note and Sam Westfall dropped, panting, beside the wagon.

Down the road came a barefoot black boy of about fourteen followed by a short-haired mongrel. Remmie's shepherd and hound rose and trotted out stiff-legged to exchange sniffs with the newcomer while the boy sauntered up to our group with his hands in his overall pockets. He addressed everyone in general, but Remmie in particular.

"Autobeel come down road yestiday evenin'," he said, "and it done kill a shoat of pappy. Man, he pay pappy five dollar, and we got the shoat too. We-all goin' have po'k chop sociable this evenin', and mammy, she ast can you-all come?"

"Oh, man," said Rome.

"We-all be there," said Sam Westfall.

"I dunno," said Remmie. "We got to get some garden sass planted sure enough and maybe it rain tomorrow."

"Pappy done got two jugs corn likker," observed the boy.

Remmie Dunlap, the teetotaler of Dee-troit, squinted at the western sky. Then he squinted at the eastern sky. "I reckon," he observed, "it ain't going rain tomorrow nohow. Freddie, you tell you pappy and mammy us Dunlaps be happy to come."

CHAPTER TWENTY-FOUR

River's End

So we have come down the Arkansas River to its mouth. We have traveled 1,450 miles from Lake County, Colorado, and dropped more than 10,000 feet in altitude.

We have passed by some of the highest mountains in the United States. We have seen the river lashing itself into white spume passing through one of the deepest cañons in the nation. We have crossed the land once called the Great American Desert—the land of cowboys and buffalo. We have traversed the fertile fields of eastern Kansas. We have crossed the old Indian Territory, passing forests of oil derricks. We have cut through a section of the fabled Ozark Mountains and entered the cotton belt. We have traveled across the whole state of Arkansas.

We have come at last to the site of old Arkansas Post—now a state park.

Stand here where de Tonty of the iron hand and the great La Salle once stood and look at the broad Arkansas flowing slowly and silvery in the bright southern moonlight.

It is difficult to remember that this is the same baby rivulet that wound down so briskly clear from the Mosquito Range above Leadville. It is difficult to remember that this is the same stream that exalts its lusty young

manhood, roaring and leaping through the Royal Gorge
of Colorado.

As you stand under this luminous sky, two miles
lower than the river's source, it is difficult even to remember how the Arkansas looked back there. It has come such
a long, long way and it is a very old, tired river now.

A few miles below Arkansas Post the tired old river
ends its course. It ceases to exist. But though its identity
is lost, its waters still move on to the sea.

Acknowledgments

First off, I must thank particularly my old friends, William M. Beardshear, of Denver, and Norman G. Fuller, of Springfield, Colorado. To supply me with data which became a part of this book, they went to more trouble than one can expect even of good friends.

Likewise, I must thank my old friends, Grey J. Tipton, of Phoenix, Arizona, former undersheriff of Cripple Creek, and Clifford M. Sublette of Denver, historian and novelist.

I must thank Henry C. Butler, editor of the Leadville *Herald-Democrat,* who gave me a wealth of material on early Leadville; my brother, Glen E. Davis, of Kansas City, Missouri; Dr. Le Roy Hafen, historian and curator of the Colorado State Historical Society; H. Phelps Clawson, curator of anthropology at the Buffalo, New York, Museum of Science; Thomas Hornsby Ferril, of Denver; Miss Ina T. Aulls, of the Western History Department of the Denver Public Library; Mrs. K. L. Pardle, librarian of the Fort Smith, Arkansas, Carnegie Library; Miss Sally Large, of the Little Rock Public Library; Mrs. Lela Barnes, of the Kansas State Historical Society; Monroe N. Work, head of the Department of Records and Research, Tuskegee Institute, Alabama; and the Reference Department staff of the Kansas City, Missouri, Public Library.

I have referred to the following books in preparing data for this story of the Arkansas River:

Early Days in Arkansas, by W. F. Pope; *La Salle and the Discovery of the Great West,* by Francis Parkman; *Hempstead's Pictorial History of Arkansas; Hallum's Biographical History of Arkansas; Makers of Arkansas History,* by John Hugh Reynolds; *Folklore of Romantic Arkansas,* by Fred W. Allsopp; *Fort Smith, Arkansas—Queen City of the Southwest,* by R. H. Mohler; *Hell on the Border,* Anonymous; *Biographical and Historical Memoirs of Southern Arkansas,* Goodspeed Publishing Company; *Legends of the Ozarks,* by J. W. Buel; *Backwoods America,* by Charles Morrow Wilson; *Life on the Mississippi,* by Mark Twain; *Autobiography of General Albert Pike; A Report on the Arkansas River Waterway,* by Theodore Brent; *The Mound-Builders,* by Henry Clyde Shetrone; *Report of the Commissioner of Indian Affairs for 1865, 1867, 1868 and 1869; Soils and Men,* the 1938 yearbook of the United States Department of Agriculture; *Kansas—a Cyclopedia of State History,* by William E. Connelley; *The Kansas State Historical Quarterly; The Raven,* by Marquis James; *The Fourteenth Report of the United States Bureau of Ethnology; The Coronado Expedition,* by George Parker Winship; *Memories of a Lifetime in the Pike's Peak Region,* by Irving Howbert; *Famous Sheriffs and Western Outlaws,* by William MacLeod Raine; *Here They Dug the Gold,* by George F. Willison; *Silver Dollar,* by David Karsner; *Histoire de (Jean) Law,* by Louis Adolphe Thiers; *Moral Theology,* by the Reverend H. Noldin, S.J.; *Abroad at Home,* by Julian Street; *A History of California,* by Robert Glass Cleland.

I have dug deeply into the files of the following newspapers:

Denver *Republican,* Denver *Times,* Denver *Tribune* (all of which are defunct); Denver *Rocky Mountain News;* Denver *Post;* Leadville *Herald-Democrat;* Leadville *Carbonate Chronicle;* Pueblo (Colo.) *Chieftain;* Cripple Creek *Times-Record;* Gunnison (Colo.)

Republican; Dodge City (Kans.) *Journal;* Oklahoma City *News;* Fort Smith (Ark.) *Times-Record;* Little Rock *Arkansas Democrat;* Little Rock *Arkansas Gazette;* Pine Bluff *Commercial;* Helena *Arkansas World.*

Index

Airplane industries, 187, 188
Alamo, the, 253
Alamosa, Colorado, 100
Alberta, 3
Allen, Eliza, 251
Altman, Colorado, 140, 141
Antilynching law, 308
Apache tribe, 192, 193
Appalachian Mountains, 207
Appomattox, 277
Appomattox, Kansas, 180, 181
Arapaho tribe, 28, 31, 40, 166, 192
Archaeology, 199, 200-202
Arizona, 158, 160, 242
Arkansas, 6, 8, 198, 199, 202, 222-239,
    242, 243, 271-289
  origin of name, 6, 7
  resources, 303, 304
  settled, 243-261
Arkansas City, Kansas, 6, 188, 194,
    295
Arkansas Post, 227, 228, 234-238, 243,
    245, 293, 314, 326
Arkansas River, 3-12, 25, 26, 39, 49-
    51, 59, 60, 157, 158, 168, 170,
    194, 198, 234-238, 249
  Coronado discovers, 8, 19
  floods, 292-298, 303, 310
  highway, 243, 290-292
  mouths of, 243, 311
  source, 6, 326
  spelling of name, 7, 8
"Arkansas Traveler," 254-260, 299
Arkansas Traveler, 302
Arkansas tribe, 6, 7, 198, 225-227,
    235, 236
Arkansas Valley, 121, 156, 157, 160

Armada, Spanish, 24
Arthur, Chester A., 111, 114, 115
Artists, prehistoric, 10
Atchison, Topeka & Santa Fe, 11, 88-
    105, 147, 154, 166, 171, 175, 195
Aztec Indians, 205

Baca County, Colorado, test tract, 162,
    163
Bacon, Sir Francis, 24
Banditry, in Arkansas, 284-289
Banque Royale, 232, 233
Barges, 292
Bassett, Charley, 178
Battle Mountain, 133, 134
Baxter, Elisha, 281-283
Beaver, 28, 48, 246, 254
Bell, Edward, 145
Bell, Sherman M., 146
Belle Point, Arkansas, 243-244 (*see
    also* Fort Smith)
Bent, William, 166
Bering Strait, 201
Bernalillo, New Mexico, 16, 19
Betsy, rifle, 247, 248
Bicycles, 133, 134, 194
Bienville, Jean Baptiste, 236-238
Big Sandy Creek, massacre, 166, 167
Billingsly, John, 245, 246
Billy the Kid, 10
Bimetallism, 214
Black, James, 253, 254
Black Hawk, 40, 45
Black River, 12
Black Rollers, 10, 164, 165
Blue-sky laws, 150
Blunt, General James G., 274-276

331